Originally a musician and songwriter, James Cook released two albums with his band Flamingoes: the critically acclaimed *Plastic Jewels* in 1995 and *Street Noise Invades the House* in 2007. Present from the start of the Britpop boom, Flamingoes toured the UK and Europe extensively, selling 20,000 records worldwide. In 2009, one of James's short stories was featured in the collection *Vagabond Holes* alongside work by Nick Cave and Man Booker-winner D. B. C. Pierre. James has written about music for the *Guardian* and *Litro* magazine among others. He lives in London.

With special thanks to

Yvonne Enright
Ian Tuton
Simon Williams

Memory Songs

A Personal Journey into
the Music that Shaped the '90s

James Cook

Unbound

This edition first published in 2018

Unbound
6th Floor Mutual House,
70 Conduit Street, London W1S 2GF

www.unbound.com

Text Design by Ellipsis, Glasgow

A CIP record for this book is available from the British Library

ISBN 978-1-78352-521-8 (trade hbk)
ISBN 978-1-78352-523-2 (ebook)
ISBN 978-1-78352-522-5 (limited edition)

Printed in Great Britain by Clays Ltd, St Ives Plc

1 3 5 7 9 8 6 4 2

To Mum and Dad, with love and thanks

Dear Reader,

The book you are holding came about in a rather different way from most others. It was funded directly by readers through a new website: Unbound. Unbound is the creation of three writers. We started the company because we believed there had to be a better deal for both writers and readers. On the Unbound website, authors share the ideas for the books they want to write directly with readers. If enough of you support the book by pledging for it in advance, we produce a beautifully bound special subscribers' edition and distribute a regular edition and ebook wherever books are sold, in shops and online.

This new way of publishing is actually a very old idea (Samuel Johnson funded his dictionary this way). We're just using the internet to build each writer a network of patrons. At the back of this book, you'll find the names of all the people who made it happen.

Publishing in this way means readers are no longer just passive consumers of the books they buy, and authors are free to write the books they really want. They get a much fairer return, too – half the profits their books generate, rather than a tiny percentage of the cover price.

If you're not yet a subscriber, we hope that you'll want to join our publishing revolution and have your name listed in one of our books in the future. To get you started, here is a £5 discount on your first pledge. Just visit unbound.com, make your pledge and type **memory5** in the promo code box when you check out.

Thank you for your support,

Dan, Justin and John
Founders, Unbound

Contents

Memoria

Memoria

Memoria

'Come As You Are', Nirvana

Intro

In the autumn of 1992 I was a twenty-four-year-old unemployed musician living in a damp Muswell Hill bedsit. Under stringent conditions – a seven-day working week – I had been writing songs with my twin brother, Jude. So far, 250 tunes had been amassed. We'd been in the Smoke for over four years, and still hadn't 'made it' yet. The prognosis wasn't good.

Demos had been recorded, dismally empty gigs endured, plans ripped up and Year Zeros declared a number of times. Several record labels had taken an interest; none had offered a deal. We were sans manager and making the kind of daily either/or decisions every penniless musician knows only too well: food versus cigarettes; amp repair versus electricity bill; proper job versus an insane artistic project that has become increasingly indefensible to friends, girlfriends and every member of your family.

Ever since writing my first callow lyrics aged fourteen, I'd been striving to develop as a songwriter, learning different instruments, mastering the studio (we recorded and rehearsed day and night at a place called La Rocka – our very own Paisley Park, only in Tottenham Hale). But up to this point there was very little to show for it. I don't mean fame. The mission was never to be famous, in some kind of *X Factor*-ish way, but to escape a Hertfordshire small town and make great records. That was the mantra. To experience those moments of glory from having created a work of art – an album – that my twin was fond of talking about. (How close the language of earnest young men who form rock groups is to that of radical fundamentalism.) 'Why don't you both just start a boy band, and get it over with?' a former girlfriend suggested, my brother and I being passably presentable. Maybe she meant something similar to Bros. But Bros wasn't what I had in mind when I first picked up a guitar. Oh, no. John Lennon and Jimmy Page were the role models, and I laboured every day to produce music that even touched the hems of their Carnaby Street garments. Brian Wilson and Burt Bacharach, too – serious songwriters. *Songwriters' songwriters*.

Yet by the end of 1992, weary and recycling each teabag a dozen times, I was beginning to question my purpose – and sanity. Four penurious years in the city had left me with a dangerously warped mind. As Kurt Cobain sang, something was in the way.

But I still liked to watch television, every now and again.

One bleak Thursday night in September, after a fully balanced evening meal of spaghetti, two fish fingers and half an onion fried in economy marge, I repaired to the sitting room to watch *Top of the Pops*. (Not a long walk: it was conveniently located only a few inches from the kitchen.) I was anxiously awaiting the debut performance of a group that had special significance for me, 'the best new band in Britain', Suede.

There was a chance, however, that my precious television – ailing for months – wouldn't survive to the end of the transmission. This was troubling: if it broke, there was no money to buy a new one. And, anyway, the shops were closed.

Suddenly, they were on. My chest tightened. Despite, or because of, the tiny white portable set with a coat hanger for an aerial, they sounded pretty good. Vital, feral, alive. Eschewing caution, I turned the volume up to ten, the noise threatening to split the cheap plastic sound-hole. The picture quality was so poor it appeared as if they were playing inside a carwash.

Through the televisual froth, the singer, Brett Anderson, sashayed in a fair impersonation of Morrissey; flicked his fringe as if he was Bryan Ferry. In profile, he revealed an impressively aquiline, almost Bowie-ish nose. He sang the words to the verses (I could only make out 'lover-ly' and 'glitter') with a Johnny Rotten snarl on his lips. The sheer ardour of his performance was entrancing. The song Suede were playing, 'Metal Mickey', lacked the regal beauty of their first single, 'The Drowners', but compensated for this with a sort of unreserved self-assurance. The kind of swagger a song can only gain when its writers have come into contact with adulation for the first time: the difference between 'Love Me Do' and 'Please Please Me'. This was a group that had been given permission to surpass themselves. *Oh Dad, she's driving me mad*, went the chorus. It could have been a line from *Carry on Matron*, spoken by Kenneth Connor. Yet they didn't seem like they were joking, especially the guitarist, a slight, bolshie looking young man (who went by the mild-mannered name of Bernard). He thrashed and writhed, and sometimes punched the top of his Les Paul.

Hang on a minute, a Gibson Les Paul?

No 'indie' musician had ever dared to play that guitar in this way – using distortion, bending notes – while wearing a wide-collared shirt. It was a flagrant allusion to the 1970s: Mick Ronson, Marc Bolan, Jimmy Page. And he was doing it on national television. This, I thought, could have serious implications for the country's youth. The drummer was pretty cool, too. Loose-limbed, smiling; at home behind his kit, like the captain of a new yacht. His name was Simon Gilbert. I had a special interest in Simon, because, only eighteen months before, he had played drums in *my* band. Let me explain . . .

The group my brother and I formed with Simon, the Shade, had been a power trio with an emphasis on tight songs rather than the long Dinosaur Jr.-esque dirges then in vogue. We'd rehearsed industriously for over six months, playing original material alongside tunes by T. Rex and the Clash. Gigs had been sporadic, yet the band seemed to have a sense of common purpose, and, more importantly, mutual reference points. McCartney's high-flown bass on 'Baby, You're A Rich Man'; Mick Jones's prominent backing vocal on 'Spanish Bombs'; Woody Woodmansy's restrained drumming on 'Five Years'. At some point during the previous January, Simon – a lovely man with a quiet smile – had sheepishly admitted he was moonlighting with an outfit based in east London, named Suede. One day he'd told me he might have to 'choose between us'. The end had come after a gig at ULU where Brett Anderson, bassist Mat Osman, and their manager – a bloke in a sparkly Ben Elton suit named Ricky Gervais (yes, *that* one) – had been ominously present. When Simon eventually left the group I recall my brother saying: 'It's OK. We'll be so big next year he'll have to throw his TV away.' A grisly irony. Now here he was on my telly, part of the best new band in Britain.

By this point in the performance I wasn't crying with self-pity, I was laughing. They'd done it! They'd breached the citadel that had proved inviolable for four years. At that moment, I felt a curious mix of envy and pride for Simon.

As the song ended, and the show cut back to the baffled presenter, a random memory assailed me. In 1991, at a lamentably unattended Shade gig at Islington's Lady Owen Arms, during a sound-system breakdown, we'd all shared cigarettes like soldiers in the trenches. (Simon, a generous guy, had always been happy to flash his 10 Benson. But then he had a proper job, selling tickets at ULU.) Yes, we'd been Brothers in Rock. Now he'd gone beyond me and made a life for himself.

Full of new plans and dreams, I braved the forbidding, tenebrous hallway where the payphone was located, and pumped in a ten pence piece. It was the last one, intended for the electricity meter. Far across London, in La Rocka's cramped office, Jude had been watching the same performance. I waited for him to pick up.

'The bastard!' a thin voice said, before I had a chance to say anything. 'He's done it.'

'I know.'

'I expect he still has his television.'

It was obvious to us both we would have to rip it up and start again. Not a single one of the 250 songs we'd written so far was as good as 'Metal Mickey'. And how cunning Suede had been in managing their influences! They had successfully repackaged the seventies for the nineties. It was 'glam', but refracted through an indie sensibility. We would have to embark on one last campaign. Yet this rupture with the past was necessary. It was what I'd been waiting for. Now that it had happened it was exhilarating, emancipating. Over the last two grim years of baggy, shoegazing and – worst of all – grunge, I'd found myself almost apologising for loving Bowie and Bolan. It had taken a number of years to realise that I naturally gravitated to British art, rather than American culture, or, to use a word not really in currency back then, Americana. Maybe it was the sense of reserve, the irony, the stylish clean lines, but from John Barry to Bryan Ferry it was mostly English artists about whom I felt an aesthetic excitement. And Bolan and Bowie, despite co-opting American cool, were unashamedly English. I quickly saw that from now on it would be possible to succeed on my own terms. All I would have to do was write some new songs with my brother. And maybe steal a new television.

The following week, a crisis meeting was called. In a moment of recklessness, we agreed to abandon all the old material and the band name. Goodbye the Shade, hello Flamingoes.

Year Zero. *Again.*

But I'm jumping ahead. Perhaps it's best I share how I got into this mess in the first place. For that I must rewind many years before Year Zero, to the early 1980s to be exact; deep into the Memory Songs that resonate there.

PART ONE

The Satellite Town

I

The Two Bs

'You Only Live Twice': Growing up in a satellite town, with John Barry and the Beatles

On the morning of 9 December 1980, I was in the Hertfordshire back bedroom I shared with my twin brother, getting ready for another school day; and listening, as usual, to *Revolver* by the Beatles. At some time after 8 a.m., my mother ran upstairs crying, '*John Lennon's been shot! John Lennon's been shot!*' She was wearing a yellow quilted dressing gown and waving a piece of burnt toast. She was also actually crying. In the kitchen, where she had been making breakfast, the news had just been broadcast on the radio. Mum's announcement was so horrifying and unexpected that I set off for school in a state of shocked excitement, not knowing if the gates would be locked, the country in national mourning.

I was twelve years old. Despite having owned the album for a few months, I knew little about the individuals who wrote the songs on *Revolver*. John was the leader; that was about it. Yet it had been long enough to side with the general consensus that the Beatles were The Best Band In The World.

I say 'owned', but in fact I had borrowed the record from my father's house (my parents were in the process of getting divorced; I spent the week at my mother's and the weekends at my father's). One Sunday at Dad's, during the handover, I asked if I could listen to *Revolver*, the only pop album in his otherwise entirely classical collection. It was in there by accident. At my parents' wedding reception in 1966, someone had pointed out that the Brahms playing on the Dansette was perhaps a little, well . . . fucking boring. A guest had been sent to buy a pop record – any pop record – and had returned with *Revolver*. I often marvel at the serendipity of this. What if they'd picked up an Engelbert Humperdinck LP rather than one of the greatest albums of the twentieth century? It's a bit like going into a bookshop looking for a novel and randomly choosing *Ulysses*.

I had always been curious about the four austere faces on the cover. They recalled the American presidents on Mount Rushmore. The sleeve seemed to be trying to communicate an air of importance, yet a second element of the design – a collage of the group mucking about and throwing camp shapes – deliberately undermined this. The cover stood out among the countless Rhine scenes and Alfred Brendel portraits (the pianist glowering satanically in his thick-rimmed spectacles, yet always looking strangely like Roy Hudd).

Dad didn't care for pop – it was the enemy of 'serious' music – but, for some reason, that afternoon he allowed me to play *Revolver*. As the first bars of 'Taxman' emerged from the speakers, something unusual happened. At the gaunt chop of the guitarist's bluesy chord, a peculiar feeling arose in my stomach. The only equivalent experience was when the local marching band had trooped around the market square of the town. Each thud of the bass drum had delivered a delicious blow to the solar plexus.

This, however, was subtly different. I sensed that the blues had something to do with the mysterious realm of sex, and to a twelve-year-old boy this was of urgent interest. It seemed wondrous to me that music – something you couldn't see – was able to provoke a physical reaction as well as an emotional one, and that sometimes the two appeared to overlap. I didn't fully understand what I was hearing, but knew I wanted to hear more. As the record progressed it became increasingly puzzling. Why did it have 'Indian restaurant' music on it? Why were there so many different musical styles? I recognised the laborious 'Yellow Submarine' from school, but the next track, 'She Said She Said', mentioned death over a tumult of distorted guitars. There were inexplicable developments in the songs: the funny chord in 'I Want To Tell You' sounded like the wrong notes were being played; as if someone had made a mistake and hadn't bothered to correct it.

My parents, who had been talking over one wonderful song after another, decided it was home time. I asked to hear one more tune. A brass fanfare blared from the speakers; then a space of a few seconds, leaving the listener suspended in anticipation. A Beatle began singing (I wasn't sure which one): he was alone; he took a ride; he didn't know what he would find there. Curiouser and curiouser. There was something new in the mix: romantic melancholy, a yearning sadness. The verse flowed into the bridge – a descending bassline – the figure that, many years later, Alex Ross, music critic for the *New Yorker*, would observe 'has represented sorrow [in music] for at least a thousand years'.[1] The sequence ended in an explosive vocal release on almost only one note. It also happened to be the title of the tune: 'Got To Get You Into My Life'.

That was enough.

The car was waiting. I didn't hear the last song, 'Tomorrow Never Knows' (probably a blessing; that would have completely blown my mind). I wanted to seize *Revolver*, confiscate it for further investigation. Perhaps it would be useful, a road map for the perilous teenage years ahead. My father agreed to let me take the record, and, in doing so, passed me into the hands of the enemy.

The day John Lennon died was marked by an uncommon display of public grief. Even the teachers at school seemed upset. Returning home at teatime, I switched on the telly to watch *Newsround*. George Martin was being interviewed; he looked ashen and angry. Before bed, I was allowed to stay up and watch the endless commentary and analysis. Then, after *News at Ten*, they showed *Help!* And there was John, as a vigorous young man, skiing, gurning to the camera, telling us you had to hide your love away. *Alive*.

During the following weeks there was a predictably intense renewal of interest in the Beatles, but, disappointingly, not a great deal of actual 'stuff' available. There were the usual books, and maybe the odd story about Paul's alleged love child in the *Daily Mail*, but you couldn't, as you can now, gorge yourself night and day on YouTube and fan sites. The best resource was *The Beatles: An Illustrated Record* by Roy Carr and Tony Tyler. A sort of proto-*Revolution in the Head*, it dealt with all the albums in chronological order. Jude and I devoured their wry observations and cryptic jokes; we could quote from it verbatim (a favourite was the final piano chord of 'A Day In The Life' described as having 'all the morbid majesty of a slamming sarcophagus lid').[2] There was also Radio Luxembourg. Every week they broadcast a Beatles Hour that played listeners' requests. Here, after lights out, we could tune in on our chunky silver Amstrad hi-fi to obscure cuts from *The White Album*: 'Piggies', 'Honey Pie', 'The Continuing Story Of Bungalow Bill' . . . The Fab Four's world was stranger than I had ever imagined.

That Christmas, there were Beatles albums under the tree.

Rock 'n' Roll Music: Volumes 1 and 2, on the MFP label, instantly became the Holy Bible, Old and New Testament. I think mine was *Volume 1: Genesis*. The *Illustrated Record* rightly states that the songs 'fit together with the appositeness of a well-chosen menu'. The authors conclude, cautiously, that it is 'perhaps the best ever Beatles compilation'.[3] Here, the sex wasn't suggested, as on *Revolver*, but overt. Every tune was awash with it – 'I Saw Her Standing There', 'Long Tall Sally', 'I Wanna Be Your Man', 'Dizzy Miss Lizzy'. The first track was 'Twist And Shout'. Although I couldn't have put it into words, something in me responded powerfully to Lennon's unhinged vocal. It perfectly expressed the hormonal agitation of boys about to become teenagers; drooling over the girls they saw gyrating unattainably on the dance floor. From here on in, I was a devout, born-again Beatle-maniac.

My brother and I received two very different presents that day: a pair of lavishly illustrated James Bond books. This was our other unlikely mania. For the past few years, we had been obsessive 007 fans, collecting everything from bubble-gum cards to wall-sized posters.

At the end of Christmas Day, I pondered how the two interests could co-exist. Bond and the Beatles. The two Bs. The old and the new. They were both part of a preoccupation with the sixties, true, but one represented square, 'straight' culture, the Establishment; the other exemplified the swinging sixties, the counterculture. However, I knew by then that the Beatles, in the 1960s, had watched each Bond film as it was released, just like the rest of the country, and Paul McCartney had owned an Aston Martin. Yet the Fabs had managed to render old, sexist colonial heroes like 007 obsolete almost overnight. Bond mocks the Beatles in *Goldfinger*, famously suggesting that it's only possible to listen to them wearing ear muffs. But screenwriter Richard Maibaum's line is telling. It betrays an uneasiness: the old guard were threatened by the Beatles. The younger generation had the upper hand, and the Establishment knew it.

What, I wondered, could reconcile the two worlds? The answer was the composer of the James Bond music. The other B wasn't Bond, it was Barry.

*

The Hertfordshire town I grew up in was Hitchin, thirty-eight miles north of London. With its market square, long-established shops, tea rooms, and a Woolworth's it was just beginning to experience the homogenisation of the high street that is now complete in Britain. (There was great consternation when KFC arrived.) The older parts were appealing, I suppose, if you weren't a bored kid on the verge of becoming a teenager, but that was what I was, and most days the town possessed a stifling, almost mesmerising ordinariness. Like Hanif Kureishi's Bromley, Hitchin felt like 'a leaving place'.[4] After meeting and marrying, my parents had settled there. Father, reserved by nature – medium build, dark hair, middle class – was a computer programmer from west London. Mother, outgoing, small, fair, working class, was a nurse from South Yorkshire. After they separated, my mum moved to a semi-detached Wimpey home on an estate, where I spent the weeks listening to Radio One, riding my bike, and watching *Grange Hill* at teatime. A fish-finger childhood familiar to many. My dad lived in a two-bedroom house on the other side of town, where I stayed at the weekends, among his books and classical records. Their only sons were two slight, shy twins, obsessed by fossils until Bond, and, finally, music came along. We were bright, and, so we were told, on the way to being good-looking. Cheekbones were not something you would want to bring to an all boys' school playground, but a good qualification for a certain job later in life perhaps . . . It was said that Jude had a rounder face; mine was longer, but, being twins, there was always an unmistakable consanguinity. People were always interested in us (although we were never 'popular'). In 1980, I had just started secondary school, a comprehensive that was experiencing a similar culture shock to the one the town was undergoing. Once a grammar in the 1960s, it still clung to its quad, its house system, its masters in gowns. On cold, clamorous mornings it had that daunting, inevitable school-smell of carbolic soap, Sellotaped-up textbooks, chalk dust, actual dust, hormones, rugby socks, and farts. In class I was already staring out at the playing field, with its fence of tall poplars, watching the never-ending white line being painted, dreaming of music – and escape.

One day in the New Year, our English teacher, Mr Wood – a sprightly Leavisite with a Jacobean beard – asked the class, 'Who or what makes the most important contribution to a film?' There was a show of hands. To our surprise, our answers were rejected one by one. According to him, it wasn't the director, the star or the location. Nor was it the costumes or the special effects. We were stumped. My hand was in the air more than most, possibly just to show off my extensive but pointless film knowledge, much of it gleaned from Michael Rodd's *Screen Test*. It wasn't the second unit director or even the third unit location scout. We were becoming desperate. What could it be? In the end, no one got the answer: *the music*.

The incident illustrates something fascinating about the effectiveness of soundtracks. A director can make the most powerful, well-shot, perfectly cast film in all movie history, but if the music is wrong it's dead. To test this hypothesis, imagine a scene from a classic film with a different score. The opening of *Taxi Driver*, perhaps – Travis Bickle's cab emerging monolithically from the mist – but instead of Bernard Herrmann's menacing brass swells, Keystone Kops music. Or the start of *The Odd Couple*: Jack Lemmon preparing to commit suicide, but in place of Neal Hefti's jaunty score (which tells us it's a comedy and Lemmon will be all right), Mahler's Fifth Symphony. In this way, it is impossible to imagine an early James Bond film without a thrilling, urbane John Barry score.

The term 'Barryesque' is now shorthand for a number of distinct musical styles: sweeping, mournful strings; raucous, sexy brass; and icy, Cold War minimalism played on obscure Russian-sounding instruments, often all in the same piece. Everyone knows this music – Bond skiing down a mountain, Bond kissing a girl, Bond walking decisively through an airport; and there it is, behind his back. Simon Winder, in his book, *The Man Who Saved Britain*, suggests that John Barry's music may have been *the reason* for the Bond films' success. This is a contentious, even fanciful notion, but one which is perhaps valid. Terence Young, director of *Dr No*, *From Russia with Love* and *Thunderball*, was once asked what he thought were the principal ingredients of the first 007 films. He answered, 'Connery, Connery, Connery.' Agreed, but with one caveat – replace that last 'Connery' with 'Barry'.

If John Barry was important, vital, even, to the Bond series, he was essential listening for a certain type of music-obsessed, Generation X kid growing up in Britain in the early eighties. Barry's work should have been difficult to find – just as there was a paucity of Beatles stuff, so there was a dearth of anything Bond-related. Before discovering the James Bond Fan Club, I had to work hard for my 007 fix. Today, one can click on thunderballobsessional.com and binge on images of rare brochures, press-books, lobby cards and artwork. Back then, the films appeared twice a year on television (it took seven years from release for ITV to show *Live and Let Die*), or there were the Ian Fleming paperbacks, with their fusty smell and yellowing, dog-eared pages, costing ten or fifteen pence each. And that was it. But one of the few things available – in Woolworth's, or Boots even – were the 007 soundtracks. I listened to them incessantly; and, along with the Fab Four, John Barry became a gateway drug into the wider world of popular music.

The two Bs had an interesting, almost contrapuntal relationship in the 1960s. Their paths crossed many times. Barry often seemed like a one-man Beatles; his creativity possessed a similar effortless energy. Their artistic and commercial trajectories matched exactly: a breakthrough period from 1962 to 1964, succeeded by an imperial phase: 1965 to 1968, followed by an apotheosis, 1969 to 1970. Barry's run of late-sixties soundtracks mirrored the Beatles' albums in the sense that each one was palpably different from the last. Just as when the Fabs found a formula they would immediately break it, Barry – by nature a contrarian – never turned out standard scores. Each soundtrack was a bespoke creation for the film in which it was to be used. And, like the Beatles, he could write quickly under pressure. The theme tune for *Thunderball* was written in four days, when the film's producers wanted the name of the movie in the song. 'Midnight Cowboy' was apparently written in twenty minutes. 'Born Free', which won him an Oscar, in ten.

It would be stretching credulity to suggest Barry's music had the same cultural impact as the Beatles', yet 'The James Bond Theme' must be one of the most recognisable melodies in the Western world. Indeed, in the 1960s, one could argue that the only serious songwriting competitor the Beatles had – in terms of actual exposure to listeners – was John Barry. By 1969, almost a billion people had watched a James Bond film: all would have been familiar with Barry's vivid, soaring melodies. The competition wasn't Elvis or the Rolling Stones, but a self-assured, softly spoken man from York.

As with Lennon, it would take me a while to form an idea of the man who'd created the music. After many hours in the bedroom, poring over liner notes and biographical snippets found in books on the Bond series, a picture began to emerge. John Barry Prendergast (he wisely dropped his last name in the 1950s) appeared to have possessed a somewhat contradictory nature. On the one hand quiet and considered, a composer of sweeping romantic scores; on the other a gloriously bluff Yorkshireman who would take part in Q and A at Bond conventions with a pint of Boddingtons at his elbow. He often dismissed his 007 scores as 'million dollar Mickey Mouse music'.[5] He called the unbreakable tenet that music in a film should always go unnoticed 'an old wives tale'.[6] Although directors liked working with him for his professionalism, he had a reputation in the industry as an intractable taskmaster, a perfectionist.

By 1966, John Barry was living like a Beatle. The success of Bond and 'Born Free' meant, as *Newsweek* put it, he was able to live 'his E-type life with his E-type wife' in a desirable part of London. There is a well-known photograph of Barry, a slight, handsome man, sitting on a Charles Eames chair in his Cadogan Square flat. Rows of LPs and a piano stand in one corner; a copy of *Cashbox* magazine lies open on the coffee table. A black Bakelite phone nestles on a white rug. He's sporting a mod button-down shirt, the sort George Harrison could be seen wearing in 1966. He looks vaguely stroppy. His expression says: get on with it. We feel like we're distracting him from his work, but want to linger. Is that a framed Goya print on the wall? Or even an original Picasso sketch of Françoise Gilot over the piano? There's an air of intellectual curiosity. A bookcase filled with hardbacks is visible above Barry's head. Paul McCartney – another 'northern upstart', in the offensive parlance of the Establishment – staying at the Ashers', across town in Wimpole Street, might have been breathing in the same cultivated atmosphere. Plays, films, books, art: all would inform the Beatles' and Barry's key work from the mid-sixties onwards.

Long before the epiphany of *Revolver*, the first James Bond film I remember watching on television was *You Only Live Twice*, on a Sunday evening in 1977. Sitting on scatter cushions, wearing loud pyjamas, a melting choc ice in hand, I recall those two hours as an episode of dissipation; an almost total sensual immersion. Not just because of the obviously risqué content, but the surface elements: the music, the set design, and, especially, the colours. Every Bond film after *Moonraker* ignores the importance of this last aspect to its detriment. Simon Winder notes the sheer 'muted tastiness' of the film stock used in *From Russia with Love*. (He dismisses the 'lurid and grainy'[7] tones of *The Man with the Golden Gun*, but he's mistaken. To my eyes, at the ABC St Albans, where I first saw it, *Golden Gun* was as glam as a weekend in Tokyo.) Barry's music seemed to intensify, amplify these colours. His limpid, Debussy-influenced score for *Thunderball* perfectly suits a film that is floodlit from below in pale swimming-pool blues and malachite greens. *Goldfinger*'s percussion-heavy soundtrack suggests the clinking of coins, adding immeasurably to the burnished glow that pervades almost every scene in the movie. Similarly, the odd cymbalom and Moog combinations in *On Her Majesty's Secret Service* are somehow of a piece with the futuristic, late-sixties orange used in that film. This is why Bond is perfect for children, or early adolescents: it's all surfaces. The plots didn't matter as much: I didn't fully understand them, and, anyway, to a twelve-year-old they were always the same.

Moreover, it's hard to believe it was an accident the films were often shown on a Sunday. I like to think that ITV was aware of the crushing banality of a 1970s Sunday, with school or work looming the next day, and felt the nation needed some escapism. A glance through the 19–25 November 1977 edition of the *TV Times* (yes, of course I still own it) reveals a stifling consumerism at odds with any young music-obsessed mind. It's the advertisements rather than the listings that are most revealing. Hoseasons boating holidays, Lulu's Freemans catalogue, home organs ('incredible value!'), Kathie Webber's cookery cards, *Birds in Autumn and Winter* by Yootha Joyce, John Player cigarettes, hi-fis, tellies, Townsend Thoresen ferries, Pontins, Butlin's, Germolene, *margarine* . . . In among this litany, it is revealed that on Sunday 20 November, after *100 Best Hymns* and *Family Fortunes*, *You Only Live Twice* was shown.

It was impossible to go back to normal life on Monday morning.

David Arnold, composer of many of the later 007 scores, suggests that *You Only Live Twice* is the perfect introduction to Barry's music. In the first five minutes, all the stirring trademarks are present: the rambunctious 'James Bond Theme', the solemn, menacing 'Space March'; the soaring, deliquescent theme tune. However, at the time, the music, always accessible – invariably memorable – seemed somehow otherworldly. Like the Beatles' music, it didn't always go where you expected it to. It's now clear that Barry scored brass instruments higher than most composers would dare; used odd harmonies and voicings, employed calculated dissonances. In my mind, the boundary between the two Bs started to blur. Helpfully, George Harrison had been investigating Indian music systems at around the same time Barry had been using Eastern European scales, on Hungarian or Egyptian instruments such as the cymbalom or the kantele. This peculiar music was like nothing I'd ever heard before. At least, it was certainly nothing like the Boomtown Rats.

But perhaps the chief link between the two Bs – and one

that I unconsciously knew, aged twelve – was Barry's distinction as a songwriter. This was remarkable in his line of work. Apart from Ennio Morricone, few film composers possessed such a melodic gift, or if they did they were unwilling to use it. Barry's mastery of classic song structure from the twenties – two eights, a middle eight or bridge, and a last eight – was equal to Lennon–McCartney. And knowing the rules, he would gleefully break them. One of the first hybrid tunes the British public would have heard, five years before 'A Day In The Life' was 'The James Bond Theme'. An instrumental that changed style halfway through (shifting from a menacing minor key guitar riff to a big-band middle eight) just wasn't done in 1962.

By 1967, the two Bs were at the very top of their respective games. In that year, Barry wrote 'You Only Live Twice', arguably the pinnacle of his career as a songwriter. Much admired and covered by other artists, it is, along with 'We Have All the Time in the World', one of a handful of songs that Lennon and McCartney might have been happy to have written themselves. The Beatles were instinctive composers; some of the more advanced chords they used often suggested by the shape their fingers made on their guitar necks. (Take the sixth chord that closes many of their early songs. An A-shaped C at the third fret can easily be transmuted to a C6 with a little accidental overlapping of the pinkie. It's possible to imagine Lennon achieving this with his fleshy digits, and deciding that he liked the sound.) Barry, with his 'music by maths' correspondence courses in composition, was almost the opposite: a cerebral songwriter. But his mournful, elegant melodies also derive from his unusual chord choices. On first listen, 'You Only Live Twice' seems to be merely F, B-flat, C. I-IV-V – the 'three chord trick', the first thing a novice guitar player learns. 'Wild Thing'. 'Louie Louie'. (Most pop music is based on the three-chord trick, which derives from twelve-bar blues structure. Using the Roman numeral system for any particular key: the I is the home chord, the IV moves it on, then back to the I, then finally, to complete the sequence, the V. Sometimes known as 'the turnaround'. And then back once again to the I: resolution. Repeat ad nauseam.) On closer scrutiny, 'You Only Live Twice' is revealed as a meticulous construction. The substitutions – the juxtaposition of majors and minors within the I-IV-V framework – conspire to create a harmony that is freighted with yearning: the archetypal haunting melody, and the perfect bed for Leslie Bricusse's existential lyric. Much of this is achieved through languid non-chord notes or 'tensions' – augmented fifths deliberately used on key words: '*pay*', or the '*live*' of 'live twice'. Sophisticated songwriting of this type – employing subtle devices to manipulate the listener emotionally – was not all that common in the hit parade of 1967. Once again, the competition wasn't the Rolling Stones.

For me, 'You Only Live Twice' is a Memory Song. A piece of music so bound up with my past it is almost a physical part of it, like an old school book. I only have to hear those unwinding strings (high on haunt factor), those first few seconds of cello, to know that in moments I will be transported magically back to another life.

In this way, perhaps most of our favourite songs become

Memory Songs. On hearing a much-loved piece of music we are aware of a hierarchy of associations, beginning with the initial connection – the time in which we first heard it – and then successive ones, until the piece is like an Old Master canvas, painted over and over. Sometimes we have to work hard to bring back the first association. When a song we are very familiar with appears on the radio it can take an immense effort of will to conjure up *that* school term, or that particular summer. But it always seems to be there somewhere inside the song, a connection that cannot be undone, no matter how many other periods of our lives have been accompanied by the tune. (Paradoxically, hated songs are often most effective at precipitating the 'first' memory. This is unfortunate, and another reason never to listen to Magic FM.)

It is often the texture or timbre, the *grain* of the music, that brings us back mysteriously, deliciously, to that first association. The Beatles' songs are especially rich in this respect as, post-1966, they treated almost everything they recorded with studio effects. How potent a madeleine is the phased backing vocal on 'Magical Mystery Tour' (*Roll up!*)? Or the picked, chorus-infused acoustic guitar parts in 'Dear Prudence'? Or Lennon's slurred vari-speed vowels on 'Strawberry Fields Forever'?

In terms of Proustian transportation back to the past, I never have to work too hard with 'You Only Live Twice'. Just a second or two of Barry's strings, or Nancy Sinatra's sweet double-tracked voice, and I'm there: sitting on those scatter cushions, melting choc ice in hand, watching an 'oriental' Sean Connery – bathed in a ghostly purplish light

– toss a stone into a volcano's lake . . . which then opens unbelievably onto the villain's empire below.

*

If one had to say which Beatle John Barry most resembled it would be John Lennon: tough, spiky, no-nonsense. But in many ways he was closer to McCartney – hard-working, professional, inquisitive; the same neatness as a composer. On the other hand, perhaps he had more in common with George Harrison: a saturnine disposition and an interest in world music. Or maybe he was more like Ringo, who returned to England when the Beatles were in India because he missed baked beans. Down to earth; a Boddingtons man. In fact, he was all four, a one-man Beatles – a beguiling set of contradictions and, in the sixties at least, an equal as a creative force.

Ultimately, by the end of that decade, a deep personal sadness seemed to be informing the work of the two Bs. Barry, who is on record as hating 'happy music',[8] had so far been able to mask what Norman Mailer called 'the wound'[9] – the unhappy childhood that shapes the artist. Lennon and McCartney both lost their mothers at an early age; Barry was, in his own words, 'a fucked-up Catholic'.[10] By 1968 the wound was beginning to show. The Beatles produced 'Hey Jude' and 'Let It Be'; Barry wrote 'Midnight Cowboy'. These affecting, elegiac songs were an apt soundtrack for the times. As the sixties drew to a close, America simmered with racial tension and anti-Vietnam sentiments; in Britain, Enoch Powell gave his 'rivers of blood' speech. Demonstrations in leafy London squares erupted into violence. Peace and love was giving way to hate and war.

And none of it had the slightest impact on me. Looking up into the blue skies of 1968–9 from the double pram I shared with my twin, I was unaware that butchery and torture on an unimaginable scale was taking place. Outside, in the wider world, on the radio and in the cinemas, the harmonica theme from *Midnight Cowboy* played. Its four descending notes – a variation on the lament figure; the ancient signifier for melancholy (with which I would later become mildly obsessed) became a fitting musical backdrop to the end of the dream.

Six months after Lennon's death, in 1981, I found myself at a convention held by the James Bond Fan Club in a west London conference hotel. At these events, members of the 007 cast and crew would participate in Q and A sessions. It was unbearably exciting for a schoolboy to have Desmond Llewelyn – Q! – a man almost certainly born in a tweed suit, sitting a few feet away, demonstrating gadgets. The same thick fingers had shown Sean Connery how to use the attaché case in *From Russia with Love*. At this particular convention, unnoticed at the back of the room, was a young, bearded Pierce Brosnan. He was accompanying his wife, Cassandra Harris, soon to be in the new James Bond film, *For Your Eyes Only*.

That June, the Royal charity premiere of *For Your Eyes Only* took place at the Odeon Leicester Square. It was here that the dream really came to an end. As a member of the fan club, I'd been lucky enough to get hold of tickets. I waited with my mum and my brother in the crowd outside the cinema, limousines gliding by, feeling insignificant and provincial. First to arrive was Roger Moore, twinkly and tanned, smoking a very big cigar. Then a huge cheer shot up. Prince Charles and Lady Diana, to be married the following month, made their entrance. In the lobby, where the stars were mingling, I set to work collecting autographs. Lois Maxwell, Miss Moneypenny, was my first scalp. Moneypenny, more matronly and broad in the beam in real life, was, nevertheless, sleekly glamorous. Cubby Broccoli, the Wellesian producer of the 007 series, graciously signed my premiere brochure, dropping ash on it from a cigar even bigger than Moore's. Only Liza Minnelli (I've often wondered why she was there, perhaps she thought it was the *Arthur* premiere) refused to sign her name. I've never forgiven her and have boycotted all her movies ever since.

The film began. I was in the front row. But something was wrong. What was this? In place of the expected John Barry score was a modern soundtrack by a fellow named Bill Conti. Someone had obviously thought that Bond should 'move with the times'. The audience were craning their necks to see Charles and Di in the royal box when a serious transgression was taking place on the screen: Roger Moore, in a chunky cable-knit jumper and a blue body warmer, was running around with Bill Conti's hideous synths in the background. In the words of Noël Coward, when asked by his friend Ian Fleming to play the villain in *Dr No*: 'No, no, no.'[11] Along with Lennon's murder, whose indelible details would continue to haunt me for years, this terrible turn of events seemed to mark the start of a new, more brutal decade.

John Barry eventually returned as the composer for three more films but left the franchise for good in 1987 (by which point the films were merely formulaic exercises in making money for their producers). The series may have run out of ideas in the eighties, but I still listen to the soundtracks to this day. In the end, the Bond collection was sold at a movie fair to buy a Fostex four-track porta-studio. Ironically, the posters bought for pennies from the back of *Film Review* and the Vintage Magazine Shop on Earlham Street are now worth thousands of pounds. At an auction of James Bond memorabilia at Christie's in 1998, I was sure (when I could actually see the vitrines through the curtain of my tears) I had once owned at least ten of the exhibits.

But with Bond seeming increasingly like a childish pre-occupation, the allure of guitars was becoming harder to resist. My dad never got his copy of *Revolver* back. What's more, the spark of the blues discovered in the Beatles was leading me to music of a heavier nature. I was ready for the Hard Stuff. It was time, in the immortal words of Jack Black, to 'Get out the Led'.

2

The Real Stairway

Jimmy Page, Led Zeppelin, and 'Ten Years Gone'

One dull Sunday in 1981, on a family visit to Birmingham, my Uncle Chessh called me into his living room to hear a song. I had just turned thirteen. Knowing I was bored, he'd decided to play me 'the greatest guitar intro of all time'. I remember how he lowered the stylus carefully onto the vinyl, then stood back, as if he'd just lit a firework.

There was a brief crackle, and 'Stairway To Heaven' began. A lone acoustic guitar passage, Jimmy Page's lucid piece of contrary motion – the descending-ascending A minor figure that countless bedroom axemen have tried to learn – emerged steadily from the speakers. It sounded antique, as if it could have been recorded a hundred years ago. With a mischievous look, my uncle left the room to allow me to listen to the rest of the song.

The introduction flowed into a second section, a development of the original statement, accompanied by a naive recorder melody. Then a singer made an entrance. He revealed that, somewhere, there's a lady who knows she can get what she wants, even though the '*stars*' are closed. This strange locution puzzled me for a moment, as the piece worked through several more changes – including the best guitar solo ever recorded – before reaching a rousing, Wagnerian denouement. I was amazed; but didn't quite know what to make of it. Had it featured the greatest intro of all time? Perhaps . . . I put the needle back to side one of the record. The lead track, 'Black Dog', was built on a diabolically complex blues riff. Instantly, a peculiar feeling assailed me, the same carnal frisson I had experienced on hearing 'Taxman' for the first time. On the album's third song, 'The Battle Of Evermore', over a backcloth of bell-like acoustic guitars and mandolins, otherworldly voices invoked archers and angels. It was extraordinary, revelatory music.

The album – *Led Zeppelin IV* – was as baffling in its own way as *Revolver* had been. Yet, just as *Revolver*'s amalgamation of conflicting styles added up to a coherent whole, so *IV*'s odd mix of *Sturm und Drang* and pastoral interludes somehow seemed to work. I stared at the cover. There was no group name or photograph, not even a title – just a mysterious image of a Victorian labourer carrying sticks on his back. On the musty smelling inner sleeve, there were merely four symbols or runes, the song titles, and the lyrics to 'Stairway To Heaven' in an archaic font. Reading them through, I discovered (with a slight feeling of disappointment) that it wasn't the stars that were closed, but the *stores*. The rest of the imagery – the hedgerows and the May Queens, the smoke rings seen through trees, seemed strangely congruent with the music having come from some distant rural past. But why had the band wanted to be anonymous? What type of people had made this music? What did they look like? Why did musical epiphanies always occur on a Sunday? To my impressionable thirteen-year-old mind, the album seemed like a deliberately unsigned artifact, an Easter Island statue or an Avebury monolith, left behind to beguile future generations.

Uncle Chessh (short for Chesshire, his surname) was a charming and knowledgeable host. A tall man in his early thirties, with shrewd, amused, alive eyes; he was more like a groovy older brother than an uncle. He explained who Zeppelin were, when they had been active, what they represented. Apparently most of their songs were about sex, or Satanism. Chessh had been to university in the early seventies, and his collection was packed with Roxy Music, 10cc, solo Beatles and Led Zeppelin. I mean packed in the literal sense, too – the albums were held in the shelf so tightly you had to prise them apart to get to the treasures inside.

I had a feeling Led Zeppelin were about to become my New Favourite Band. (Is there any greater feeling in the world? It's like the beginning of a love affair. You want them all the time, over and over.) Yet surely Zeppelin were 'Heavy Metal'? Hard rock. Would that mean I would have to embrace the entire genre? I wasn't sure I wanted to spend the next year with Whitesnake logos on my school bag, and no girlfriend. Even more pressingly, was 'Stairway

To Heaven' – by common consent their best song – the band's greatest achievement?

*

There is a wonderful moment in the film *It Might Get Loud* where Jimmy Page, The Edge and Jack White are sitting around exchanging ideas and jamming. By this point they've got to know each other quite well; you can see Edge thinking: this is going splendidly, I'm holding my own here. I've sold *x* million records; I can sit and talk informally with a legend like Page. Jack White is thinking: this is cool, I've sold *y* million records; I can kick it with of one of my heroes, when suddenly Page starts playing the riff to 'Whole Lotta Love'. The two younger men are reduced to helpless fan-rubble in the presence of their idol. It is written on their faces that they used to practise this riff as boys in their bedrooms. They are both smiling, as if witnessing the revelation of a long-lost alchemical formula.

It's not surprising that guitarists refer to Page as 'The Guvn'r'. For me, Jimmy Page is the best guitar player in the world. He is also one of my favourite songwriters and record producers. That his talent in these latter fields is often overlooked is fairly predictable; Page's dazzling gifts as a guitarist are what he'll be remembered for.

During the film, we're shown Page's engagingly childlike enthusiasm for the vinyl of his youth. In a study lined with records he digs out a copy of Link Wray's 'Rumble'. As soon as the song begins, the famous Cheshire cat grin spreads across his face. Halfway through the tune, Page points out that the vibrato on Link Wray's amp increases, becomes 'more intense'.[1] This is what made Page a great producer: he was alive to the nuances of texture that make a record. More importantly, he praises the 'profound attitude' in 'Rumble'. This notion would be useful later when I tried to reconcile a love of Zeppelin with the Clash and Manic Street Preachers. It was clear that great music on its own wasn't enough: there had to be *attitude*. This could be expressed by a vocal inflection, the clothes the band wore, what they included on a record; what they left out. It always seemed that Zeppelin, alone among their contemporaries, had that primitive punk spirit, that attitude. Page's virtuosity was always less important than his vitality, his rock 'n' roll sensibility. Indeed, live, he was often the sloppiest of the guitar greats, but somehow greater for it. He was willing to sacrifice precision for excitement. It came as no surprise that Zeppelin used to cover Eddie Cochran's 'Something Else', a song also reimagined by the Sex Pistols in *The Great Rock 'n' Roll Swindle*. Further, Plant and Page used to visit the Roxy in 1977 to see the Damned, the only prominent members of the old guard to do so.

Later in the film, The Edge shows Page how to play U2's 'I Will Follow'. Jimmy asks The Edge if he's 'sure about that C?' (The bass under the riff moves jarringly from E to C.) When The Edge replies in the affirmative, Page tries it again and agrees that, yes, it *does* work, in fact it's 'roaring'.[2] The Edge declares that it's 'punk', adding that maybe Jimmy has a 'bit of punk rock' in him . . .

Just as there had been a dearth of Bond stuff, there was a noticeable *lack* of Zep. Back in 1981, the only picture of the group I could find was a smudgy photograph in an old pop annual, part of a quiz at the back of the book. It seemed as if they were sitting on a sofa in a line, but I imagined that they were on their own private jet after a gig. Later, I discovered this was true. What a wild, excessive life they must have lived! What enormodomes they would have played! They *looked* like a band: an insular unit, a cadre that had experienced much together – a four-man us-against-the-world cell. But the main impression, aided by the graininess of the image and the gig-sweat drying on their faces, was that they looked dangerous, sexual – utterly debauched.

Around this time, something that had happened a few years earlier came back to me. One balmy summer's night, in my mum's lounge, sitting with her by the open window, I asked: 'What's that sound in the distance?' She replied: 'They're having a pop concert at Knebworth.' I now know that it was Zeppelin. Knebworth was ten miles away, yet they were still audible. I would like to say it sounded like distant thunder, sweet devilish melodies on the breeze, 'the hammer of the gods'. But it was more like the rubbish collection at 6 a.m.: remote, stop-start, muffled, annoying. It's a shame, as it is probably the closest I'll come to experiencing Led Zeppelin in concert. This distant memory, the picture in the pop annual, and the album session at my uncle's, was, for now, all I had to go on.

Then, one Saturday afternoon, *Pop Quiz* – the far more innocent predecessor of *Never Mind the Buzzcocks* – showed a clip of Zeppelin playing 'Black Dog'. The fact that it was from a movie, *The Song Remains the Same*, shot on 35mm Eastman Color and not the usual video, elevated it to the glossy immortality of Bond or *Star Wars*. So *this* was what they looked like. The two frontmen shimmied around the stage with a fluent grace, a carnal agility not usually associated with white Englishmen. They possessed that easy facility for movement great dancers have. Under the lights and in the dry ice, they seemed completely relaxed – gods with the world at their feet. Apollo, and a diabolic Pan in strange, dragon-design bell-bottoms. Sometimes they would tilt their heads together and smile in an almost homoerotic celebration of the noise they were creating. Thrillingly, the song being played was one of the tunes I had first heard at my uncle's, the one with the tricky blues riff that fights against the drums. The following week, with all my pocket money, I went out and bought a Led Zeppelin album: *Physical Graffiti*.

The summer of this purchase was dominated by Culture Club, ABC, the Associates, and an emerging new group called Duran Duran. During this time, I listened exclusively to one band: Led Zeppelin. It was a very hot summer. I wore Dunlop sneakers, wide blue jeans, a collarless shirt, and a heavy, padded green army jacket. My hair was an unfashionable approximation of Robert Plant's, circa 1968 (any longer and the school would have intervened). The sweaty, deeply uncool combination of these fashion choices, and my lamentable hairstyle, ensured I wouldn't have a girlfriend for many, many years. But at least I had my Zep album.

A decisive leap from *Led Zeppelin IV*, *Physical Graffiti* is an inexhaustible source of pleasure. Its fifteen songs fuse an impressively diverse list of musical genres. Hard rock, pop rock, blues, bubblegum pop, funk, fifties rock 'n' roll, folk, and Indian classical. In the ferocity of some of the playing, the album even prefigures punk (John Lydon was allegedly a fan). It is one of the great eclectic records by a British band at the peak of their career, part of a lineage that includes *The White Album*, *London Calling* and *Parklife*. It is a team effort: Jimmy Page – the controlling intelligence behind the project – is wizardly throughout; Robert Plant's vocals are miraculous, his phrasing and timbre perfect; John Paul Jones – using his experience as a musical director in the sixties – excels as an arranger and multi-instrumentalist; and John Bonham, keeping his head down, just *pummels*.

But then, he doesn't.

Pummeling is only what it sounds like. Bonzo was simultaneously the heaviest and lightest of drummers. For a big man from the Midlands he was surprisingly light on his feet. Listen to the early live version of 'I Can't Quit You Baby' from the Albert Hall. The first chord – a massive D9 – is propelled by a kick-drum strike so thunderous it hits the back of the hall like a howitzer shell. We can hear the decaying Italianate venue shudder as it bounces off the Dress Circle. But it is the fluid footwork that follows – impossible kick-drum clusters and unexpected accents – that demonstrate his paradoxical lightness of touch, the 'swing' that he became famous for. He was twenty-one at the time, and already the best drummer in the world.

Physical Graffiti is an apt title. Most of the music is gloriously visceral. The first track, 'Custard Pie', forcefully requests our attention. Like 'Black Dog', it is extraordinarily heavy – the purposive riff is archetypal machete-Zep in Page's favourite key of A major. But there is something else in the bleached-out sound picture that accosts us. It is the tinder-dry, middle-less oddity of the mix that exerts a sort of suffocating forward pressure. This is what it feels like we're up against, listening to 'Custard Pie' on big speakers . . . As the song fades, we're presented with an example of Page's attention to detail in the studio. Before computer-automated mixing desks, the producer would manually push the faders up and down, adjusting the elements of the sound as the track progressed. This allowed the music to breathe; lent it a living, dynamic quality – made it appear to contain peaks and troughs, rather than just progressing in a straight line. At 3.40, after yet another of Plant's lubricious exhortations, Page nudges the fader on Bonham's floor-tom for two savage, booming deep hits that threaten to sink the entire mix. It's a marvellous moment, a lovely surprise for the listener. Page excelled at these tricks. He often used Plant's voice in a similar fashion, 'ghosting' it behind a guitar phrase for extra effect. ('Whole Lotta Love': the strangled '*yeuah!*' just before the orgasm of the solo.)

The intended centrepiece of the album was 'Ten Years Gone'. It was Page's favourite on the record; he had quietly high hopes for it. That it was immediately usurped in the fans' affections by the panoramic 'Kashmir' was not surprising. The latter song's mesmeric riff in ascending half-steps, its sparse yet lush mix that has so much space it's almost 3D, its dazzling Eastern string colourings, its ensemble playing that is taut yet free and breathing – all generate a cumulative effect that is epic, intoxicating. Given all this, it was inevitable that 'Kashmir' would become 'the new Stairway'.

'Ten Years Gone', however, was a more modest proposal. It was originally intended as an instrumental with three distinct sections until Plant came up with the lyric. The song begins with a simple two-chord pattern: a seesaw between a reflective A9 and a mild, questioning F6. Then, after a discursive foray through a jazzy E-flat diminished and a couple of breezy major sevenths, a dramatic motif – revealing the guitar to be in a drop-D tuning – announces the beginning of the song proper.

The riff that follows forms the body of the song, and is one of Page's loveliest cyclical sequences. It incorporates the lament figure – the stepwise chromatic descent – but unlike 'Stairway To Heaven', where it is obvious, here it is hidden slyly in the middle of the chord, starting on the seventh and descending to the fifth.

Plant's lyric, one of his most celebrated, strains for poetic effect (whereas 'Kashmir' succeeds spectacularly without trying). It doesn't matter; we forgive the lines about eagles for a couple of killer punches later in the tune. The song is generally accepted to be about Plant's first girlfriend. She asked him to choose between her and his music; he chose music. Ten years later, he's beginning to have regrets.

The emotional core of the song, its high point, is the middle eight. Here, the yearning music and the lyric are in perfect congruence. Plant asks if we ever needed somebody. Indeed, whether we ever needed anyone *bad*? And Page, in one huge, swooping backwards pick-stroke hits a resounding, elegiac Dadd9. This tremendous, startling, rich chord – and the line that precedes it – is the first punch.

The second blow follows soon enough. After mourning his mistakes for a few more lines, Plant finally gets down to business; what every teenager is preoccupied with: losing it. His strangely nasal, keening Black Country voice informs us it was his girlfriend's first time, too, and that he knew she 'would'. It is a slender reference amid all the courtly love, but it's there, like a hard-on through albescent denim.

The song, and its middle eight in particular, personified something that had been troubling at the time: the dichotomy between love and lust. Like many sensitive teenage males, with no sisters, and an inmate of an all-boys school, I was engrossed by an idea that had originated in the Bible: love serves others; lust serves itself. How could one reconcile the impulse to idealise the opposite sex with one's baser instincts? This is what concerned me in my sweltering bedroom, in the summer of 1982.

Finally, as the song begins its fade, teeming layers of overdubs – Page's rococo 'guitar army' – complete the sound picture. Bonham and Jones, unobtrusive and adroit throughout, continue to play with an almost jazzy dexterity. After 'Stairway To Heaven', Page was always trying to write another epic piece that would showcase all four of their talents. Which song would become 'the new Stairway'? Was it 'Kashmir'? 'In The Light'? 'Achilles Last Stand'? The jury was still out, smoking weed.

One thing painfully apparent back then was how uncool my love for 'Ten Years Gone' made me. Long before the rise of today's heritage rock industry, in which Zeppelin hold an elevated rank, there was a bleak period when it was virtually illegal to like them. The band had never been fashionable in the seventies; by the early eighties they were almost an offence against the hip, a kind of shorthand for the excesses of the previous decade. Many in the media were eager to pillory them. There is a lamentable YouTube clip of Jimmy Page and Roy Harper being interviewed for *The Old Grey Whistle Test* in 1984. They're halfway up a mountain; Page has a nearly empty bottle of wine at his side. He would have just turned forty, his hair shorter and betraying traces of grey. The interview is ostensibly to promote their new projects but feels more like a stitch-up piece of broadcast journalism. The sniggering tone of the interviewer, Mark Ellen, implies that these shambling old men with their guitars are all washed up, now that music played by young guns on synthesisers is what the people want. The bucolic setting, chosen by Harper, is a gift for Ellen, who is keen to cram in as many references to 'getting your head together in the country' and 'seventies rock stars' as he can. Harper reprimands him: 'Seventies rock stars? Eighties, nineties more like.'[3] Perhaps Harper, ever the wild-eyed seer, could see the future. Page, on the other hand, appears diffident. He refers to himself as 'a craftsman, nothing more'. But then, emboldened by the wine, and Harper's rather feeble swipe at Frankie Goes To Hollywood ('Bannock Goes To Frankieburn'), he suddenly denounces the new bands as 'Herman's Hermits with computers'.[4] Page usually comes across in interviews as a likeable fellow – modest, reflective and, above all, generous to other artists. Here his courtesy falters; but there was good reason. (And not just the bottle of red from what we imagine is an extensive cellar.) Page simply thought he had made music that would last; that was as good as the Beatles, and was puzzled as to why it was no longer valued.

These were his years in the wilderness. *He* couldn't see the future, of course – Zeppelin's critical rehabilitation during the nineties; the induction into the Hall Of Fame (US 1995, UK 2006); the veneration of a new wave of artists; the astonishingly steady year-on-year sales; the triumphant show at the O2 in 2007 where over 20 million people applied to see a single concert.

Finally, towards the end of the interview, at the bottom of the screen, a facetious message flashes up: 'Out of Touch'. It is a terribly unfortunate coincidence. 'Out Of Touch' is the title of a Hall and Oates song, the leader in the 'video vote'. But it could be a summation of the nation's, or at least Mark Ellen's, thoughts on Jimmy Page in 1984.

The show cuts back to the studio to reveal Depeche Mode flipping the peace sign and saying 'Neil' (a reference to Nigel Planer's hippy character in *The Young Ones*. People did this a lot to anyone male with long hair around this time). The group blandly concede that Zeppelin 'did their thing at their time'. I recall watching this as it was transmitted – stoned, long-haired, girlfriendless – and thinking, with the characteristic certainty of youth: I know which side I'm on. At that age one defines oneself by what one hates. I couldn't see the future either. The present was all there was: a gaudy hi-tech melange of drum machines, hairspray, hi-top trainers, Howard Jones, and definitely, absolutely, no guitars. To use a six-string in Orwell's year was to be Luddite or 'rockist', according to the *NME*, and other arbiters of cool. The idea of there being a 'retro' era to come was unthinkable, nonsensical. I now think that this was down to one unassailable fact. The eighties were the last truly forward-facing decade. There seemed to be a quaint, almost Victorian belief in 'progress' – that we wouldn't be needing these old guitars now that a more efficient instrument, the synthesiser, had rendered them obsolete.

The year after *The Old Grey Whistle Test* interview, *The Song Remains the Same* was screened at Stevenage ABC. I'd managed to get a girlfriend by then; I took her to see it. I recall she giggled dreamily at Plant's packet, visible through the tightest pair of jeans ever worn. The flares and – there's no other word – *blouses* had dated so quickly. I couldn't have chosen a more anomalous film. It had only been shot twelve years earlier, in 1973, but it may as well have been an Elizabethan costume drama. The Beatles had often looked outrageous, but Zeppelin's seventies livery of kimonos and dragon suits was astonishing. Hanif Kureishi calls the Beatles' psychedelic clothing 'gloriously non-functional',[5] signalling their 'creativity and the pleasures of drug-taking'.[6] The same could be said of Zeppelin's attire, except it seemed all the more shocking and rebellious to me in the mid-eighties. It reinforced the notion that clothes could be transgressive, especially if they ran counter to prevailing tastes. Clothes could convey attitude, could broadcast your identity. And seriously mess up your fertility.

*

Ten years on, walking through sunny Camden at the height of Britpop, I noticed two long-haired fellows being interviewed by a camera crew. They had that aura of having once been famous, and were surrounded by a crowd of onlookers. Drawing closer, I realised it was Page and Plant. Confrontation with one's adolescent heroes is a disquieting experience. My heart was beating faster, I wanted to get a better look; but didn't want them to disappoint me. There was a danger that the golden gods of *The Song Remains the Same* could be exposed as mortal. And so it proved. In the unforgiving natural light they looked immeasurably older. Certainly, Plant's face had coarsened, like a rugged actor's – Sean Connery or Kevin Spacey perhaps. (This *coup de vieux* had started in his twenties. The just-right Plant of 1973 was, only six years later, the craggy man of 1979.) Pagey was still using the hair dye; it would be many years before the dignified silver-fox look of today. But they seemed happy in each other's company, smiling and telling jokes. I left them to it, and rushed back to tell my brother.

Making my way home that day, I thought about the songs on *Physical Graffiti*. It is axiomatic that music is associated with the season in which we first hear it. In my mind, the album will always be connected with a never-ending early adolescent summer. (Apologies if you first heard the record in Moscow during a particularly savage winter.) Titles such as 'Down By The Seaside', or the Shangri Las and summer moons of 'Kashmir' seem to reinforce this. Certainly, 'Ten Years Gone' basks in that eternal sun of dwindling childhood. Moreover, I realise now that Plant's assertion as the song's fades – that he was never going to leave his paramour – was not an unrealistic promise to a girl he hadn't seen for ten years, but a recollection of what their innocent younger selves *used to say* to each other. Like Joe Buck's memory of his sweetheart's words to him as they make love in *Midnight Cowboy*: 'You're the only one Joe, you're the only one.'[7] It is unbearably poignant. It has the complete ring of truth to it; and is one of the reasons why, for me, 'Ten Years Gone' will always be 'the real Stairway'.

3

Bowie's Nose

Pin Ups, the Velvets, and 'The Jean Genie'

Fast forward. A long way forward. In August 2013, aged forty-four, I took the time to visit *David Bowie Is* at the V & A, the first survey of a pop star's work ever held at the museum. On display were guitars, posters, set models, costumes, album sleeves, handwritten lyrics – all manner of curios and relics from the great man's personal archive. In among the tat and ephemera there was even Bowie's coke spoon.

Attendance was healthy. In fact, it was so busy that some exhibits were frustratingly obscured by backs and heads that seemed in no hurry to move. Who were these people? Who were *we*, moving through each room as slowly as folk in a post office queue? Some were tourists, wearing confounded or pleasantly surprised expressions; some bored, indifferent kids with an excited dad, showing off his knowledge of a pop icon who must have seemed as distant to them as Queen Victoria. These fathers were like me, and we exchanged furtive glances. We knew every word of every song piping through speakers into the hot, stuffy rooms.

And despite the air con, it *was* hot. This, and the solemn tempo imposed by a crowded exhibition, slowed the heart rate. Just when I thought I was flagging – Bowied out – I turned a corner into an enormous high-ceilinged space. (Ian Rankin, interviewed on *The Review Show*, called it 'a cathedral'.)[1] It was dark, and people lolled on sofas as if in anticipation of something. Suddenly, a huge video screen crackled into life. Bowie's face, nine metres high – higher even, it seemed – flashed up. He was singing 'The Jean Genie'. A surge of excitement like a drug rush hit me. That dirty, bluesy riff, the E major chord that goes straight to the balls, was thundering out at top volume. My heart seemed to start beating to its rhythm, quickening, sliding easily into its groove just as it had done every time I'd heard it in the last thirty years. What was this? I'd never seen this clip. Or had I? The unexpected excitement had precipitated a second of confusion, a senior moment. I had seen it only once before, on YouTube. It was recently unearthed BBC footage from 1973, long thought to have been wiped. The cameraman had kept the only copy because it showcased a fish-eye lens technique he imagined might find him work. He'd recently found the tape in his garage.

The fish-eye frames flashed up now: the band squeezed into a silver globe like a gigantic bauble on a Christmas tree. A stick-Mick Ronson and a stick-Trevor Bolder, improbably stretched and distorted. Then a wide shot, with 'pushed' LSD colours – effervescent greens, vivacious reds. These effects are now so overfamiliar one barely notices them anymore, but I was seeing them for the first time. The camera zoomed in to reveal a copper-haired Bowie, shirtless under a striped, wide-lapelled bum-freezer jacket. Below this: loose blue peg slacks, and platforms. He was moving effortlessly to the music, diamante earrings brushing his neck. In one hand he held a pair of maracas, in the other a harmonica. His eyes fixed you. Every head in the cathedral had turned and was now concentrating avidly on the performance, even the jaded teenagers. This is a proper pop star, kids! I felt like shouting, but suppressed this dad-like thought and was pulled back to Bowie's eyes. They were cold, and the absence of eyebrows made his black, unreadable, coked-up stare even colder.

Above almost anything else, I associate 'The Jean Genie' with cocaine. Many years earlier I'd attended a stag party that had started at nine in the morning. A full day's activities had been planned: paintballing, go-karting, water-skiing – the usual. We had our work cut out. It began at the Trocadero in Piccadilly Circus, all of us playing video games and snorting huge lines of chang in the gents (we were a classy bunch of bucks). I had to leave early for a gig, and, on the way, in the car, 'The Jean Genie' came on the radio. At that moment, I got it. Just as D Mob's 'We Call It Acieed!' only makes sense on MDMA, or 'A Day In The Life' was designed for tokers, 'The Jean Genie' is best appreciated on a big fat baby's arm of chisel. (I don't take drugs anymore, by the way. Not even in Bowie's honour.) Indeed, only madmen coked to the eyeballs could have created that urgent, persistent heartbeat of a riff. It precisely re-creates the feeling that overcomes you in a public place when the first line is revving you up, but you know you have to keep it together. It's controlled, contained – but only just. All you can think of is the next line. Which comes soon enough, in the form of the euphoric release of the chorus, a monumental B chord, the V.

In pop, the Chord of Euphoria is the V. (It's used to create the building introduction of 'Twist And Shout' – 'Aaahh!' – pushing, begging to be resolved, especially when a bluesy seventh is added.) The excitement is so intolerable there's only one place to go: to the I, the home chord. 'The Jean Genie' takes you back down to the I gently, via the stepping stone of the IV, but then you have to face it: the filthy, mean riff, the home chord of E. Prowling, insistent. Your mind on the next line.

After watching the clip another three times, I decided to return to the exhibition, and real life. One's forties could only go downhill after this. Hearing Bowie sing 'The Jean Genie' had stirred many teenage memories; most, but not all of them, golden . . .

*

The guy who turned me on to Bowie, who introduced me to 'The Jean Genie' at the age of sixteen, was a lower-sixth-former named Duke. (Not his real name: he was known by that handle because of his obsession with The Thin White Duke.) Rangy, smart, self-confident, a year older than me, Duke was about to embark on his final year of studies. His school uniform was a black army greatcoat (called 'Christiane' after the Bowie soundtrack to the cult film *Christiane F.*), assorted chiffon scarves, aviator shades, and costume jewellery, which he continually moved up and down his long, luminously pale forearms, a sort of displacement activity while he talked. His hairstyle, when the holidays allowed, was a Hendrix–Dylan 'fro of black curls. (Think *NME* writer Charles Shaar Murray, circa 1974.) Completing this outrageous look were tight blue jeans and a pair of black Converse hi-tops – the only concession to the group he semi hung out with, 'the Metallers' or 'the Rockers', as they were known. (Duke was far too much of an individualist to belong to any youth tribe.) On anyone else this get-up would have seemed a risible affectation, but Duke pulled it off through sheer force of personality. He was a genial guy, but had a sharp tongue you wouldn't want to be on the wrong side of. He didn't suffer fools. Add to this his working-class credentials, and the fact that he stood over six feet, meant the hard kids left him alone. What he had in abundance was charisma. He would crack open a silver Zippo with a long thumbnail, fire up a Marlboro Red, and in the fading haze of lighter fuel pull the smoke forcefully into his lungs. This made his already Bowie-ish nose flatten, like certain photographs of David singing. Duke sparking up always made me think of the *Ziggy Stardust* soundtrack sleeve – Bowie on fire, and the line about time taking a cigarette from 'Rock 'n' Roll Suicide'. After the fag was lit, Duke would start chuckling about something, an infectious gathering titter, somewhere between a giggle and a cackle, and you knew you were about to hear some scurrilous story or other.

The first words Duke spoke to me – yelled, rather, from the passenger window of a passing car – were, 'I'll bring something to make it worth your while!' It was a week before my sixteenth birthday, the end of summer 1984, and I was walking up the road to my father's house from the off-licence. I looked up just in time to see a head of black curls flash past. It was sticking out of a yellow Mini Cooper, packed to the roof with what appeared to be about fifteen Rockers. He'd seen me with a bag full of booze, deduced my party was that night, and invited himself on the promise of some free whisky. Ah well, that's the house smashed up then, I remember thinking. (I was living mostly at my dad's by now, looking after the house during the week while he was away working in France.) I'd been vaguely aware of Duke – seen him around – an older music head. But I hadn't spoken to him. He was L6, I was fifth form, and upper years seldom socialised with lower.

That night, he showed up with the Rockers, as threatened.

They barged in, changed the music . . . and started drinking peacefully from tetra-packs of cider. It turned out the Rockers, like that other youth tribe Goths, were essentially a gentle breed, into their music, drink and smoke. As Duke sipped his Jack, he proceeded to tell me about all the bands he'd seen live. The Alarm, Marillion, Bauhaus, Hanoi Rocks, the Cramps, Bowie . . . I was amazed, not just at the quantity, but the multiplicity. Surely, in order to belong, you had to like only one type of music and stick to it, cultivate an identity? Not so. For Duke, there was no such thing as a guilty pleasure (he was thirty years ahead of his time; nowadays it seems everyone has an eclectic taste). All music was there for the taking, and, as a consequence, he lived all his musical lives simultaneously.

Exhaling a cumulonimbus of Marlboro smoke, Duke casually took a ten of diamonds from his coat pocket. The Alarm's Mike Peters had thrown the card to the audience at the Hammersmith Palais, during 'Where Were You Hiding When The Storm Broke?'. Duke had slipped backstage and chatted with the band after the show. My jaw must have dropped. I knew he was probably embellishing a bit for me, to impress the younger kid, but it didn't matter. When would I go to concerts in London and hang out with the band? It seemed like a fabulous world of grown-up licence. After a summer recovering from the O levels, and the sixth form looming ominously, I badly needed to believe a fabulous world of grown-up licence might someday be mine. With my brother, I had spent the holidays getting smashed and stoned every night, a six-week saturnalia that had been a reaction to five long years of toil. I'd somehow gained eleven O levels, but at a price. I was burned out, and didn't relish the thought of another pile of textbooks. Furthermore, hampering any academic ambitions was a new obsession: our band, a three-piece power trio (completed by the school's star drummer, a kid with the unlikely name of Desmond), already rehearsing and recording demos. We'd christened the group Fly Agaric, after the hallucinogenic mushroom, a name that had once caused the owner of a local rehearsal studio to raise an eyebrow and say, 'I wonder what sort of music *you lot* play.' We'd both started on guitar, but somehow I'd ended up on bass. I was the singer, though, and this was fine by me. Some of my heroes were singer-bass players: McCartney, Brian Wilson, Jack Bruce (no, not fucking Sting). I was writing, too. The compulsion to put words on paper had begun at thirteen, around the same time as prolific self-abuse. Managing both habits was, by now, like holding down two jobs. As the summer of '84 came to an end, I'd been writing lyrics and music seriously for two years. Moreover, a clear objective had formed: the band would one day move away from Hitchin and make records.

Live appearances, however, had been scanty. Somehow we'd been allowed to play the school concert (it's hard to overstate the blasphemy of this act in a space where we normally sang hymns), but, apart from this, and a best-forgotten shambles at a Christian Youth Club, we were a bedroom band. It was useful that I was acting as custodian of my dad's house in the week; we could rehearse and take drugs in peace. The only disadvantage was that his home had swiftly acquired a reputation as a party venue, and this had become a source of tension over the summer. My father didn't approve of the band, and suspected large quantities of marijuana were being smoked. The words 'layabout' and 'haircut' had been aimed at my spotty, long-haired head. And this wasn't the only family discord. On the other side of town, at my other home, things weren't much better. My mother had remarried, and her new husband, a lanky ignoramus from Barnsley, would lash out with a hand or foot – or belt, even – when he suspected you of 'cheeking' him. Calling him my step-dad aroused murderous feelings in me. I didn't know which was worse – living at my mum's or my dad's. But I did know one thing: it would all end in tears, probably mine.

Back at the party, Duke was still talking. He revealed he was also in a band, named A Roomful of Psychopathic Psychiatrists, and they played a song, 'Billy's Paranoid About Rivers', a reference to one of the band members, PsychoBilly. 'I'll introduce you – you'll love 'im!' he shouted over the music. I wasn't sure I wanted to meet this dangerous lunatic. Finally, Duke announced he hated school more than anyone else, and was going to write for *Sounds*.

My head was spinning, and not just from the cider. The party was animated now, everyone drinking and pogo-ing to AC/DC's *Back in Black*. The guitars came out. Duke looked on, cackling, as my brother – a shit-eating, Page-like grin on his face – played a wild feedback version of 'Whole Lotta Love' on his knees. I kept rhythm on a gut-string Spanish guitar. Then Duke walked on *his* knees in the full lotus position, his party trick apparently. That he did this to the accompaniment of 'Have A Drink On Me', while smoking a cigarette, is astonishing even now.

For days afterwards, I hoped Duke would call. But it turned out he didn't socialise in the week, instead staying at home, 'playing records'. It was a week later, at one of Hitchin's many underage-friendly pubs, the Sun, that Duke finally resurfaced. I was sitting listening to my contemporaries talk boringly about the imminent sixth form, when I caught sight of a tall figure in black. This apparition moved through the bar, Hendrix hair restrained by a headband, plastic jewels visible over the cuffs of his greatcoat. There was a murmur of amusement from the lager-swilling rugger players present at this guy dressed like a rock star for a night down the pub, but I was thinking: what a dude. With him was a diminutive, polite-looking kid in an Aran sweater. Intense, animated, agreeably unassuming; I vaguely knew him to be an upper sixth former, studying the sciences. It was PsychoBilly.

No way. It couldn't be . . .

But apparently everyone in A Roomful of Psychopathic Psychiatrists had the 'Psycho' prefix; it wasn't an indicator of personality. There was even a PsychoNicky. ('I'll introduce you – you'll love 'im!') It was here that Duke admitted A Roomful of Psychopathic Psychiatrists wasn't really a proper band. However, he knew Jude and I had a group that actually played instruments, and offered to roadie for us. (There was a rumour of a gig in Chelmsford.) Instantly, we continued where we'd left off. Music, music, music. It transpired Duke wrote lyrics, too, or poems, rather. What were they about? 'Ah, you know, anti-parent, personal break-up, that type of thing,' he said, looking down at the Guinness he was stirring with a long finger. We agreed to swap our stuff. When Billy – who preferred to be called Bill – joined the conversation I instantly warmed to him. He possessed a formidable intelligence, and a wild enthusiasm for music that surpassed even mine. Strange-sounding groups were his thing: Psychic TV, the Fall, Blood and Roses, Current 93, the Milkshakes. But also esoteric female artists such as Kate Bush, Anja Huwe of Xmal Deutschland, and Cosey Fanni

Tutti from Throbbing Gristle. I could scarcely breathe with excitement. We left at closing time, shades on. It was all arranged. I was going to teach Duke guitar, and he would write our first review for the music papers.

Walking back to Duke's council flat that night, where he lived with his dad, past the town's large Victorian cemetery, I discovered his parents had split, too. This was mildly surprising; divorce wasn't as common then as it is now. I told him about the time our English teacher had asked the class if anyone had parents that were separated. The only two people to show their hands were me and my brother. It was getting heavy at home, I said; something bad was going to happen soon. By unspoken agreement, we steered the subject back to the safer waters of music. Duke raved about Bowie, and Hanoi Rocks – his 'pet band'. Then the Smiths, and Dead or Alive. Abruptly, he started laughing the laugh. What was funny?

'I saw them at the Palais, and Pete Burns was wearing this leotard. 'e was posing away at the front when one of 'is nuts popped out, and stayed out 'til the end of the gig. The front row was in stitches, man. Burns was oblivious.'

We woke the dead with our laughter. This kid was completely on my wavelength. And the fact that he was hanging out with a fifth former was more than slightly flattering. I took my leave and walked home, my mind reeling. That evening there was a coolness to the air, a fresh autumn note already. The new term would soon be here. A thousand stars were above, and as many possibilities ahead.

Apart from music, Duke's other enthusiasm was books. It

had been exciting to discover words were as important to him as they were to me. One man had fostered this interest, our head of English, Mr Wood, the Puckish, intense Renaissance man who'd asked the class about film music. For the past three years he'd been steeping us in Eliot, Lawrence, Shakespeare, Dickens, Henry James, Conrad. The canon. My brother and I were already readers, but Mr Wood had somehow converted the rest of the class. He'd made Eng. Lit. seem as exciting to a bunch of disinterested schoolboys as rock music; such were his energies, his innate talent for communication. Along with the beard, Mr Wood wore Lennon specs, and a floppy rug slightly shorter than John's on the cover of *Let It Be.* Although his tastes were classical ('How are you as a class for opera?'), it was rumoured he was an *Abbey Road* nut. This is not to say he was a groovy, down-with-the-kids teacher; he wasn't. Indeed, the lack of this affectation was one of the reasons he commanded respect. His classroom was always immaculately silent. There was an alert, unflinching intelligence at work behind those avid, penetrating, grey-blue eyes that made you careful how you trod around him. The only acknowledgement he gave our extra-curricular predilections was a droll remark once, when handing out textbooks: 'If you ever feel like a *Hamlet* and marijuana party, these notes might be useful . . .' His teaching strategy was unique: he treated us as equals, and took care to praise and encourage everyone, even the nuggets at the back. It worked. We raised our game. It was a relief, too: most of the other teachers – a grim collection of sports obsessed oddballs and boy-gropers – dealt in sarcastic put-downs and arbitrary cruelties. In short (and he was rather short), he was our Miss Jean Brodie.

One day, at the start of the Third Year, Mr Wood had strolled into the classroom with a gleam in his eye, and said:

'This term I'd like you all to write a novel.'

There was a stunned silence.

'Really, sir? Won't that be a lot of work?' said someone, at the back.

'Yes, but it will help with your understanding of some of the texts on the syllabus.'

'Oh. OK. Can it be about anything we want, sir?'

'Yes, any subject you like. But as I've said to you before, with creative writing, *it's best to write about what you know*.'

We ignored him. My brother's effort was an occult yarn set in the Channel Islands, with the still hilarious title 'Fear of the Goat'. There's probably an upper limit on how good a novel entitled 'Fear of the Goat' written by a thirteen and-a-half-year-old can be, and I don't think he exceeded it. My friend Ian Carter's offering, more of a novella, was a fantasy based on his favourite group, Queen, in which he became a member of the band. Written in biro, it filled a small exercise book. I went one better and set mine in the Vietnam War. How hard could it be? In the name of research, I found Betamax copies of *The Deer Hunter* and *Apocalypse Now*, and wheeled the enormous school TV and VCR on its trolley into the English block for lunchtime viewings. It was a good excuse to avoid the freezing, violent playground. A doss, to use the parlance. Every night after school, instead of bashing the bishop, I bashed away on an old, black iron typewriter. ('The Imperial Typewriter Co. Leicester'. How I wish I still owned it.) I used a lot of Tipp-Ex. The result, for some reason, was a dismal, cliché-ridden conflation of all the war films I'd ever seen. It didn't matter; it was all writing. Perhaps some of the discipline needed to complete the novel would find its way into the songwriting. That was the plan anyway.

Around this time, Mr Wood put my brother and I forward for a national short story competition. When, after some kind of mistake on the part of the judges, Jude won first prize and I second, he bought his first electric guitar with the prize money: a Westbury Standard in burgundy, with double DiMarzio humbucker pick-ups, and a beautiful unbound rosewood fretboard. The only snag was he couldn't hear it. For weeks the Westbury lay in its plush purple coffin, thrillingly lifeless. (The scratchy sound of a chord played on a non-plugged-in axe still gives me a shiver of excitement.) The next step had to be an amplifier. That Christmas, a black fifty-watt Laney combo, the size of the old school telly, sat under the tree. Soon, I'd saved enough pocket money to buy myself an electric (a Fender Bullet, cream with a white scratchplate, a proper Fender case, the works). But there was still only one amp. The problem was solved by plugging two guitars in at once. By the time we played in front of Duke at the party, my brother was an accomplished blues lead guitarist, and I was pretty mean on rhythm, the result of many guitar lessons and many more hours of practice. Despite this, the band had yet to really play live. I settled for posing in gig gear. It was harder to move like Jimmy Page than he'd made it look . . .

But something was bothering me about Led Zeppelin by now. As great as Plant's lyrics sometimes were, often they weren't, and the music suffered as a result. I wondered if there was a way of combining literary ideas with rock music. Had a songwriter attempted it before? One had, and I discovered him in an unexpected way. A happy task in the first depressing week of term was covering our textbooks with brown paper, after the old jacket had been stripped. It was a means of protecting the book, but could also be a way of broadcasting one's identity. The copy of *Simply Physics* I inherited bore a sleeve I was reluctant to dispose of. 'Fizikz For Simpletons', as its previous owner had scrawled under the title (in my imagination I see a third-form long hair with a fat tie and a smug smile, a bit like that photograph of Tony Blair in his school uniform), was covered with beautifully drawn band logos. Pink Floyd, Led Zeppelin, ELP, Hawkwind, the Grateful Dead, Genesis, Yes, Van der Graaf Generator, and one moniker that leapt out but didn't really cohabit with the others: the Velvet Underground. It was easily the coolest name for a group ever dreamt up. It suggested a dark, sensuous space; maroon or plum in colour, the inside of a drinking den or brothel, or some forbidden part of the subconscious. Knowing I had to find out what they sounded like as soon as possible, I cycled to David's in Letchworth – a bookshop with a damp-smelling music department at the back –

and started searching. Eventually I found a Polydor Best Of on tape, the one with the band photograph capped by sprocket holes, like a film frame.

The album began with 'White Light/White Heat'. It knocked me down. The music was a revelation; nothing like I'd expected, or heard before. The song was going in and out of time, was out of tune, and badly recorded to a shocking degree. It sounded like the jams with my brother plugged into the same amplifier, yet was accomplished in some elusive, indefinable way. The people who had created this noise were clearly self-aware, surely self-taught musicians, with a frame of reference far beyond merely other rock music. Everything about 'White Light/White Heat' was magnetic, even the forward slash in the title.

Elsewhere on the album, during 'I Heard Her Call My Name', the guitarist was playing like a man unhinged. It didn't seem as if he was following any recognisable scale, just placing his hands at random on the neck of the loudest guitar ever recorded. And the words . . . the singer, Lou Reed, threw them away as if he didn't care, yet they were clearly good words (*that* was attitude). Only later did I discover Reed's aim had been to attempt in pop music what novelist Hubert Selby Jr had achieved in literature, with *Last Exit to Brooklyn*. One song, 'The Gift' was even a short story, obscured by the band playing a riff of unwavering, single-minded repetition, punctuated by brief, alarming disturbances: feedback.

And no one I knew had heard of them. (This was crucial to the Velvets – the conviction that they are your band; that they speak just to you. Indeed, I've just demonstrated it – 'the Velvets'. Sounds slightly knowing and proprietorial, doesn't it? Like calling Joni Mitchell 'Joni'.) Lou Reed wrote songs with a literary sensibility, a punk attitude (before punk), and, in every picture I could find in the weeks to come, looked cool as fuck. I'd just discovered my New Favourite Band.

No one, apart from Duke, of course. Two weeks after the auspicious meeting at the Sun, I found myself in another of Hitchin's underage drinking taverns, the Red Hart. That night it was heaving. As I elbowed my way through the crowd, choking on smoke and hairspray and hormones, I spied Duke and Bill in a corner. With them was a kid I didn't recognise. He was wearing a cool, cream raincoat and a fine pelmet of spiked blond hair. When I reached the table, he fixed me with a level stare. His blue eyes were hooded behind thick frames, Michael Caine in *The Ipcress File*. 'Are you armed?' he asked, with high seriousness. I told him I had a bottle of Smirnoff back at the house. Duke cut in, 'This is PsychoNicky!' The young man in the raincoat dropped the severe look, and smiled. 'Call me Nick,' he said. But it seemed everyone called him Spike, because of the hair.

We drifted (a very Duke word, 'drift') up to my dad's house: me, Duke, Bill and Spike. It transpired Spike, who was from Codicote, one of the nearby villages, also had impeccable taste in alternative music: Cocteau Twins, Billy Bragg, Echo and the Bunnymen . . . I realised I'd seen him a couple of mornings in the upper sixth house, wearing the cream raincoat and a pair of brown brogues, shaking out a long umbrella. He'd seemed worldly, urbane even. The upper sixth were afforded liberties I could only dream of. Music was allowed. They drank *coffee*. There were ripped sofas, and Andy Warhol biographies scattered about. Something was always being smashed up with a cricket bat. That autumn, freedom smelled of Mellow Birds and drying umbrellas.

Halfway up the hill to my dad's, Duke said, 'Hey, you know Bill's into the Velvet Underground.' I was stunned. Surely no one else on earth had heard of them? It turned out he knew all the track names; his favourite was 'Sister Ray', a song I wasn't even aware of. 'If you like Lou Reed,' said Duke, 'I'll lend you *Transformer*. Bowie produced it. I can lend you his stuff, too.' I couldn't wait.

Spotting the Rockers in the Beer Garden – a semi-circle of benches at the top of Tilehouse Street – we stopped off to freeload their cider. I was finding out more about Duke. He claimed he was celibate, after Morrissey, and suffered from an incurable book kleptomania. We talked about Bauhaus, the band, not the art movement. (At the time I was starting to model my image on their guitarist, Daniel Ash. The green army jacket was long gone.) Just as we were leaving, a Rocker asked, 'Can I crash at anyone's pad?' Duke replied, 'How about your own?'

The following week, I cycled to Duke's council flat to teach my first guitar lesson. In his bedroom I tried to tune the untuneable wreck of a guitar. Then, after managing to impart a few basic chords, we repaired to the sitting room to listen to how it should be done: Daniel Ash, and the master, Hendrix. Just as Jimi's version of 'Gloria' was fading, Duke Snr walked in from work, singing.

'G – L – O – R – I – A! We're not all squares you know! I liked 'im when he was still alive and thought 'e was brilliant then.'

Shorter than his son, slightly stout and immediately likeable, Duke's old man was a gracious host. He insisted I stay for tea – bangers and mash, which were divine. Then he kicked off his shoes and we watched *Only Fools and Horses* together. As I cycled off into the crisp, early September night, 'King Volcano' and 'Voodoo Chile' in my head, I couldn't help but contrast the warm welcome with the cold set-up I was going back to. A dismal rhythm had been established: the tense weekends at my mum's with my stepfather, the weeks at my dad's, making sure there were no roaches left in the coffee cups.

As the autumn half-term drew near, the evenings settled into a routine of records, jamming, and smoking weed, followed by the comedown of school the next day. No one seemed to be doing a stroke of work. One morning, finding Jude slumped in a study booth, asleep after a night's dissipation, I noticed something had been left for me under my chair. A plastic Sainsbury's carrier, from Duke. The bag was bursting with albums, and a folder containing a sheaf of his poems. What was in The Bag? To the best of my recollection, this:

Bauhaus, *Burning From the Inside*
Simon and Garfunkel, *Wednesday Morning, 3AM*
Joy Division, *Unknown Pleasures*
Marianne Faithfull, *Broken English*
Lou Reed, *Transformer*
Hanoi Rocks, *Two Steps from the Move*
Paul Simon, *There Goes Rhymin' Simon*
The Pretenders, *The Pretenders*
David Bowie, *The Rise and Fall of Ziggy Stardust and the Spiders From Mars*, *Pin Ups*, *Aladdin Sane*
The Hollywood Brats, *The Hollywood Brats*
Cocteau Twins, *Garlands*
The Cramps, *Songs the Lord Taught Us*
Free, *Fire and Water*
Japan, *Assemblage*
Crass, *How Does It Feel to be the Mother of a Thousand Dead?* (7" single)
Elkie Brooks, *Two Days Away*

Yes. Anyone who could have Crass and Elkie Brooks in the same collection had to be some kind of deranged genius. The records swiftly became the soundtrack to the new term, and, out of all of them, the ones I played most were the Bowie albums. *Ziggy–Pin Ups–Aladdin.* Oddly, my favourite was Bowie's album of covers, *Pin Ups*. In July 1973, he'd taken the trouble to reimagine a set of songs by British pop acts from 1964 to 1967.

The album is not highly thought of in the canon. I knew this even back then, because, helpfully, there was a Bowie

Illustrated Record as well as one devoted to the Beatles. The authors, Roy Carr and Charles Shaar Murray, strafe it with disapproval, but occasionally they recognise its merits. 'Everyone actually sounds inspired, and Ronson positively dazzles,' they write.[2] This is one of the reasons I loved *Pin Ups*: it's a great guitar album. (It would be many years until I heard Ronno's staggering version of 'White Light/White Heat', an outtake from the *Pin Ups* sessions. How I wish I'd known it at sixteen.)

It would be foolish to suggest *Pin Ups* is an equal to *Ziggy Stardust*, yet to my mind it forms the central panel of a triptych that is just as important as *Low–Heroes–Lodger*. Everything the critics dislike about the album, I like. Bowie's crooning vocal on 'Here Comes The Night'; his vague, wistful reading of 'Sorrow' (the *Illustrated Record*: 'dreary', but as teenager I could relate – he sounds as if he's savouring his sweet sorrow, secretly enjoying it); the slow version of the Who's 'I Can't Explain' that my brother and I would play many years later with Flamingoes on European radio shows.

Charmingly, Carr and Shaar Murray suggest making a tape of the originals, and even supply catalogue numbers so the vinyl can be hunted down at record fairs ('It'll cost ya!'). How different things are today, and how much less interesting. I could make that compilation in an hour, at no cost at all, and without leaving the house.

As well as many of Ronson's finest moments, *Pin Ups* includes some of Bowie's greatest singing. On the penultimate track, an apocalyptic reading of the Who's 'Anyway Anyhow Anywhere', the *Illustrated Record* submits that drummer Aynsley Dunbar is 'on towering form . . . and Bowie matches him with a vocal of *berserk power*'.[3] This is the reason I think I really loved the album. It spoke to me directly about my experience, in a tone I could understand at sixteen. Although Bowie sang it as a twenty-six-year-old, his address was actually to his fifteen-to-sixteen-year-old self: the Bowie of the Konrads and the King Bees. *Pin Ups* was the right record at the right time, a mirror to the adolescent operatics, the dramatic pace of change at that age, the sense of confusion, and that feeling of desperately wanting to run away. The 'changes' that Bowie had sung so eloquently about on *Hunky Dory*. Perfect for a teenager sick of school, mired in domestic chaos, assailed by hormones and homework.

The song titles seemed to set out a familiar weekend sequence: 'Friday On My Mind', 'Here Comes The Night', 'Don't Bring Me Down', 'Sorrow', 'I Can't Explain'. And girls named 'Rosalyn'. Let's not forget girls named Rosalyn. There was a fifth former that I and just about everyone had the hots for, Rosie – short for Rosalyn. Petite, vaguely posh, chestnut-brown eyes – a danger to any teenage male within a ten-mile radius. Some time that autumn, in the upper sixth house, Spike casually revealed that Rosie fancied Duke. A quiet smile formed on Duke's lips. He considered the remark for a moment, then said, 'I can handle it.' I was inconsolable for at least a weekend.

But there was a new feeling to contend with, alongside the excitement, boredom, and confusion, and one quite unexpected: nostalgia. The song on *Pin Ups* Bowie left to last was a reinterpretation of the Kinks' 'Where Have All

The Good Times Gone'. It must have held special significance, as it's the only track on the album to have a transcription of its lyric on the insert. Written in 1965, the song seems to be lamenting the end of the sixties before they have even properly begun. Bowie attempts to match Ray Davies' tone of world-weary revulsion, and successfully captures the teenage conviction that everything is changing – for the worse. Only the week before Duke delivered The Bag he'd told me, 'fifteen was such a good year. I started going to concerts, smoking dope, and lost my virginity. Seventeen and everything's gone wrong.' How can you be nostalgic at seventeen? But you are. It is one of the authentic hallmarks of youth.

If one could distil the essence of 'Where Have All The Good Times Gone' it would be: couldn't we just go back to how it was? No. Why not? *I can't explain*. But things had been going wrong for a long time and were about to explode. The tension at home (both of them) was at tipping point. Ronson's methodical, grinding, boot-boy power chords seemed to be of a piece with this, like words punctuating a beating. Where. Have. All. The. Good. Times. Gone? And the lines about the parents in verse three – daddy not needing any toys, mother needing no boys – these were especially poignant, appearing as they did over the bridge's descending C–A minor–G sequence.

And there they were again: the melancholic descending lines of the lament figure. They were all over *Ziggy* and *Aladdin*, too. The cliché asserts there's no accounting for taste, but I was beginning to wonder why I was attracted to them. Why do some people like jazzy, happy major sevenths and others prefer bluesy sevenths, or sad, descending lines? Perhaps the preference for melancholy came from Mailer's 'wound', the well of sadness that all children of divorce carry.

Although Britpop was many years away, *Pin Ups* marked one of the first stirrings of the backwards looking, nostalgia-fixated culture that would prevail twenty years later. Indeed, *Pin Ups* could be seen as Bowie's Britpop album. The Who, the Kinks, the Yardbirds . . . there are no American artists covered; all are from the United Kingdom or the Commonwealth (the Easybeats were Australian), all favouring tight three-minute pop songs.

Sitting in my mum's lounge, taping *Pin Ups*, staring at the sleeve – a nearly submersed Bowie looking directly out, intense, imploring (*do it, run away*), a languid Twiggy on his shoulder – I would dream of escape. When would I be free of the school? And know-nothing pricks like my step-father? When would I get my leg over? No progress of any sort was being made on that front. I did a lot of thinking about Bowie's nose. Despite his androgyny, it was a man's nose. My own tilted femininely upwards, and I hated it. Like all teenage boys, I wanted male secondary-sexual characteristics, as many as possible please, and soon. I felt like Morrissey, waiting for nature to make a man of him yet. Yes, Bowie's nose was certainly something to covet.

The *Pin Ups* sleeve recalled, in an odd way, a photograph I'd found in another Bowie book: the fabulous, decadent Terry O'Neill shot from '75, Bowie and a visibly aged but still glamorous Elizabeth Taylor in Beverly Hills. It looks as if they are dancing. Liz is wearing his fedora, one motherly arm around his shoulder, feeding him a drag of a cigarette – the symbolic baton of fame that she's passing on (fame takes a cigarette . . . ?), that must have happened in a split second, and O'Neill astutely knew he must capture. Bowie looks down, with an expression of unbearable sorrow. Liz looks sad, too, but leavens this with a strong maternal indulgence. Bowie's nose, in profile, is as elegantly curved as the wide front wheel arch on a 1930s Chevrolet. In contrast, his nose on *Pin Ups* is sharp, straight, avian. It fascinated me how it appeared to be different in each picture, like the different voices he used in songs. Typical of Bowie, even his nose was a chameleon. I would lay the books and record sleeves out to compare them. Like that other compelling pop hooter, Lennon's, it would change over the years, in Lennon's case – and more than likely Bowie's – from the amount of charlie that had gone up it. The only drug I could find was dope from the friendly Rastas on Nightingale Road. ('Good weed! Good weed!') No one I knew had seen, let alone taken, cocaine. Class As were off the menu, for the time being at least. For now, all I could do was dream of that fabulous world of grown-up licence.

*

I'm not sure if it was after my first acid trip, or my stepfather beating me up in the front garden with the neighbours looking on, that I decided to leave school for good. It must have been towards the end of October, at the very least. The casual violence that had been taking place for years erupted that autumn, and took a darker turn. My stepfather had made his masterpiece. After this outrage, I would contrive to spend as little of my life in his company as I could. Around the same time, as something of a counterbalance, all heaven broke loose. The LSD arrived suddenly from the nearby villages, Superman tabs – fierce visuals – and if I couldn't find these, mushrooms from the misty fields on the periphery of town. In any event, the violence and the drugs, the accelerated pace of this turbulent period, led to a drastic decision. One late autumn afternoon, on a Hitchin playing field named Pinehill, the sky a red, buckling edifice (no acid had been taken, it just looked that way), I made a pact with my brother: we would leave the school and form a band in London. It appeared there was nothing to lose.

A few days later, Mr Wood came round to have a word. He sat in my mum's lounge with tea and custard creams, and told me I was throwing my life away. His intentions were good, but I didn't care. I was going to London to play rock 'n' roll. It seemed as if everyone was against me, that other adolescent staple. I'd even managed to alienate friends in my own year – I wasn't socialising with them anymore, and it had become yet another source of conflict. 'You hero-worship Duke,' one of my old mates said. But . . . you guessed it, I didn't care. For the shortest, most fleeting time it would transpire, I'd found myself an alternative family, something certain to place against an uncertain present, and even shakier future. We called ourselves the Desperados: Duke, Bill, Spike, Jude, and me. Roaming the cold town in long coats, the bonfire air thick with Silvikrin hairspray, hair gel and Marlboro smoke. A gang. OK, we were the least scary gang in north Herts, but it was still a gang, a posse, a crew. All I needed were my muckers, the Desperados. It was to be short-lived. To my great surprise, I found a girlfriend (alas, not Rosie), and I left the guys to it, carousing the weekends away.

The only other refuge from the storm was music. Masterpieces were casually being released every week. *Rattlesnakes* by Lloyd Cole and the Commotions, *Treasure* by Cocteau Twins, *Hatful of Hollow* by the Smiths – all within a thirty-day period. As a result, education became an irrelevance. The teachers at school already had me down as a drug-taker and a layabout (some eleven-O-level layabout), part of 'the lunatic fringe', as they inventively called it, so why not leave? And, anyway, I had a new teacher. Bowie told us we could throw the homework on the fire, if it was bringing us down. For years, I'd been collecting 'teachers', older figures that opened windows onto possibilities, or demonstrated that there were different ways to live. Some were artists: Lennon, Jimmy Page. Others relatives or friends – Uncle Chessh, Duke. Some were actually teachers: Mr Wood. Even the hirsute third-form head who'd written the Velvet Underground on his textbook was a sort of teacher. And now Bowie.

Following the rupture of leaving the sixth form, my dad made it clear we were not welcome in his house until we came to our senses and returned to school. For a night, my brother, always more rebellious than me, slept rough, and Duke lent me his icy bed, while he kipped on the sofa. To our elders and betters we were 'going off the rails', but I knew exactly what I was doing. I'd made my career choice at the age of twelve, when I'd first heard *Revolver*, and was mystified when others admitted they didn't know what they wanted to do after leaving school. Music was becoming the only thing worth engaging with. The song that sustained me during this chaotic period was 'The Jean Genie', from The Bag's *Aladdin Sane*, and I would sneak down after lights out to listen to it on headphones. My heart ticked to its colossal rhythm. It wasn't just in my blood, it *was* my blood. The big city world it conjured up – cool bars, cracked actors, neon signs – beckoned. And Snow White. I knew what *that* was a euphemism for. The years spent dreaming of playing loud, wild music to an audience – usually during the desolation of double Physics – were at an end. Now I was taking the first breathtaking step to making it a reality. Yes, I'd decided what I wanted to do. Fuck school! I was going to be an artist, a writer, a musician – in a rock 'n' roll band!

4

The Idea of Autumn

Mike Scott, the Waterboys, and 'This Is The Sea'

Of course, I went back.

Brokering a deal with my dad, I returned to the sixth form on the condition I could still live in his house. I couldn't stay at my mum's after what had happened in the front garden; that much was clear. It was a strategic move. Something is always lost in a retreat, as Napoleon once said. But more is gained. Fly Agaric could rehearse for free, and I could write songs in peace. Many were being stockpiled for the next demo tape. The London plan remained intact. Indeed, this desideratum became all-consuming, the motor of my days.

Although moving to the capital had been temporarily postponed, I finally realised my ambition of going to gigs there. During the autumn of 1984, I travelled up to the Smoke for a cluster of shows – three in quick succession. The first was Echo and the Bunnymen, at the Hammersmith Odeon. For Ian McCulloch – 'Mac' – their lead singer, it must surely have been a big deal, treading the same boards as his hero, David Bowie. Just over a decade previously, the Dame had resigned from live performance on the very spot Mac was standing. Except it would have been if they hadn't adopted an unusually democratic stage plan. The group appeared in a straight line: Pete de Freitas, behind the drums; Will Sergeant, the guitarist; Les Pattinson on bass; then Mac. I've never since seen a band deploy this configuration. It was oddly thrilling.

Mac radiated nonchalance ('Anyone got the footie results?'), and beseeched us to stand – 'It's not a soddin' school assembly' – but looked inimitable. Pineapple hair, short-sleeved checked shirt, stonewash jeans with a turn-up, white socks, loafers. Tab on. (Reading that back, I realise I've just described Paul Calf, Steve Coogan's student-hating, northern yob alter ego. But, honestly, that night Mac was the epitome of the cool lead singer.) His cohorts were equally impressive. Wearing a Brian Jones bowl cut, Will Sergeant sent wave upon wave of coruscating top-end from his Vox Teardrop out into the auditorium. His stacks of sixties Fender amplification were a hip reference to Television: the inner sleeve of *Marquee Moon*. Pete de Freitas, using brushes but sounding as powerful as a sticks player, was astonishing. I walked out into the sharp October night, ears ringing, head bursting with magic: 'Zimbo', 'The Killing Moon', 'Stars Are Stars', 'Never Stop'.

The second gig was R.E.M., at Dunstable Civic Hall. Not exactly London, admittedly, but a different county at least. After many hours negotiating Bedfordshire's arcane bus system, my brother and I found ourselves waiting in front of an empty wooden stage, a platform more used to stuffy middle-aged councillors than America's most hotly tipped alternative group. Staring at this void was unusually compelling. Back then, these darkened, mysterious spaces held a strange fascination: the drum kit wreathed in dry ice, the red lights on the amps glowing like tail lights in fog. It was theatre, the stillness intensifying the anticipation of the spectacle to come. That evening, R.E.M. played to fewer than a hundred people, all of them huddled at the front of the capacious hall. As a result, the performance felt like a private gig. Singer Michael Stipe had strained his neck the previous night, and didn't venture from the centre stage hot spot, yet was spellbinding. I recall his extraordinary hands, large domed thumbnails visible from his idiosyncratic mic-technique. After a stately version of the Velvets' 'Femme Fatale', the band leapt into jerky New Wave-ish motion. Peter Buck, the guitarist, was a tornado – Wilko Johnson with a Rickenbacker instead of a Telecaster; yet with shapes all of his own, soon to be copied. Several songs in, someone hurled a plastic beaker of beer onstage. Half of it splashed over Buck's shoes. Without malice, or missing a pick stroke, he bent it like Beckham. The cup hit the front row where we were standing, soaking us.

Gigs in those days could be violent, cathartic events, somewhere between a street demonstration and a barroom brawl. 'Chicken dancing' was in: rotating on one foot while the other kicked and flailed, both fists punching the air. Audiences still spat at bands – chronologically, the era wasn't far from punk. I recall the Alarm's Dave Sharp, his face glistening with gob as he tried to play his electro-acoustic in 'Where Were You Hiding When The Storm Broke?'. At one gig, a drum-stick thrown from the stage struck me just below the eye. With blood pouring, I made my way to First Aid, then pinched the cut together on the train home, because a girl in the third row had told me that way it wouldn't scar.

After the R.E.M. show, I queued for autographs, the only time I've done this for a band. (I must have forgotten my bad experience with Liza Minnelli.) Backstage, Peter Buck was seated in the centre of the dressing room, holding court like a department store Santa. He was loving it. Not loving it, and standing alone in a corner, was a mute Michael Stipe, visibly wincing every time he was asked to sign someone's album sleeve or t-shirt. The awkwardness of his body language, his dislocation from the fans and the rest of the band, was unnerving. He was easily the shyest person I'd been in a room with, and, being a teenager, I'd been in a lot of rooms with a lot of shy people. In hindsight, however, with road experience of my own, Stipe's withdrawn presence was understandable. It must have been a drag doing a UK tour with neck strain, chatting, signing autographs. Some nights you could do without the hassle.

Realising I had nothing for the band to sign, I found an empty B&H packet on the floor, and pulled out the inner gold strip. When my turn came, Buck, and the no-less-loquacious rhythm section, decided to have some fun. Was it a chocolate wrapper? Foil from a Champagne bottle? Gold leaf?

'What's your name?' asked Peter Buck, good-naturedly. I told him. The scrap of paper came back, now a piece of real gold.

To Champagne James, Peter Buck

Gold man! Bill Berry

Au Chocolat, Mike Mills

Finally, I approached Michael Stipe, an encounter I'd been dreading. He scribbled quickly, with those unforgettable fingers. Zero eye contact. When I was outside the dressing room, and could breathe in relief, I looked at the autograph.

½ M$%^^&("*

The third gig was the least impressive, but the most auspicious. One chilly evening in November, waiting for U2 to appear onstage at Wembley Arena, I found myself idly watching the support band struggle through their set. Seated in a tier stage-left, close to the action, I saw everything in profile, as it were. The lead singer was wearing leather trousers, and brandishing a Gibson Les Paul similar to the one Mick Jones used to play in the Clash. His chestnut-coloured hair was coiffed into an impressive rock-star shag-pile; and his nose had an upward tilt, uncannily like my own. He was singing something about hearing the Big Music, after which he would never be the same. The noise they were making was rapturous, incandescent, exhilarating. The U2 fans couldn't have cared less, talking in their seats like farmers at a livestock market, but I sensed the band had something I needed. I immediately decided it was an injustice they were dying up there on stage. The front-man seemed to share this sentiment – even from twenty yards away one could feel him bristle at the audience's lack of interest. Finally, the band played a long, curious, narrative song about World War Two, into which the singer poured his soul.

When the tune finished: nothing. Tumbleweed. Only myself and a few others whistled and cheered. At this, the singer did something unforgettable. He cocked his head, turned on his heel, and walked purposefully offstage. He then proceeded calmly down a concrete gangway, Gibson slung upside down across his back, rock 'n' roll-outlaw style, and vanished out of sight. Wow. That was a gesture. A fuck you. But also a challenge: are you with me or are you not? Are you in or are you out?

I was in.

The singer was Mike Scott, and his band was called the Waterboys. They had just released their second album, *A Pagan Place*, and were promoting it on U2's *Unforgettable Fire* tour. A few weeks later, I borrowed the record from a friend, then illegally taped it, as was the custom in those days. On the sleeve, Scott peered enigmatically out from beneath the shag-pile, one eye only visible. He certainly possessed all the qualifications necessary for the job of windswept, romantic rock singer: fine cheekbones, full lips, scarily taut jawline, and that strangely vulnerable nose. Furthermore, as had been hinted at live, Scott's voice was a revelation: forceful, moving, yet wistful. Every so often, for emphasis, he would emit a trademark 'Whooo!' – a sort of uninhibited Native American holler. There was almost too much to admire in Mike Scott's voice. The secure top notes – high As – of 'A Pagan Place' were particularly impressive.

Few facts about the band could be gleaned from the sleeve. I knew from an interview in an old issue of *Sounds* that Scott was from Edinburgh, now living in west London, and that the Waterboys were a fluid collection of associates rather than a 'proper' group like U2 or Led Zeppelin. On the back of the cover was written, quaintly, 'For information send S.A.E. to: 3 Monmouth Place, Off Monmouth Rd, London W2.' I considered it for a moment. No, best to wait for the next album, which would be out soon enough, certain to be a masterpiece, and learn about the band from the surfeit of press it was sure to receive.

A whole year passed – with more of Bowie's changes than it's possible to recount here. Autumn 1985. No mention of the Waterboys in the music papers. I was seventeen by now, an upper sixth former, walking the carbolic corridors of the school with an affectedly world-weary gait, a copy of *The Penguin Book of English Verse*, and a mullet. Exiting through the gates one splendid, blowy September afternoon, reading the *Melody Maker* (the habit of religiously reading the music press, especially the *MM*, had been established this year), I noticed a tiny News In Brief. The Waterboys were about to release their third album, *This Is the Sea*. The oddness of the idiom, and its inherent romantic quality, was immediately exciting. It had a great deal to live up to with a title like that. Not this is *a* sea, but this is *the* Sea.

I bought a copy on the day of release. Vinyl, of course. The sleeve, in ravishing black and white, displayed the same artfully cultivated mystique, but this time there was no eye contact; instead, Scott looked down, attaching a feather to his jacket. The pose was a direct reference to the cover of Marianne Faithfull's *Broken English*, the wrist canted at exactly the same angle. On the inner bag were lyrics, and copious illustrations. There was also a list of all the instruments used beneath each song. A bellzouki had been played on one tune. What on earth was a bellzouki? I was intrigued. On the back cover, Scott wore dark glasses, and peered intently over his piano at something just out of reach. Anthony Thistlethwaite, the sax player on *A Pagan Place*, was be-scarfed and be-shaded. And there was a new recruit: someone called Karl Wallinger, a geek in Lennon specs, enigmatically sniffing a wild flower. They looked cool as hell. What would the Waterboys have for us this time?

This Is the Sea, released the same week as Kate Bush's *Hounds of Love*, is one of those albums that critics throw the word 'masterpiece' at. For once, this is not an exaggeration. It is a perfect collection of songs, faultlessly executed, and, although not concept-driven, as side two of *Hounds of Love* is said to be, has an integrity of sequence; a will of its own, a flow. Aptly, the theme of the final, eponymous track is regeneration – the ending of an old life and the beginning of a new. Scott presents us with a simple idea: the unhappy past has faded, become irrelevant, and the far larger, more important present is here, right now. *That was the river; this is the sea.* Furthermore, there's a chance you *might* have a future, but, ultimately, it's up to you. Life's what you make it. What a freeing, hopeful idea! This could have been trite, homespun wisdom if it wasn't for the music's huge elemental power, and the darker, conflicted undercurrents of the lyric. The song allows that past events don't just vanish, they have consequences that intrude on the present. Yesterday mingles with today, making it harder, as each year accumulates, to make decisions. Indeed, the narrator (if one reads the lyric as inner dialogue, counsel to oneself, not a friend) is trawling through his memories, trying to identify where he went wrong. He is stuck, and can't just throw the past away. If only he could . . .

If you are familiar with the song, you will know that much of its power comes from the lyric's uncanny ability to describe all your life's crucial turning points as and when they happen. 'This Is The Sea' is a song about regeneration that constantly regenerates itself. The words always seem to fit the situation or dilemma precisely, like a mathematical formula. In this way it is perhaps the definitive Memory Song, where one can look back at the layers of memory, when and where the song was one's companion, on which dark nights of the soul. I can truthfully say this has occurred during every major event in my life. It may have been the end of a relationship, a friendship, a job, or time spent living somewhere, but the song's lyric always represented it perfectly. At seventeen, the train in the fifth verse that you could catch if you hurried was the transport that would take me to London. I imagined I needed to get a move on; that time was running out.

After this verse – the drop, or lull where the band 'take it down' – the song begins its ascent to a kind of summit. A gathering instrumental wave of frightening power, a giant breaker threatening a tsunami, starts to rise. The sound picture becomes dangerously engorged, Scott repeating the same phrase over and over. It builds and builds until it cannot build any further . . . Then it breaks, and there is calm. Scott had been true to his promise. The album's title track *was* the sea, an ocean of personal meanings and connections, but also oddly mimetic of the sea itself, its dreadful power. And how unexpected and pleasing it was to discover that last unruffled line, the quiet injunction to *behold* the sea. Accept change, it seemed to say, marvel at it; don't ask why. Such is the song's strength, if I sit down to listen to it now, I still come away dazed, altered in some way.

Some of the effect, it has to be said, arises from straight musical repetition. Back in 1985, if you'd suggested Mike Scott was a Velvet Underground fan I may not have believed you (he was a Bowie-phile and Lennon-head also, but I didn't know that either). There were many bands beginning to use the Velvets as a template then – shades, turtlenecks, feedback – but the Waterboys were not one of them. Instead, he took their quintessence. In the sleeve notes to *This Is the Sea*'s 2004 reissue, Scott states that from the Velvet Underground he learned the power of the two-chord song: 'The glory of sustaining a single dynamic intensity for an entire track.'[1] 'This Is The Sea' uses double-tracked twelve-string acoustic guitars, playing a simple E to A sequence – I to IV, then back to I, and so on – to create a rolling, repetitive tide of sound. Each guitar is 'hard-panned' (i.e. separated, so one is heard in the left speaker, the other in the right). Consequently, they spark against each other, talk to each other almost, one accent complimenting another. Over this, Scott layered multiple tambourines playing 'disciplined rhythms', as he called them – the triplets that drive the song. From this simple, naive palette emerged a distinctive, sweeping, quixotic sound, one at odds with the cynical airbrushed eighties; something no other artist was attempting at the time.

If his musical influences were sometimes well hidden, Scott was, ironically, one of the great 'portal artists'. Like Bowie, Scott's work often alludes to, or quotes directly from, another artist or cultural figure. In this way they are, in a benevolent teacherly way, the portal to another body of work, a new world. Just as *Aladdin Sane* references Jung, Benny Goodman, Che Guevara, the New York Dolls, Marilyn Monroe, and Jean Genet via 'The Jean Genie', *This Is the Sea* alludes to, among others, Yeats, Joyce, the nineteenth-century English artist William Strutt, and Sylvia Plath (the album's title is a direct quote from 'Berck-Plage'). And not forgetting the name of the band. The Waterboys, I was delighted to discover, derived from Lou Reed's *Berlin*.

There were punk citations, too, the Clash in particular. The band are everywhere in the Waterboys' frame of reference, especially the earlier songs. 'Church Not Made With Hands' from *A Pagan Place* features a galloping 'I

Fought The Law' intro, a piano playing sixteenth-notes à la 'Rock The Casbah', and a binary 'siren' guitar motif at its fade, reminiscent of 'Police On My Back'. Pure Mick Jones. (I should have known, really, when I'd spotted the leather kecks and the Les Paul at Wembley.) Patti Smith was in the mix, too. Smith wore a brooch of a horse on her blazer jacket; Scott wore an anchor, and the song 'A Girl Called Johnny' originated from Scott's teenage meeting with her. The shag-pile hair was Mike's version of Patti's version of Keith Richards' original. Not having heard of her until the Waterboys dropped into my life, I decided to investigate. From Patti Smith, there was a direct line to Blake, Rimbaud, Baudelaire . . .

Scott also led back to an author who, fittingly, had written about an actual portal to another world in *The Lion, the Witch and the Wardrobe*: C. S. Lewis. I knew the book; it had been read to us by our form teacher as we sat cross-legged on the carpet of our classroom at junior school. But I knew little about the man. A made-for-television biopic of Lewis's life, *Shadowlands*, was shown around this time. I watched it solely because Scott had referenced the title in the first line of 'Church Not Made With Hands'. From the film it transpired Lewis had written an autobiography, *Surprised by Joy*, which I found in a dusty Hitchin bookshop. In this wonderful, short book I discovered a marvellous phrase. As a young man C. S. Lewis admitted to often feeling an almost nauseating thirst for '*the idea of autumn*'.[2] Without any further explanation I knew precisely what he meant. It perfectly summarised how I felt at seventeen, an earnest, bookish adolescent, thinking himself a rock star, at all times longing for the season of melancholy and decay, loss and falling leaves. Keats' mists and mellow fruitfulness. Good job the Waterboys were the New Favourite Band that fall, and not the Style Council. *This Is the Sea* was the apposite soundtrack – autumnal music par excellence.

The press profile I'd hoped the album would achieve was starting to build. A fabulous single, 'The Whole Of The Moon' had attained a respectable chart placing – twenty-six – and as a result the band were starting to divide Hitchin's small community of aspiring musicians. (You were either in, or you were out.) On the cover of the *Melody Maker*, Scott had revealed a sideburn. It was an affront to the clean-cut pop faces of the day, two fingers up to the wine-bar bands, the Wham! wannabes. In the same photograph, the top three buttons of Scott's shirt were undone. Shirts in the eighties were to be fully buttoned at all times. The transgression was the subtlest of code, Masonic almost, a faint visual recognition signal of 'our people', but all the more powerful for it. There were hints in the music, too. Perhaps I imagined it, but wasn't Scott's 'see-ea yeah!' in verse four of 'This Is The Sea' a direct quote from Zeppelin's 'Custard Pie'?

An episode one day in the town's guitar shop perfectly illustrates this polarity. The short-haired fellow behind the till was in one of the many local bands – outfits with names like Surface Tension, or the Passion Theory – jazz funk combos infested with tasty geezers in Pringle sweaters. Level 42 fans. His group didn't wear Pringle but played a harder style of funk, and were called the Good Time Boys. I couldn't have come up with a better eighties antonym of 'Waterboys' if I'd tried. That decade was about hedonism; summery, pastel colours; a particularly nasty, Tory, philistine set of values. The Waterboys were inward, autumnal, defiantly poetic. As with Led Zeppelin and Depeche Mode, I knew which side I was on. The Good Time Boys wore ankle-length leather coats with the sleeves rolled up, and covered 'Get It On'; not the fleet-footed T-Rex original, but the Power Station's pompous slaughtering.

I'd only asked for a pack of Ernie Ball strings, heavy gauge, when he embarked on a tirade:

'You know the one band I can't stand at the moment are the fucking Waterboys, and that "Hole in the Moon". Absolutely hate them. Saw their video on *The Tube* last night. That's everything that's wrong with music at the moment that is. Just fucking hippies. Awful. Who let them back in? Him with his earring, long hair and sideburns. What year does he think it is? 1973? You probably like them, you and your mate, what's his name, Duke . . . ?'

And so on like that, until I zoned into a dream. Yes, the video was rather fine, Scott with the anchor jacket, Ovation acoustic held high, spinning round and round on his heel as the music reached one delirious climax after another. I saw myself onstage, throwing a few Scott-like shapes. When I came to, the peroration was still in full swing.

'. . . Fuckin "The Hole in the Moon", what does that mean?'

'Er, actually it's "The *Whole Of* The Moon",' I replied.

'Whatever.'

'Can I have the strings please? And my change . . . Thanks.'

Around this time, I started wearing fishermen's caps, blazer jackets, open-neck shirts. I even bought a pair of leather trousers (PVC, actually, from a rare trip to Camden Market), and for a while thought they were a perfectly acceptable addition to a young man's wardrobe. As well as being an homage to Mike Scott, the trousers were a nod to two other Scottish artists, Jim and William Reid of the Jesus and Mary Chain. The best of the groups to take the Velvet Underground as their model, the Mary Chain released their masterpiece first album, *Psychocandy*, two months after *This Is the Sea*. The only group I ever wrote a fan letter to (never sent), I had become besotted with them. Along with their image, and their turbid melodies that ran beneath ear-splitting layers of feedback, there was another reason to be attracted to them: the Mary Chain were a group led by two brothers. There had been numerous brother groups ever since Don and Phil Everly harmonised their first couplet together. The Beach Boys, the Kinks, the Bee Gees . . . These bands hold a special fascination for the public as they are usually fraught with conflict, the time-honoured 'sibling rivalry'. It seems all groups that decide to save money on the Musicians Wanted ad in this way are doomed to suffer from the malaise. My brother and I were no exception. The eleven O levels we had each attained weren't an accident, but the result of intense competition. Furthermore, twins are competitive in a way conventional siblings are not. Being regarded as equal, there is a constant struggle to be the centre of attention. Jude was singing by now, too, and although we shared a common purpose – the band – there were heated arguments about musical direction, the set list, what to wear on stage. We couldn't agree on anything. (Apart from dispensing with our surname – a very eighties affectation.) And because there was no older brother, no Noel, to have final say, the fights would last for days. It's usually said there is one dominant and one passive twin. Granted, but they are not always the same guy. They change places over the years, take it in turns. With male twins it is often like kings. For whatever complicated set of reasons, one abdicates and allows the other to take over. The twin that has stepped down bides his time until he finds a way to seize control again. One can see this power play being enacted not only in brother bands, but groups led by equally talented songwriters. The most obvious, and striking, example being the Beatles: John's early dominance weakened by a failing marriage and his dependence on LSD; Paul sees the leadership gap he's been waiting for, and steps in. At the time, as self-elected chief songwriter, I was in the ascendant; got my way more often. This would not always be the case, however.

One advantage that twins – with their unparallelled closeness – have over ordinary siblings, or tight songwriting partnerships, is they are less fissile. It was harder to divide us, as the decision to pursue a music career had been made by a committee of two equally obstinate minds. While an older–younger sibling dyad may have been hampered by conflicting priorities, we closed ranks. It swiftly became clear that a band of brothers – twin brothers – was a sturdy power base, a cell of two.

Us against the world.

Gazing at the sleeve of *Psychocandy*, taking in the titles and the writing credits – Reid/Reid – I would dream of the day I'd share a similar attribution with my brother.

Jude/James.

No, hang on, shouldn't that be James/Jude . . . ?

But even that was OK – John and Paul had had a similar tussle.

In October, to mark the album's release, the Waterboys headlined the Kentish Town Forum on the *This Is the Sea* tour. This time Scott, still wearing the leather kecks, a Lou Reed sunburst Gibson 335, a fisherman's cap, and the greatest haircut he would ever have, owned the audience. Opening with 'Don't Bang The Drum', the first track on the new record, Mike Scott demonstrated to those of us plotting to form a group how it should be done. Two hours of beauty, abandon and heartbreak followed. 'This Is The Sea', appearing towards the end of the set, felt like a religious experience. I exited feeling as if I had just witnessed the best live band in Britain, if not the world. Which, of course, I had.

The same month, we played our first proper gig at a local village hall, in Pirton. We bludgeoned ineptly through the Waterboys' 'Medicine Bow', and the Velvets' 'I'm Waiting For The Man' before a crowd of our peers, including

Duke, Bill and Spike. There was clearly still some way to go.

The experience only sharpened the desire for the band to get better, and escape to London. There was something in the way, however: university. Further education at this point was a pressing and conflicted question, one that could be evaded no longer. Like Tommy Wilhelm in *Seize the Day*, I was 'eager for life to start. College was yet another delay.'[3] But there was opposition to this youthful impatience. Mr Wood, and an old boy, Rob Newman, had been mentoring us for Cambridge. Wood had introduced the future comic, novelist and activist to the class the previous autumn, at the start of the sixth form. Charismatic, ridiculously handsome, four years my senior, Rob occasionally visited in the holidays, down from Cambridge, where he was reading English Lit. at Selwyn College, to scribble lyrics for songs my brother and I had written. He was supposed to be helping us with our exams, but sometimes we just ended up jamming. (Music was important to Rob, especially the Clash. He gently chided me for my schoolboy enthusiasms, the Alarm in particular. 'The poor man's Clash.' But I was too young for the Clash, like an Oasis fan who had never heard the Beatles. Strummer and Co. were the property of old punks, the generation just before me. My very own Last Gang in Town was the Alarm, although I was beginning to realise the older cool kids thought they were a bit of a joke.)

Rob – who had attained his place through merit rather than privilege – admitted to being bored by Cambridge. He stayed in his room, like the character in 'The Whole Of The

Moon', planning his next move. All of this didn't exactly make university an appealing notion in 1985. Moreover, I had an uneasy feeling Cambridge would be bad for the street cred. There was no Radiohead at this point, and I wasn't aware of Nick Drake. All the musicians that mattered to me were from ordinary backgrounds, like myself. Not many had gone to university, let alone Oxford or Cambridge.

In the same month as the Waterboys concert, my mum drove us up to Selwyn for the interview. I spent forty minutes with Shakespeare scholar Wilbur Sanders – venerable, patrician, terrifying – talking passionately about Gerard Manley Hopkins. (The choice of the tortured, neurasthenic Hopkins was telling.) A few weeks later a letter of acceptance arrived. Jude passed, too. However, when we deliberately sabotaged the entrance exam by not revising a month later, Mr Wood wrote to me. I found the letter the other day, in a dusty old folder. He insisted Cambridge wouldn't be all that bad, we could still do the music and acquire a degree at the same time. It's an affecting, sincere, non-pressuring, non-judgemental, yet firm appeal, with an invitation to dinner at the end. But I'd already decided on the path to be taken.

*

Twenty-six years later, in autumn 2011, I switched the TV on one night, and there was Mike Scott, on *Later . . . with Jools Holland.* Cocky Lennon-stance, well-cut suit, Bowie 'Space Oddity' twelve-string. He and the Waterboys were halfway through 'Mad As The Mist And Snow', a song from Scott's album of Yeats' poetry set to music. With its wild punk energy, references to Cicero and Homer, and Scott's incomparable voice, I experienced the same tremor of excitement as when I'd discovered the group all those years ago. They were still hungry. Coldplay were on the same show, and, in the rock 'n' roll vernacular, the Waterboys blew them off stage. It was hard not to smile – in Scott's attitude to the bigger, more feted band, I recognised the same singer who had stalked off U2's stage at Wembley in '84.

Something was noticeably absent, however – the throat-shredding 'Whooos' of the past. He uttered one, but it seemed designed to save his voice. Had he been to a vocal coach? If so, I could empathise. Some years ago, not being able to survive a gig without a torn larynx, I took a couple of lessons in an effort to save my voice. My teacher was the distinguished jazz singer Ian Shaw, a large, friendly man in his mid-thirties, invariably dressed in black, who could sell out Camden's Jazz Café when he played one of his infrequent shows there. We spent an hour a week at his Brixton home, concentrating on breathing. Shaw himself was then taking lessons from his mentor, Tony Bennett. They would conduct the sessions in Bennett's New York apartment, high above autumnal Central Park, the whole of the Big Apple laid out before them. As he told me this, I got the thirst, the yearning for the idea of autumn (it was summer, which helped). I could see the yellows, golds and taupes, the russet and orange carpet, a fantasy of New York learned from Woody Allen films.

Sitting at the piano, Shaw taught me to breathe from the

diaphragm, thus avoiding the throat, and preserving the voice. He said he'd been coaching Paul Young, who'd been concerned about losing his trademark Sam Cooke rasp. Shaw had warned him he'd lose it altogether if he didn't stop using effects from the larynx. 'By the time I finish with you, you'll be singing like a Sunday School vicar,' he'd said to Young. (I tracked down Paul Young's later records; he was.)

At the end of the final lesson I casually asked Shaw if he'd ever done any session singing. He said he'd sung on the Bodyform ads, back in the eighties.

'No way,' I said, 'that's a black American woman, someone like Loleatta Holloway!'

'No, it was me, on one of them at least,' he said with a confident smile.

'Go on, then, prove it.'

At this, Shaw, still sitting by the piano, threw his head back and let rip.

'WOOOOOAAAAH BODYFO-ORM! BODYFORM FOR YOOOOOOOOOOOOO!'

'OK, OK. It was you. I believe you. Mind your throat . . .'

*

Back in 1985, autumn had given way to winter. Snow covered the dead leaves, banked up in all the lanes leading out of Hitchin.

There are many references to snow on *This Is the Sea*. One of my chief memories from the time is listening to the record at my father's, the snow falling outside in perfectly vertical lines, reading and rereading the album's *Melody*

Maker review. It was a rave, and concluded: '*This is the sea, and this is the one*'.[4] Would a newspaper ever write anything like that for my music? I wondered. There was intense longing for London, but also fear of it. Everything was set to change. The old small-town life would soon be ending; the river emerging into the sea.

But not for a while yet.

5

Born Sandy Devotional

'Stolen Property', Love (not the band) and the Triffids vs the eighties

One day during the sixth form, in the hot summer of 1985, our class teacher told us we couldn't know much about love because we were far too young. I glanced over at my friend Mike. He'd put his pen down and was looking at me. Couldn't know much about love? Here was Miss Nicholls, a spinster who had unwittingly gained our life-long contempt by admitting she wrote poetry in her spare time, telling us we couldn't know much about love.

I'd just broken up with the girl of my dreams. Mike – tall, blue-eyed, angularly handsome – had been through a similar experience. We were men with broken hearts. Yes, we knew a thing or two about love, all right.

Now that we were both single, we'd be down the Red Hart every Friday night, drinking Stella to ease the pain, and staring desolately at girls our age, most of them wear-ing whatever Madonna was in that week. I suggested that, with my dark hair and his blond hair, we'd have a sort of Butch and Sundance thing going on. The Hitchin Girls' School lower sixth wouldn't stand a chance.

After a single rejection, we would return to our seats and watch the older boys move in. At the end of the evening, we'd head back to my dad's house for coffee, spliff and fried-egg sandwiches. Mike would be driving his mum's huge battered boat of a Citroën, 'I'm Waiting For The Man' would be pounding out of the stereo, and both of us would be talking querulously about our exes and our other favourite subject: music.

Mainstream music had reached what we hoped was some kind of final nadir in the mid-eighties. (It would get worse; thankfully we didn't know that.) Despite this it was hard to envisage a future where records wouldn't have synthesisers and clattery drum machines. It was like trying to picture peacetime during war. And it was a war: the charts were the enemy, but we knew we had God, or at least Morrissey, on our side.

But 'good' music was around if you were prepared to look for it. John Peel and *Sounds* weren't exactly obscure sources, and Mike was a regular subscriber to both. He liked to bring round records he'd heard on Peel's show and enthuse about them. I got to hear all kinds of odd bands in this way: the Del Fuegos (one great song: 'Nervous And Shaky'), the Jazz Butcher (no great songs, but one great title: 'Bath Of Bacon'), and the Fuzztones (*only* great songs, especially '1-2-5', a demented garage rock classic). During one of these sessions he pulled out an album with a gaudy red and yellow cover. It was *Raining Pleasure* by an Australian group called the Triffids. Apart from the Velvet Underground, my favourite bands at the time had settled into a loose rank order: the Jesus and Mary Chain, R.E.M., Cocteau Twins, Echo and the Bunnymen, the Waterboys, and the Smiths. Most of them had made, or were in the process of making, their Big Record with a Big Producer. The self-produced Triffids, in comparison, sounded tinny and thin. Still, they name-checked their local off-licence on the back of the sleeve and that was cool.

The following week, Mike bought two tickets for their Croydon Underground gig. It was July, the month of Live Aid, the high-water mark of the eighties. After enduring the Talking Heads-y support band (we always watched the support band) the Triffids walked on stage. They looked strange and slightly uncool. All of them were different shapes and sizes, and there was a fellow with glasses seated behind a pedal-steel. But they also wore fantastic shirts, Cuban heels and had sixties sunburst guitars. This last detail was crucial. I remember seeing Johnny Marr's vintage red Gibson 335 on the Smiths' *Top of the Pops* appearance for 'What Difference Does It Make'. It declared: I am against the eighties and its dreadful shiny new guitars.

We were right at the front. Close enough to see the greasy fingerprints on the singer's 1960s Fender Jazzmaster. From the first deafening, trebly chords of the opening song, to the final splinter of white noise as the last song collapsed, the Triffids were a revelation. They were a thrashy, *trashy* rock 'n' roll band – an eighties manifestation of our beloved Velvets. This was more like it. At the time, most indie bands were offering a soft Byrds-ian jangle. Primal Scream (who, ironically, went 'rock' later) were the epitome of this type of approach. We had seen them at Nottingham Rock City a few weeks earlier, supporting the Jesus and Mary Chain (Bobby Gillespie appeared in both groups that night). Someone had placed a small ad in the *NME* along the lines of: Look out Nottingham, there's gonna be another riot. We cowered at the back hoping for some punk rock thrills, but only the Mary Chain delivered. The Triffids, then, were the answer to our rock 'n' roll prayers.

As a singer-in-waiting, I always concentrated on the front man. My teenage diary records that he looked like a) he had been up for three nights tripping, and b) Iggy Pop. Now I knew as well as the next indie kid what Iggy Pop looked like, and it was nothing remotely close to the tall, craggily handsome singer-songwriter of the Triffids, who was called David McComb – a very un-rock 'n' roll name. So why the comparison? I hadn't properly grasped it, but they shared the same mixture of erudition and aggression. McComb's stage persona was very masculine but in a hip, non-eighties way.

It was two in the morning when the lights went up. We'd missed the last train home. In an act of sheer bravado we (OK, Mike) approached McComb, who wasn't in the dressing room doing lines like a rock star, but sitting beside the stage.

'We were wondering if you could give us lift into London, 'cause we've, ah, missed our train,' asked Mike, hopefully.

McComb looked us up and down with a charming smirk and said:

'You look like a couple of nice boys!' It was then I remembered we were both smeared in eyeliner.

Sensing our embarrassment, he added, 'We were going to ask if we could have a lift with *you*.'

True, he had announced they needed transport back to London during the gig, but I'd assumed he was joking. Surely bands that had been in *Sounds* had a limo waiting to take them back to their hotel?

No lift forthcoming, we made our way back to King's Cross on night buses. By five in the morning we were in a Wimpy Bar, watching the pimps and the working girls, feeling cool in our shades. Yes, it was going to take four hours to get home, but this was an adventure, right? I could imagine McComb doing this sort of thing for inspiration. He seemed like the kind of writer who was interested in the seamy underbelly of city life. Hadn't one of the songs from the gig mentioned heroin?

I still have the set list from that show. It reads: *Chicken*, *Hell*, *Life*, *Prop*, *Lonely*, *Seabirds*, *Rain*, *Jesus*, *Pony*, *Waste*, *Stolen*, *Field*, *Water*, *Monkey*. As a list of intriguing nouns, verbs and adjectives it's pretty impressive; as a list of great songs it's faultless. I didn't realise it then, but McComb had completed nearly all his key work.

There was one other lasting impression from the gig: McComb looked uncannily like my friend Mike. I don't think I told him this, but if I had he would have cherished it as the highest possible compliment. Looks and image were important to us. If someone had 'got their image together' they were all right. We were both Bowie fans – it was Mike who had completed my Bowie education with tapes of the later albums, *Lodger* being a particular favourite. We minced around the school in waistcoats and eyeliner, thinking we were the hippest of hip cats, a beating never far away.

The Triffids were inspirational that night, but they didn't become the New Favourite Band. They were just one of many good groups on the live circuit at the time. From the music papers, I learned they'd moved here from Perth at the end of 1984, in the footsteps of Melbourne's the Birthday Party. They were also a brother group – the guitarist was McComb's older sibling, Robert. In the autumn they appeared on *The Tube*, playing an excoriating version of 'Hell Of A Summer'. Although an old song, it was part of a promotional drive for a new album the music press kept insisting was on the way.

Nearly a year passed until we saw the Triffids again. ULU, 1986. Bizarrely, Zodiac Mindwarp and the Love Reaction were supporting (we always watched the support band). After the dry ice had cleared, the Triffids drifted on stage. Once again, we were right at the front. They opened with a tune called 'Chicken Killer'. McComb began by slashing almost artlessly at the first chord (a full fat G major, one of the most satisfying open chords to play), but the volume his Roland Jazz Chorus amp was kicking out, and his attitude, were breathtaking. They played a new song my diary misnames 'Buried Deep In Love'; a short 'Field Of Glass' that contained 'Sympathy For The Devil'; 'Raining Pleasure'; 'Jesus Calling' (McComb: 'This is about one of my heroes') and 'Beautiful Waste' as an encore.

A grand design was emerging. Like all great groups, each member had their own image and identity. David McComb was the captain, his brother Robert a studious lieutenant on guitar and violin. Martyn Casey, the bass player, another lieutenant, always smartly dressed in a denim jacket over a tucked-in shirt; Jill Birt, the keyboard player and second singer, tiny, but quietly fierce in DM shoes and print dress; and Alsy MacDonald – concerned yet nonchalant behind his drums. Finally, Graham Lee, seated and bespectacled, the sober anchorman, completed this odd collection of people. (Later in their career, Island Records tried to coerce McComb into going solo – a fine example of major label wrong-headedness. If ever a band was the sum of its parts it was the Triffids.)

There were details to savour, too. The three cans of Red Stripe on each amp as we anticipated their arrival onstage; the way McComb ambled on to fix up his effects pedals when he could have asked a roadie to do it for him; the way Jill Birt sang the words to her song from an exercise book, and how the look of genuine terror on her face made the audience will her on.

I was starting to fall in love with this band. So when the hell was their new record out?

A fortnight later, on the day of release, Mike called at my dad's house with a copy. The cover – an aerial shot of a beach with a receding tide; bad lettering – was a reminder that record sleeves weren't their strong suit. The title, however, more than compensated. It was mysterious, evocative

– magnificent. *Born Sandy Devotional.*

From first listen it was clear everything had been radically improved: the songwriting, the playing, the sound. There had always been a possibility that when they abandoned self-production they would make a great album, and *Born Sandy Devotional*, produced by Gil Norton, turned out to be it.

Side one, in old money, begins directly on the first line of 'The Seabirds', and the surge of Graham Lee's pedal-steel feels as if you're swooping down to the beach on the cover, and into their world. Every successful songwriter eventually creates a unique universe into which the listener can escape. McComb's was his native landscape, the sun-parched tip of Western Australia. *Born Sandy Devotional* is the indie-rock equivalent of Nicolas Roeg's *Walkabout*, a harshly physical world, a realm of the senses. An arena of dust, death and wide open roads, where emotionally tortured characters could dramatise their lives. McComb, a literary songwriter with diverse tastes – Fitzgerald, Heinrich Böll, Flannery O'Connor – had had a go at this before. Several of his early songs, 'Red Pony', 'Raining Pleasure', contain writerly references to sensuality and an extreme climate. But this was a focused attempt at sustaining these themes for the length of an album. Of course, this was unbearably exotic for a kid from the Home Counties.

Essentially, you could reduce the Triffids' milieu to 'the beach'. This should, in theory, have increased their crossover appeal. For a while, in the eighties, it seemed as if everyone wanted to be on a beach. In the summer of 1986, Owen Paul's video for 'My Favourite Waste Of Time' showed him walking hunkily along a beach in a denim shirt. Back then, the girls we knew divided boys into hunks or wimps. We were definitely wimps (although I can hear Mike's voice stating emphatically: speak for yourself, Jim). If you were an indie kid, and owned a few Cure records, then the beach was the most hated place to be. Morrissey's line about the dreaded sunny day from 'Cemetery Gates' is the perfect expression of this. No, McComb was on a very different beach to Owen Paul. It was the same beach all romantic outsiders in music have walked on, from Nick Drake on the *Fruit Tree* box-set to Ian McCulloch on the cover of the Bunnymen's *Heaven Up Here*.

The emotional landscape is just as well drawn. Designed as an open letter to a departed lover, the record sometimes sounds as if it's a concept album about sexual jealousy. It goes through all the miserable stages. *Born Sandy Devotional* is a 'devotional' to one person, but also a vicious, spiteful phone call made late at night when pissed. ('Love includes every emotion: hatred, guilt . . .'[1] McComb said in an interview at the time.) It is the testimony of someone trying to accept a betrayal, and the failure of a relationship.

Even though it was over a year since being dumped by my dream girl, I still wasn't over her. In fact, my infatuation had grown to startling proportions. My diary was becoming ever more histrionic and morbid, full of adolescent pain, rage and despair. In short, the exact emotional terrain of *Born Sandy Devotional*. Yes, I was ready for *Born Sandy Devotional*, even if the world wasn't.

This would all be fairly heavy going and unconvincing

if it wasn't for two things: first, the voice. What a magnificent, monstrous instrument McComb's voice is. Like a preacher's stentorian bellow, it is designed to leave the listener in no doubt as to who is IN THE RIGHT. Only occasionally does it border on camp or melodrama. Second, the quality of the songwriting. These were the tunes I'd heard in Croydon the year before, now honed in a recording studio, yet losing none of their power. The album's centrepiece is 'Stolen Property'. From the strings that snake and swell around the opening bassline to the final resigned phrase, it's an astonishing piece of music, their 'Idiot Wind'. McComb uses this epic backcloth to collect his turbulent thoughts into some kind of order. For him, it was, to use that embarrassing nineties idiom, 'closure'. No one called it that then. He was just sorting shit out in his head.

The first time I really listened to 'Stolen Property', concentrating on the lyrics, was a pivotal experience. It was the last day of the sixth form. Mike and I were lounging on sunny Windmill Hill – the vantage point that overlooked the whole of the town; cans of Red Stripe open, Marlboro Lights glowing, Ray-Bans on, *Born Sandy Devotional* drifting from the tape player. Hoping girls would walk by and notice us. Hoping *she* would walk by. The song began reassuringly enough, the simple E to A sequence a close relation of 'This Is The Sea'. In fact, you could hum the opening lines of that song over the intro to 'Stolen Property', and I often did. McComb was eulogising his departed love once more. Presently, Graham Lee added a soaring embellishment on the pedal-steel: F-sharp to A-flat, and the music rose; seemed to ascend to a sunlit upland. A lavish, romantic atmosphere was in place. But then, quite abruptly, McComb went on the attack. Using his preacher voice, he was now referring to her as his property, invoking the schoolboy phrase *finders keepers; losers weepers*, and implying she had all the emotional intelligence of a child. Uncomfortably, I realised he was, well, *slagging her off*. I knew you could harbour these thoughts in real life, but could you express them in a song? In a *love* song? Apparently you could. I was on a different sort of upland now, and it wasn't a sunny one: it was the outraged moral high ground of the cuckold. There was a rumour going around that my beloved had taken up with a twenty-year-old roofer named Gary, who drove a Vauxhall Viva. A hunk. I hated him. Yes, he had *stolen her from me*. Incredibly, it had taken me a year to comprehend this. She was gone, and wasn't coming back any day soon. But just as I became convinced that a crime had taken place, the band took it down, and McComb, in the most tender, baffled, bereft voice sang:

Let her run away.

It was a devastating moment. He was finally accepting that he'd passed through 'denial' (another queasy word) and was approaching 'closure'. But it still hurt; he still loved her – that was the reason for the anger. I realised that a good song could contain these contradictions. McComb once said that what he looked for in a song was 'a kind of inaccessible truth, an unresolved core of strange beauty'.[2] Which is exactly what he achieved on 'Stolen Property'.

Looking back, *Born Sandy Devotional* seems like a very grown-up record for a kid to be listening to. But, then again, it's precisely the sort of thing a bookish, angst-ridden teenager *would* listen to. Never once did it strike me as odd that McComb, a grown man, should be singing about this stuff. Maybe it should.

After the end of term, Mike and I headed to the South of France for, of all things, a beach holiday. We listened to the album every day, along with the Go-Betweens' *Liberty Belle and the Black Diamond Express*. It finally cured me of the girl, and I had 'closure'.

*

The Triffids were typical of the sort of Fender Jazzmaster-playing, Cuban-heeled-wearing, floppy-fringe-flicking critics' band that the future generation of Britpop musicians were exposed to in the 1980s. *Born Sandy Devotional* was one of those albums, like the Woodentops' forgotten classic *Giant*, that was common currency for music press readers at the time. I bet Noel Gallagher owned a copy. Although Britpop was largely a conflation of sixties and seventies influences, all its key players grew up during the eighties, all read the music papers, and all were affected, however subliminally, by the bands of the day. Moreover, to have allegiances to these groups was to be part of a dispossessed minority. I certainly thought so, listening to Radio One week after week, feeling the old order badly needed to be overthrown. Hang the DJ, as Morrissey sang. Pop music meant something in those days; one had to take a side, it wasn't just another leisure option, as it is now. Consequently, much of the impulse behind Britpop began around this time. Like a patient opposition party, guitar/alternative/indie music was sitting out the eighties until it saw its chance to seize power. (This mirrored the politics of the day: Thatcher, a convenient, even reassuring enemy for the left, prevailed for the entire decade, just as synthesisers – the guitar's natural enemy – did in the mainstream.) When would 'our' bands be on *Top of the Pops*, asked many an indie kid back then. It would be some time yet.

In the years that followed, we saw the Triffids three more times – at the ICA, the Boston Arms in north London, and, finally, the Kentish Town Forum. We were far away at the back, and the immediacy, the sheer visceral assault of their sound, just wasn't there. McComb looked slightly lost, throwing shapes on a little parapet at the front. Island were trying for the big push. The next album, *Calenture*, seemed disappointing in comparison with its predecessor. I didn't buy the follow-up, *The Black Swan*, and after that it was over, the band broke up. Mike stayed more loyal, acquiring the solo records McComb released throughout the nineties. Whenever we met there would be a Triffids conversation. There were dark rumours circulating in the music industry. McComb was ill; he was a junkie living in Tufnell Park; he'd given up music. But we were busy getting on with our lives, and the Triffids were becoming part of the past.

Despite this, their influence was subtle and pervasive. Years later, needing a name for my own group, I took Flamingoes from Roxy Music, but also wanted an exotic creature or thing like the Triffids. Flamingoes didn't sound anything like the Triffids, but it's the small things . . . even later still, needing a new bass, I bought a sunburst Fender Precision, with a tortoiseshell scratchplate. Peering at the inner sleeve of *Born Sandy Devotional*, I realised it was identical to the one Martyn Casey used to play.

Nothing stays with you like the music you loved between the ages of fifteen and nineteen. And 'Stolen Property' will always remind me of desolate heartbreak.

I'm glad it was Mike who gave me the news. After all, it was he who introduced me to the band. We were having a pint at the Camden Falcon, in 1999, when the conversation turned to the Triffids.

'You know he's dead, don't you?' said Mike.

'Who's dead?'

'McComb – he died in a car crash in January.'

I hadn't listened to the Triffids for years, but this was shocking. (It turned out McComb had actually died at home from complications, a few days after the accident, and two weeks before his thirty-seventh birthday.) It was one of those moments when you feel a small part of your youth die. January? But it was March now. Why hadn't I seen any obituaries or tributes? The answer was simple: the Triffids 'failed'. They are a testament to the futility of being in a band, but also to the nobility: to do all that careful work, to commit your life to music, when so few groups are remembered. They didn't become the Australian R.E.M., as predicted; McComb will never have an airport named after him like John Lennon, although he should. *Born Sandy Devotional* will never be in those '100 Best Albums of All Time' lists, despite the Triffids being a 'critics' band'. *Born Sandy Devotional* is equal to *Blood on the Tracks*, but, much as I love Dylan, he is someone else's artist, while McComb is mine.

Incredibly, *Born Sandy Devotional* still sounds magnificent today. The gorgeous lustre of 'Estuary Bed' and the wearily optimistic 'Tender Is The Night' sound as thrilling now as they did in 1986. Plus, it retains its mystery. *Born Sandy Devotional*: what a title. McComb once said he wanted something like *Blonde on Blonde*, 'A sort of law unto itself.'[3]

Essentially, it's a relic, a memory, and shouldn't be disturbed. *Born Sandy Devotional* is the sound of a summer and the start of a friendship. Over the years, I've trawled through the diaries, the yellowing cuttings, the set lists and the tickets. I've scrutinised my tape covers of earlier Triffids albums in Mike's backward-sloping hand. When he put his pen down and looked at me in the classroom that day, maybe we didn't know as much about love as we thought. Obviously, we knew nothing at all. But *Born Sandy Devotional* was as good a textbook to start learning from as any, and it was written by a fellow who knew just a bit about love.

6

In Every Dream Home a Headache

Roxy Music, two more Bs, and 'If There Is Something'

Sometime in 2005, finding myself back in Birmingham for an afternoon – not visiting Uncle Chessh, but killing time before a band interview – I ducked into the Museum and Art Gallery. The first exhibit in the building gave me a shock. There, in a vitrine, was Brian Eno's feather costume from the gatefold sleeve of Roxy Music's *For Your Pleasure*. It felt like bumping into an old friend. (A friend that had shrunk: it was tiny, like those miniature suits of armour in the Tower of London.) Memories of my Roxy life, my nineteenth year, returned unbidden. The garment, part of an exhibition of stage outfits, was a fabulous rayon, satin, silver-thread and feather creation, designed in 1972 by Carol McNicoll, Eno's then girlfriend, an artist and ceramicist. It was the attire that had cemented Eno as a flamboyant, eccentric presence in the public imagination. For some reason I'd assumed the feathers were peacock, but on reading the information card below it appeared they were in fact cockerel. Black cockerel feathers – how devilish! And how entirely appropriate for the mischievous, impish Eno.

The costume – and Bryan Ferry's space-age Elvis one-piece, designed by Antony Price – had leapt out from *For Your Pleasure*'s sleeve, the focus of many hours of study during my year of Roxy. These outfits, already over a decade old, seemed vividly compelling, refreshingly artificial in 1987, the year of *The Joshua Tree* and all things authentic.

January '87 was slow and frozen, with no clues as to how the next twelve months might proceed. It had been over two years since the convulsion of '84. Friends were slipping off to university, saying how 'heroic' I was for not going, and good luck with the band and all that. I was signing on; living at my dad's. My parents were getting on with their lives, in their separate houses. My brother and I had talked the talk; all that was left to do was act – move to London. This was proving troublesome, however. We had no contacts in the city, no idea how to gain a foothold there. For the time being we would persevere with the old band in the old town, until a way in was found.

The group was now called the Stormboys (not hard to spot which band was its chief influence), an exciting four-piece pop-rock combo available for entertainment bookings in the greater north Herts area. Most weekends, though, would be gig-less, spent alone with a Chinese takeaway, writing songs, and watching *The Tube*.

One Friday, the show broadcast a montage of Richard Hamilton's pop art collages backed by a Roxy Music song,

'In Every Dream Home A Heartache'. The images were a welcome injection of glam in a bleak, drab January, but what really startled were the lyrics. A stupendous narrative, icily intoned, with a pleasing reversal in the first verse, where the singer mentions heaven then immediately questions its existence. He expands: apparently the only course of action, faced with all this luxury, is to *pray*. It suggested a kind of Graham Greene-like religious crisis in the narrator's troubled mind. Certainly, this was no ordinary songwriter. The next day, I got on my bike, and once again headed for David's in Letchworth, returning with a copy of the band's second album, *For Your Pleasure*. After two songs I knew they were not just the New Favourite Band, but my dream band – some sort of ultimate realisation of everything that was achievable in pop.

Where to start? The name perhaps. The collocation of 'Roxy' and 'Music' was fascinating. Apparently, Bryan Ferry, their songwriter and leader, had wanted just 'Roxy' but an American group had already taken it. Suffixing the dry 'Music' (with its overtones of classical music) to the sexy 'Roxy' was a mark of genius. It correctly suggested that the band would juggle a number of opposing ideas, antithetical elements that would somehow sit in harmony. A coherent, fully-orchestrated marriage of graphic design and sound.

Plus it looked great on the page, in a block of text. All those 'ys'. *Bryan Ferry and Roxy Music*. So very stylish. And *Bryan Ferry* – a great name for a singer, like *Billy Fury*.

I had been vaguely aware of Ferry as a bloke in a pastel

blue suit crooning Lennon's 'Jealous Guy' on TV a few years previously, after the murder. Then, with a jolt, I recalled a clip from *The Old Grey Whistle Test* that had been shown around the same time. Ferry singing a song with the improbable title 'Ladytron', in a lurex tiger-stripe bomber jacket, scrunching up his eyes – menacing, other-worldly. It seemed incredible they were the same man. The clip was ten years old then, but still felt futuristic, revolutionary. This unsettling visitation from another planet must have been filed away as too far out, but now I was ready. The mannered phrasing, the tight vibrato – like a male Edith Piaf – suddenly made perfect sense. Here was a singer-songwriter who combined all my preoccupations at nineteen – music, words, art – *and* he got to date the best-looking women. And if we're going to talk about portal artists . . . Allusions and puns abounded in the lyrics and sleeve design. Marcel Duchamp, Humphrey Bogart, Dorothy Parker, Aubrey Beardsley, Busby Berkeley, Nabokov, Nietzsche, Nijinsky . . . A dizzying mix of modernism and revivalism: pop art mixed with art nouveau, art deco. Roxy unearthed whole eras to investigate: the twenties through to the forties, Hollywood, Glenn Miller, the fifties . . . And, in the resolute crotchet playing of drummer Paul Thompson on 'Do The Strand' – soul. Stax and Motown. Ever since Phil Collins's dismal cover of 'You Can't Hurry Love' in 1982, the country had been in the grip of a Motown revival. (Later in 1987, Terence Trent D'Arby would monetise this trend with spectacular success. Only ABC came close to Roxy's vision that year, with the sublime 'When Smokey Sings'.) I was not immune, and was devouring the Supremes, Marvin Gaye and the Temptations at a furious rate. But Roxy broadened the palette to include earlier black artists: Earl Bostic, the Ink Spots, the Platters, the Drifters. Ferry had served apprenticeships in soul bands, and, as a result, black music was in Roxy's genetic material, from the descending 'I Feel Good' basslines in 'Do The Strand' to the vocal nods to the Four Tops in 'Street Life'.

But what was ultimately compelling – and confounding – were those antithetical elements. A cerebral, ideas-band that was also frivolous, sexy. A stylish, seemingly throwaway group that made emotional, even melancholy, music. An ensemble of apparently heterosexual musicians who flirted with homosexual or androgynous imagery. The apotheosis of this was the gatefold sleeve of *For Your Pleasure*. Ferry looking down, smiling, throwing an Elvis shape, as if it was all a bit of a lark, instead of all meticulously planned. And the elfin Brian Eno, wearing the feather costume, the intellectual core of the group, yet dolled up like a Hollywood starlet.

Other, not of this world.

Meanwhile, back in that world, the Stormboys were recording yet another demo tape, this time at a real studio, in Letchworth. Driving up in the snow, trying to find the address and getting lost in a housing estate, it became awfully apparent that the studio might be 'residential'. And so it proved. The engineer, a tall, boss-eyed chap in a dressing gown, greeted us cordially on his doorstep and led the way into the freezing one-up two-down. We set to work.

In the living room. During a vocal take, the local paper, the *Hitchin Comet*, plopped through the letterbox. Then a pipe burst, sending water everywhere. Our visually impaired engineer phoned his parents. During this, all my bass parts were successfully wiped. Finally, we exited with tape copies on strange hypnotherapy cassettes, the guy still consulting the manual. It was not, from the many rock books I'd read, what I thought the recording process would be like.

Intermittent live work followed. Bedford, Dunstable, then Harlow's the Square – a proper gig with printed tickets and a ceiling-mounted 'flying' PA, but, alas, no audience. Sometimes the long-coated silhouettes of Duke, Bill and Spike would be visible in the audience. But more often than not we played badly, and drunkenly, to an empty room. After one of these debacles, Spike found me 'backstage' and uttered two words: 'Pop star.' But I knew our energies could be better spent elsewhere. It was clear the move to London would have to be effected immediately. To add to the sense of drifting in the wrong direction, my new Roxy-influenced vision for the band seemed completely out of step with the times. In March, U2 released *The Joshua Tree*, sales of which rapidly overtook every other album by a guitar band that year. Almost overnight, they become the biggest group in the world. The songs were on the radio every ten minutes, oleaginous DJ Gary Davies proclaiming them to be his favourite band. The record was deemed so important, *World in Action* devoted an hour-long special to it. There was a choice that year, or so it seemed: Stetsons, stubble, and leather waistcoats; or feathers, mascara, and lurex tiger-stripe bomber jackets. Apart from the release in the same month of Prince's peach and black phantasmagoria, *Sign of the Times*, Roxy Music were the only beacon of light.

My need for more Roxy, more of their sublime songs, and for information about the band, was insatiable. The only book available was *Roxy Music: Style with Substance* by Johnny Rogan, the biographer Morrissey later said he hoped would die in a pile-up on the M3. It's an often snide read, depicting Ferry as a serial womaniser and clothes horse. (Referring to Ferry's obsessive dating of the Roxy album cover girls, Rogan accuses him of 'nympholepsy', a word I had to look up. Nympholepsy *n.* Ecstasy or frenzy caused by desire of the unattainable.) But the backstory was there: the band were comprised of artists and intellectuals, as suspected; and Ferry, like Bowie, had been a mod in his youth. It was also clear that Ferry was not really a literary writer, but had taken his love of wordplay from Cole Porter.

Typically, the only friend that was into Roxy was Bill, and over cups of tea at my father's house we would discuss the lyrics to his favourite song, 'Strictly Confidential'. Bill loved this dark tale of schizophrenia, but sometimes it was hard to make out the words. I was just taken by a writer who would use the conjunction 'nevertheless' in a pop song.

Rogan also examined the troubled relationship between Roxy's two Bs – Bryan and Brian. It was now clear that the best groups, or at least the most interesting, had at their core a kind of twin relationship. Indeed, the most famous of these dyads – Jagger and Richards – was even nicknamed The Glimmer Twins. (Elvis had a twin that died at birth. Imagine if the other had lived. Imagine *their* band.) By now I owned the first, eponymous Roxy Music album, and there in the gatefold were the two Bs, facing in opposite directions, dressed in similar, but differentiated big-cat outfits. Tiger-stripe for Bryan; leopard spots for Brian. It reminded me of my mum colour-coding my brother and I when we were younger. Red for him; blue for me. A convenient way of giving each twin a shot at a separate identity (inevitably we were referred to by a collective noun: 'the boys'. To my ears it sounded almost as bad as 'the clones'), and maybe a means of ensuring she didn't mix up which one was which . . .

In any case, the power struggle between the two Roxy Bs was fascinating. During their most fertile period – 1972–3 – Brian swiftly overtook Bryan in popularity: audience, press and, apparently, female admirers. Bryan needed primacy – he saw Roxy as his group. It was the old story: this band ain't big enough for the both of us. Brian left before he was sacked, in July 1973.

None of this was relevant to the music, of course. The first, eponymous LP was, if anything, superior to the refined, muscular second act. Here, the most glaring example of antithetical elements being juggled was the disparity between a sleeve that looked as if it had cost thousands of pounds to produce, and music that sounded as if it had been recorded for twenty new pence. Music writer Ian Penman points out that the 'bad' production suits Roxy's decadent image – it sounds as if they're playing in an empty ballroom.[1] It was also of a piece with the Velvet Underground's low-fi values, another major Roxy influence. I remembered the glossy, airbrushed sleeve from Uncle Chessh's, next to his 10cc albums, and wrongly imagined the music it contained to be of a similar lustre. I could now, with all the dole time on my hands, study the sleeve and revel in the amount of care and attention that had been put into it. How Ferry's expression is an analogue to Kari-Ann Muller's, the model on the cover: lips parted, teeth bared, ecstatic, animalistic. How the group's logo echoed her mascara and lipstick. How each band member was assigned a different colour background for their photograph. Ferry had chosen for himself a fetching Flamingo-pink.

From the first line of the first song, 'Re-make/Re-model' (the forward slash a nod of allegiance to 'White Light/White Heat'), it seems Ferry is preoccupied with memory. Looking back, he concedes, is a self-defeating pastime. Yet he was aware that the wellspring of his creativity was his childhood and adolescence, and, like Lennon in 'Strawberry Fields Forever', cleverly locates musings on the past in futuristic settings. The most complete realisation of this is the third track on *Roxy Music*, 'If There Is Something'. (Bowie, who regarded Roxy as his only peers in 1972, covered the song during his Tin Machine period.) One of their strangest hybrid songs (aren't all early Roxy songs strange hybrids?), it begins as a parody of a Country and Western tune, before Ferry, inhabiting the same predatory persona of 'Ladytron', steers it into more sinister terrain.

In a torrid vibrato, he reels off a bathetic list of homely comforts he can provide for the object of his desire: a cottage, a rose garden, an allotment (a startling ruralism at odds with all the flash). The hoarse edge of violence to his voice should have been enough to make her run screaming for the hills. Behind this, without the listener noticing, a descending bassline, with a classic lamenting shape has emerged. A . . . G . . . F . . . E . . . priming us for a switch from musings on an idealised future to a meditation on the past. Memory lane.

The instruments melt away, one by one, leaving just piano, bass and Paul Thompson's sinuous shuffle to sustain the track. We can hear the squeak of his kick-drum pedal. Urgent anticipation has been created – an expectant hush, the musical equivalent of a spotlight on an empty stage. What would happen next? With Roxy you never knew. Ferry's vocal re-entry is the most extraordinary piece of singing in the entire Roxy canon, and one Bowie took care to duplicate in his reinterpretation. His voice cracks, almost girlishly, to produce what can only be described as a screech. Perhaps he wanted an effect similar to Marvin Gaye's astonishing 'yeah!' in the second verse of 'Trouble Man', the greatest scream ever recorded. If so, he came close.

The lyric evokes a past lover, or friend, or family member, even; we aren't sure which. But in the image of the girl with a ponytail, shaking her head, perhaps vividly laughing, Ferry is taken back to some significant moment in the past, when he was younger, and, in doing so, takes us back, too.

It is all too brief. After a few moments, the other instruments return for a valedictory coda. As the song rides out, Ferry – confident we're with him now – takes us on a tour through a glorified version of Yesterday, an all-out wallow in nostalgia. Admit it, he seems to be saying: your youth was a better place than where you are now, everything was more abundant, colours more intense, hills higher, trees taller. Everyone, in their own personal mythology, will have specific trees here. For me, it's the line of bare, upward-rushing poplars on the school playing field, always visible from the prison of double Maths, seen in ravishing winter sunlight.

A symbol of freedom, escape.

*

As 1987 drew to a close, a new feeling of ennui and frustration descended. Duke, Bill, Spike and Mike had all left for university, powering ahead with their lives, leaving me and Jude behind in the small town, with our pop dreams. Roaming a deserted Hitchin on cold nights, cans of Tennent's Super stuck to our mitts, we would talk strategy: we gotta get out of this place, or go mad trying. On these desolate unpeopled evenings, the town seemed almost abandoned; an old film set on an empty lot. My brother was now working in a steel castings factory, and had moved into a bedsit near the railway station. This became our HQ, the nerve centre of operations for the mission ahead; spaghetti bubbling on the two-burner stove, *Aladdin Sane* on his music centre, the windows misted against the chilly night. On one of these evenings my mother came round unexpectedly, with two plates of cold chicken under foil for us, and announced she was separating from her second husband. She'd finally given him the boot. I was elated, though it was painful seeing my mum, pale and fraught, putting a brave face on it, but finally admitting defeat. But at least she was out of the clutches of the man we had long called 'the Bastard'. She said she was thinking about moving back up north, back to her roots. A new, lonely chapter was opening up for her.

During this time, I lived inside my Roxy albums, especially the first one, *Roxy Music*. At the end of the second side were two songs that seemed perfectly to encapsulate life at this moment, two pieces so contrasted they could have been the work of different bands. The first, 'Sea Breezes', has more in common with Vaughan Williams' *Ten Blake Songs* than anything in rock. In a plaintive falsetto, backed by Andy Mackay's forlorn oboe, Ferry seems to be contemplating a journey, or a dislocation from the past, a move he must make alone. After a while, this reverie accedes to an atonal middle section, with restive, then frantic Velvet Underground guitar. When Ferry's vocal returns it is disjointed and anxious; the singer fearful of his newfound isolation. Johnny Rogan, writing about this passage in *Roxy Music: Style with Substance*, calls it 'a new period of loneliness, real and devastating'.[2] It was this section that terrified me. Was this what lay ahead in London?

The second song – the last tune on the album – couldn't, on the face of it, have been more different. 'Bitters End' is a light, camp tango, with party chatter background noise, and verses awash with pink gin. But then, in the song's middle eight, doubts and fears creep back once again. Against a heartbreaking Earl Bostic saxophone, set low in the mix and washed in reverb for added emotion – Andy Mackay 'overblowing' to create distortion – Ferry enters the confession booth once more. This time, however, there is merely resignation at the loss of meaning and identity. The desperation of 'Sea Breezes' has all but evaporated.

These last two songs I came back to again and again, for their lonely end-of-the-pier atmosphere, and for a weird sort of consolation. What *was* waiting for me out there in the malign big city? Madness? Ruin? Daytime TV and a crack habit? Yet even though all my friends had left town, I realised I did have one left, a fellow traveller, a (sorry to invoke Dire Straits) brother in arms: Jude. I wouldn't be doing this on my own. And our resolve was stronger than ever. Yes, I still lived alone, rattling around my father's house, the lights on all night, filling notebooks with stage costume designs, song titles, album running orders. But at least I would have someone with me for the next stage. Furthermore, over the last year, I'd worked out what I really liked in music: a certain Britishness, or Englishness. U2, the band of the moment, the outfit everyone was trying to copy, seemed to want to be an American roots group. I occupied a diametrically opposite position. All my favourite bands were from England, Scotland or the Commonwealth. Ferry, despite his fixation with US culture – Studebakers, Andy Warhol, forties Hollywood – was as English as Noël Coward, would never dream of singing in an American accent. The echoes of hymns and music hall in the Beatles' songs; Bowie's use of the affectionate, mollifying 'luv' in 'Rock 'n' Roll Suicide'; Ferry's spectral 'ta-ra' at the close of 'For Your Pleasure' – broken into a thousand pieces by Eno's synthesised delays – all these English things I loved, and wanted to try out myself, as a recording artist.

November. The last gig in the diary, at the old Red Hart, came and went. It was a sad moment, breaking up the Stormboys; bidding farewell to drummer Desmond. Now we had to somehow form a new group in the capital. Merely dreaming about it was no longer an option. I knew what I wanted us to look and sound like: early Roxy Music. Cockerel feathers and leopard spots. The week before, glue drying on my hands from sticking up the gig posters, a headache from the freezing night, and a police caution to my name, I wondered what the next step would be. With all commitments fulfilled, there was nothing left but to take the great leap into the unknown. I started packing clothes and records. At the Hart I'd told everyone I was going to 'get to London'. Now, in the words of forgotten mod band Secret Affair, it was time . . . for action.

PART TWO

The City

7

The Long Hot Summer of the Clash

London, Joe Strummer, and 'Train In Vain'

Eighteen months later.

On a freezing March night in 1989, I made my way alone through the streets of Camden to Dingwalls, a London music venue. I was early for Birdland, the band I was planning to see. Finding the building at last, hidden around a corner in the Stables Market, I decided to ask a member of the taciturn door staff what time they'd be on.

'Excuse me . . .'

'Ten forty-five. No DHSS concessions.'

How did he know I was on the dole? With no money to kill three hours in a pub, there was nothing for it but to roam the icy pavements. I'd been a Londoner for ten months.

Heading up Camden High Street towards Parkway, I noticed four good-looking peroxide-blond boys in long black coats walking towards me at speed. They were huddled close together against the cold, a many-legged insect becoming larger and larger by the second. It was Birdland! Stepping aside to avoid a collision, I asked them what time they would be on – stupidly, as I knew this already. They ignored the question and babbled furiously as one.

'Start a fight! Smash the place up!'

'Er, you want a riot?' I asked, taken aback.

'Yeah, punch someone! Smash the place up!'

'Brilliant!' I said, slightly unsure whether it was.

Then there was a second of silence where I couldn't think of anything else to say, but they were already moving off, an excitable, four-headed creature, speaking its own private language.

Later, standing smiling in the queue, I went over the details of the episode. Could they possibly have been, as my mother would say, on drugs?

The only riot that night was onstage. Birdland went berserk, a flailing mass of blond hair and black jeans, flash-bulbs discharging at their feet every other second. It mattered little that they had few songs of their own, and that these were laughably bad: they played mostly covers instead. They thrashed through an unrecognisable version of Television's 'See No Evil', followed by Patti Smith's dubious 'Rock 'n' Roll Nigger', the guitarist bellicosely jabbing his white Strat into the singer's side. Finally, the bass guitarist smashed his mic stand over, sending it slicing into the front row, narrowly missing my face. The drum kit followed, inevitably, booted over Keith Moon-style. And that was it. Twenty minutes of sweaty mayhem, but every one breathlessly exciting. I'd screamed myself hoarse.

Birdland, another band fronted by two brothers, had

been hyped in the music papers, notably by journalist Chris Roberts as part of his 'Blonde' movement (a loose collection of his current favourites – the Darling Buds, the Primitives, etc. – all of whom featured a singer with blonde hair.) It was a mark of how thrill-starved I was that I'd go to see a tenth-rate indie-punk band with no songs, and a sign of how desperate the press were for the new Great White Hope that they would put Birdland on front covers. (They wouldn't have to wait long for the next saviours.) But it was the group's image, attitude, and the sense of jeopardy; the notion that twenty minutes of heart-racing excitement was worth two hours of dull-witted musicianship that had forced me out into the barbarous cold.

My first address in London was Coleridge Road, Finsbury Park, N4. Since the demise of the Stormboys, I'd been taking the train from Hitchin to work temp jobs, a day here, a week there. Then one day, Bill – studying Biology at UCL – said there was space on his sofa in N4, if I needed it. Suddenly, there was a foothold in the capital, albeit a precarious one.

In many ways it was perfect. The first sight that greeted me each morning was the imposing flank of a landmark of rock lore, the Rainbow Theatre. Roxy Music had supported Bowie there in 1972. It was also where the audience had torn up the seats at a Clash gig, 9 May 1977; a night Joe Strummer, their singer and leader, once cited as his best memory of the band.[1]

My brother had begun working as a cycle courier, and sometimes flashed past on Oxford Street as I walked the other way, lugging a bag of clothes. I'd found a delivery job for a firm called Sleeves that sold shirts to 'people too busy to leave the office and go shopping'. (Poor buggers, Sleeves. They didn't see the internet coming, did they?) The job became an education in London's geography, walking the streets with a bag of French Connection polo tops on my back, 'Somewhere In My Heart' by Aztec Camera, or Yazz's 'The Only Way Is Up' streaming out of shops. It was the 'summer of love'; Acid smileys were appearing on walls, pirate radio stations starting up across the capital, playing the new sounds. With my brother, I made pilgrimages to the *Ziggy Stardust* phone box on Heddon Street, and the Abbey Road zebra crossing, complete with a predictable argument as to who would be first in line, i.e. John, i.e. the leader. That initial summer in London was freighted with hope. But with both of us living in different parts of the city, working many hours, the focus on the band had become dangerously diluted.

In May, a compilation, *The Story of The Clash, Volume I*, was released, and this time I was ready. The Clash had always felt like someone else's band, but now I wanted to make them my own. After deliberately ignoring them for so long, I could at last discover what all the fuss had been about. Once again, music from a distant era seemed more vital, more relevant than anything from the present. After nights spent smoking and boozing with Bill and his mates – many of them Rockers from Hitchin – I would find myself on fuzzy mornings, getting ready for work, listening to the Clash. I played 'Career Opportunities', a song that accorded all too well with experiences of DSS interviews, being coerced into wildly unsuitable jobs in the Forces. I played 'The Magnificent Seven' to convince myself I hadn't sold out. The lyric described in grim detail the early starts, the cold water splashed on the face that brings you back to an awful place. The hours of employment dragging; the minutes jerking. I played 'Train In Vain', because it made me feel good.

The other lesson in London's geography came from the Clash. Their songs were – quite deliberately it seemed – crammed with references to the capital. A mythological A–Z: Hammersmith Palais, Brixton, Streatham (on the bus), all the pleasures of grey London Town. There was a flavour of the city's diversity, too: Notting Hill carnival, reggae, dub, traditional Irish music. And in a pre-echo of Britpop's rejection of American culture, they identified a weariness with the US hegemony. When the Clash had written 'I'm So Bored With The USA', in 1976, the TV listings were dominated by American shows. *Starsky and Hutch*, *The Six Million Dollar Man*, *Charlie's Angels*. I remembered these programmes well, sitting on the scatter cushions as a boy, wondering if this was all there was to aspire to. Instead of America, the Clash sang about their own backyard.

Two superb documentaries, Don Lett's *Westway to the World* and Julien Temple's *The Future Is Unwritten*, feature the band members talking about their experience of London, and how it affected their songs. Mick Jones is interviewed on the eighteenth floor of a tower block, Wilmcote House, W2, where he grew up with his gran. 'All you got to do is look out there to write a song,'[2] he says, grinning, gesturing to the London skyline at night, the familiar orange and yellow lights in the blackness. But it is Strummer, still cool in his forties, who truly inspires. 'When you hear a great song you know someone's torn that piece out of their life,'[3] he says. Strummer certainly sounds as if he's done this on the first Clash album. But if he could come across as angry, callous even, in the early songs, there was a sensitivity at work, too. In *Westway to the World*, a smiling Strummer recalls the bad live review from *NME*'s Charles Shaar Murray that had wounded him, and eventually inspired 'Garageland'. He wryly quotes from it: 'The Clash are the sort of garage band that should be speedily returned to the garage, preferably with the motor running . . . '[4]

By the time I escaped to London, in early summer 1988, Strummer had resumed recording after a long hiatus. There was a new album on the way, *Earthquake Weather*. Interviewed by *Sounds*, he humbly accepted he was on page 18 now, not the cover. I read the piece, skiving from the job in sunny Hyde Park, where Strummer had once worked, 'Cutting the verge that never ends',[5] as he put it.

There was, as ever, a frustrating paucity of information about an artist I was hungry to learn about and from. Then, one evening at Bill's, on some yoof TV show, Strummer appeared, being interviewed in a west London skate park. He still looked great – Gene Vincent leather, casual white shirt, bootlace tie, quiff and a kiss curl – and seemed to utter inspirational soundbites effortlessly: 'I'm not interested in musicianship, but in somehow getting your personality, your individuality through your instrument.'[6] The fresh-faced presenter, in an American baseball jacket, nodded along. There was unexpected humour, too. While in full flow about the old days, Strummer accidentally spits on his interlocutor.

'Sorry,' says Joe, and carries on speaking.

'It's all right,' says the presenter politely, wiping himself.

Strummer tries to continue but starts laughing, realising he needs to comment.

'I gobbed on you, sorry. It's the memories.'[7]

As the clip ends, Strummer graffities some band posters (he writes 'let's groove' over forgotten dance outfit Habit), before hopping on a 31 to Westbourne Grove, still the rebel Rocker, still hipper than anyone else.

Although Joe was the chief inspiration in the Clash, the tune that recalls the first summer in London is actually one by Mick Jones, 'Train In Vain'. It is the slightest of songs, bolstered only by handclaps, harmonica, a shiver of tape-echo delay, and a shaker that arrives towards the end, to add some jalapeño heat. It's all about feel; Topper Headon's drum introduction sits perfectly, is neither too fast nor too slow. The restless octave riff in A, achieved by stabbing, and 'damping' the strings, underscores the urgency of the lyric. The key lines for me, at nineteen going on twenty, a'swim in a strange new city – giddy, insecure, afraid – were the ones in verse three about having a job that didn't pay, needing new clothes, a place to stay. There is a suggestion of the lament figure in the bassline, too, developed later in the bridges: D–C-sharp–B minor. It's slight, but it's there, lending the song the yearning it needs. But, ultimately, it's the eager appeal of Jones's vocal that is compelling. He's asking for solidarity, for someone to stand by him, for belief when no one else believes. A peculiarly male vulnerability snakes through the song, a nakedness, a hint of desperation even.

There was only one disappointment: no mention of a train.

I spent my days on trains. Rising early to the sound of Radio One, I'd head for the Victoria Line, change at King's Cross, emerge at Tottenham Court Road, note the soft, discouraged, bluish sky, and buy the *Melody Maker* at the newsstand. Then I'd pack the bag in Sleeves' tiny office, and set off for the first drop. The Fire Station on Stoke Newington High Street usually, a gritty road, long before its Crouch End-ification. Then Liverpool Street, Goldhawk Road, Holborn Circus – taking cheques from office workers in chinos, the bag becoming gradually lighter. Then back on the train. Being underground for so long would play strange tricks with the eyesight. Coming up for air at Blackfriars station, emerging beside the Thames at water level, the sun would burst on the surface, blindingly.

Soon I could find my way around the Tube system with my eyes shut, like a salmon swimming upstream. But it wasn't wise to become too confident. Sometimes, taking a wrong turn, you could find yourself facing oncoming traffic, as it were. It was terrifying, the pleasure the mob took in crushing you. And the concomitant pleasure you took in defying them.

For a break I would drop in at Bestie's, off Baker Street,

run by a certain George Best. You could see him on the bar's payphone at midday, toxic bloat hidden by a full beard, glass of Pinot Grigio in hand. A soft, smiling, bemused presence. It was around the time of the disastrous, drunken interview on *Wogan*. He was lost, but there remained an ineffable air of greatness about him, a bearing that bespoke past glories.

After this I'd kill an hour in John's Café on Chalk Farm Road, an old Strummer haunt. It was opposite Rehearsal Rehearsals, where the Clash used to practise. Here I could read the *Melody Maker,* and string out a strong, sour tea.

London in 1988 still had a whiff of the 1970s. You could smoke on buses, and, until the year before, on the Tube; the ban was only put in place after the 1987 King's Cross fire. The IRA were still active. Pubs closed at three and opened again at six. Not much was open at all on a Sunday. No Tesco Metro at the end of the street (almost certainly still a pub). Earnest young men in holey jumpers and crumpled shirt collars sold *Socialist Worker* at Tube exits. London in the late eighties was still quaintly politicised – a Citizen Smith-like idealism – before everyone gave up in the face of the globalised super-economy.

After a small, provincial market town, the metropolis came as an overwhelming shock. Sometimes I wonder if it would be easier for a teenager today, used to surfing the web. In 1988, London *was* the internet, a rapid, bewildering succession of violent, erotic images, all of them transient and unsatisfying. And then the contrast when you returned to your bedsit, and it was switched off.

Every day you met the world head-on: litter, dog shit,

delays, confusion, overcrowding, graffiti, ever-present opportunities for violence. Sordid odours of sweat and stale urine on the Tube. Entire carriages of commuters nodding out over their *Evening Standards* ('Theatre-goers are getting used to stepping over bodies in the Strand . . .'), the first kids of my age begging.

The crazies, the public drinkers, the babblers: these were the real surprise. Satellite towns have their eccentrics, maybe the one tramp, but in London they seemed to be on every street corner. Thatcher was in the process of throwing open the mental hospitals (notably Friern Barnet in north London) on the pretext of 'Care in the Community', but really just to cut the NHS bill. Once, sitting in John's Café, a mentally ill man in his sixties whispered in my ear as he left: 'I feel safe with you in office.' It became a catchphrase with me and my brother, a stock answer to everything, working just as well as a greeting or an adieu. But although we made fun of them, more often than not it was ugly and dispiriting, seeing these sick people in need of help.

Dance music was in the ascendant; Acid House the new sound. Only the slightly contrived Transvision Vamp, another of Chris Roberts' Blonde groups, referenced the Clash (well, the guitarist wore white jeans anyway). At least Acid was vaguely anti-establishment, I thought, listening to Radio One each day. Rave culture aside, it was business as usual. Stock Aitken Waterman, Miça Paris, Phil Collins in *Buster*. And a new group, fronted by twins in Levis 501s, Bros. Wherever I went with my brother from now on people would feel compelled to make a remark. Once, needing somewhere to rehearse, we found ourselves in a squat on King Henry's Road, Primrose Hill. A guy at Sleeves had told me there was a battered white upright we could routine songs on. When he opened the door he said, inevitably, 'So you're the new Bros then.'

By now I badly needed a place of my own. But with no connections and little money, how to go about finding one in the labyrinth of London? I began by looking at shop window ads in Camden, then the *Evening Standard*, then *LOOT*, then the *Ham & High*, finally finding a bedsit to rent on the Archway Road. When I was shown the room, the door opened on a scene of devastation. There were dozens of Bob Dylan albums scattered everywhere, as if two fans had had a terrible fight over which was best, *John Wesley Harding* or *Nashville Skyline*. Still, if a music nut lived there, perhaps it would do for me.

When the day came to install my stuff, the landlord, Pan – a sleepy Greek guy with perma-white stubble and an off-white roll neck, like an extra from *The Guns of Navarone* – came round to help.

'Is this your first time away from home?'

Indeed it was, I said, both of them. All I had were my books, vinyl, denim jacket and jeans, a black and white TV, an old Suzuki acoustic, my father's Olympia typewriter, and the three-tier white bookshelf he'd made out of old beams salvaged from Gospel Oak priory. That dated from when *he* had lived in London, in 1966.

The first evening in my new place, I switched off the lights, wiped two spaces on the steamy window, and gazed into the night. Who, or what, was out there? There were lofty, flourishing trees, a milky maroon sky, an aeroplane – just two red lights – cutting across and vanishing into cloud. Orange shapes, the windows of the houses opposite, diffracted in the raindrops on the pane. So many people in their tiny boxes. The trees swayed gently as I smoked into the night, listening to records. So this was London, my new home.

The Tube ran below the house, and from 5 a.m. the crumbling Victorian structure would tremble every few minutes, as if in the grip of earthquake aftershocks. I quickly got used to it.

Pan was cool, said he didn't mind if the rent was late now and again. That Christmas, there was even a bottle of dangerous looking red wine for me. I kept if for emergencies. As the legend on an off-licence further down Archway Road read: 'A day without Troodos wine is a day without sunshine!'

By early 1989, however, when I braved the freezing streets of Camden to see Birdland, any glamour London may have had was starting to fade. One winter in, the work drying up, I started signing on again. To earn extra cash, we were auditioning for pub gigs, terrifying sheds in Edmonton, doing our duo thing as the landlord did his tax return on a table, or groped the barmaid. After a couple of cans of hard lager, we'd brazen in with two acoustics, and give them our 'Ziggy Stardust'/'I Fought The Law'/'Suffragette City' medley. On the night of the gig itself, the plug was sometimes pulled. We were too real for them (or maybe just too drunk). The little money made from these sorties supplemented a meagre dole.

In May, the band the press had been waiting for finally arrived. This is where Britpop begins, with the release of the Stone Roses' first album. Without having heard a note, I bought the record on the strength of a review by Bob Stanley in *Melody Maker*. He concluded it was 'simply the best debut LP I've heard in my record-buying lifetime'.[8] The songs were indeed as miraculous as he claimed, instantly canonical. At this stage, the group possessed faultless instincts: Ian Brown's harmonies formed counter-melodies as memorable as his lead lines; the capo-ed, *Revolver*-esque guitar figures and lucid production from John Leckie lent the record a chiming brilliance. They'd certainly listened to the Beatles, and Led Zeppelin ('I Am The Resurrection' – John Squire and Mani in tight unison, crunching down on the riff that fanfares the coda). There was a confrontational attitude that was exciting, too. Sometimes they mentioned the Clash and Situationist politics in interviews. And, of course, they looked tremendous.

But, most importantly, it was here that, for some British groups at least, the prominence of *songs* over mere riffs or noise began. For the past year, the music papers had favoured abrasive American outfits such as Butthole Surfers and Sonic Youth. The Roses, with their orthodox song structures and Beatles-y harmonies, were set to become the new template.

One Sunday evening around this time, idly watching something called *Night Network* on the black and white television, a chap came on and performed an impression of Morrissey, then one of Rick Astley. They were both pretty good. Who was this imposter, then, this new Rory Bremner? He looked maddeningly familiar. The presenter, Tony Wilson (yes, that Tony Wilson, head of Factory Records), said, 'And more of Rob Newman later.'

Come again?

Of course. Something about the eyebrows, the profile, the camber of the nose . . . I flashed back to autumn 1984, the first meeting, a week into the sixth form, when Mr Wood had introduced him to the class. 'Gentlemen, this is Robert Newman, he's going to be helping you with your *Hamlet* essays.' Before us stood a movie star: Montgomery Clift in 1956, an almost embarrassingly handsome, smiling young man. He passed impressively among us, making astute comments and wry asides.

Towards the end of the lesson, he got round to me. I must have told him I was writing poetry because he asked, 'Come on, what's her name then?' He was looking at me expectantly, smiling, eyebrows raised, with something the deeply charismatic always have: you are the only person in the room. 'Ah, they're more lyrics, really,' I said. But this only piqued his interest. Did I have a band? What type of music was it? Just then, our conversation was cut short by the bell.

Back watching the show, while other guests talked, someone out of camera range was singing 'London's Burning'. Rob had always venerated the Clash – it *must* be him. After an agony of waiting it was confirmed: 'Stand up, Rob Newman.'

Rob was marvellous, cutting Wilson down, but all the time endearing himself with an innocent, 'who me?' demeanour. He was intensely watchable.

'So, how long have you been doing impressions?'

'Thirty to thirty-five years now.'

'Was your first love impressionism?'

'No, the Clash.'

When the show ended, I dashed outside, found a phone box and called my brother, who was by then living in a bedsit himself, in Harlesden. (Eighteen years of co-habitation in Hitchin, plus nine months sharing a womb, meant that we always lived separately in London.) This was indeed a spur, a galvanising event. Jude had once held a debate with Rob as to who would appear onstage at the Hammersmith Palais first. Now Newman was on TV, and, according to Wilson, writing for *Spitting Image* and Radio Four. It was time for furious activity.

One thing the Clash had projected was the notion of an all-or-nothing struggle. 'Death or Glory', as the *London Calling* song has it. Perfect for idealistic, zealous young men, eager for their own moments of glory. Having made the difficult move to London, the pressure was now on to make it. With the added stress that there was nothing, certainly no degree, to fall back on. Moreover, my parents had moved to different parts of the country, my mother back to Yorkshire, my father to Kent. There would be no 'going home to Mum and Dad', although I knew that their doors would always be open.

Since landing in the Smoke, a permanent base to rehearse and record had been urgently required. Studio time was expensive, as we'd discovered when we recorded a demo at Redshop Studios, near Highbury and Islington. We had booked time there solely because it was where Mike Scott had made the first Waterboys album: there was a framed record sleeve, even the piano on which he'd played 'A Girl Called Johnny'. Eventually, my brother found a place under the railway arches at Camden Road station, Bonny Street Studios: a no-frills joint with maimed blue carpets and ancient amps, woodwormed with cigarette burns. A shabby rehearsal room was situated upstairs, but downstairs was a clean, compact eight-track recording space. It was this we had our eyes on.

Bonny Street was run by a gentle older guy named Pete. He seemed ancient to us, but was probably only around forty. Soft-spoken Pete was the archetypal ageing ex-hippy guitarist, hair already whitening, flannel shirt, jeans, and sandals in the summer. A north Londoner, he'd seen the Beatles at the Rainbow, and Zeppelin at the Fishmongers Hall in Wood Green, December 1968. In 1975 he'd had a chance to audition for the Clash, but at the last moment had opted to see Bob Marley at the Lyceum instead. It was a great war story: the thought of Pete in the Clash when he was such a lovely, calm bloke was unimaginable. Indeed, for a veteran rocker, Pete who neither drank nor smoked, seemed to have only two vices: supermarket ready meals, and the odd biscuit or two, which he kept in tins or Tupperware secreted around the studio's office.

From now on we would run up rehearsal and recording bills, then pay them off by 'looking after' – taking bookings and payments from the bands. Soon, my brother was working as a part-time employee, a trusted key holder, opening up in the morning, locking up at night. Two other fellows were already doing this, Scratchy, a rarely seen silver fox in a battered leather jacket (a modest chap, too, it transpired. It was years until I discovered he was Barry 'Scratchy' Myers, the Clash's on-tour DJ. So that was why there was a huge Clash flight case at the studio.) The other was Chris Sheehan, a young New Zealander. Unutterably cool, guitar-cable-thin, sleepy red eyes, an almost catatonic presence, Chris was the first heroin user I'd met. He'd been a platinum artist down under in the Dance Exponents – they had supported Bowie on the *Serious Moonlight* tour – and was now trying to eke out a living while working on his own stuff under the name Starlings. He'd seen the Triffids in Melbourne ('out of tune and drunk'), and played guitar on Curve's first recordings. He was making progress towards a deal with Anxious, Dave Stewart's label.

This was heady, exciting stuff. Now *was* the time for furious activity. No drugs (couldn't afford them anyway), no television, no distractions, just hours spent alone with a guitar, in exile, writing songs. Other instruments, too. I began learning the saxophone, my teacher allowing me dole rates, or even exempting payments when money ran out. A target was set: to finish three songs a week. In 1989 I wrote thirty-one songs, enough for a double album, or three single albums (if, that is, a record label had sanctioned such a thing). Jude was writing at an even faster rate.

The Clash, like the Beatles, were unusual in that they had more than one singer-songwriter, just like our group. In fact they had three – Paul Simonon sang his own tune, 'Guns Of Brixton'. A decision was made to start at the start, to embark on a proper study of the devices used by Lennon, McCartney and Harrison, then move on to the Clash. Arrangements, instrumentation, number of chords, subject matter, first or third person, tenses; all would be investigated. The funny chord in 'I Want To Tell You' wasn't a mistake, it was a dissonant poly-chord, G sharp 7 diminished against E7, and was there because the protagonist's feelings were discordant. The resolution to the home key of G in the bridges of 'A Hard Day's Night', on the word 'home', was intended to underscore the narrator's domestic bliss. The curvilinear verse melodies of 'Get Back', the lines about 'Jo Jo', were a way of grabbing the listener's attention – the rise on the set-up; the fall on the pay-off. There was plenty of time, in the Archway bedsit, over uncountable roll-ups, to investigate this – and to marvel that the Beatles did it all instinctively.

And not just the songs, the records, too. It was clear, from my own limited studio experience, that a good tune could easily be ruined by a bad recording. Writing a decent song was merely the start of a perilous journey towards what would hopefully be a great record. (When people say a great song they often mean a great record.) Much could be learned from the Beatles' relaxed approach, their sense of play, of fun. One thing always noticeable was the sheer number of ad-libs, the 'heys' and 'yeahs' that were left in. Has anybody counted them? Probably. Not just the deliberate whoops, like excitable schoolboys on the last day of term, before and during a solo (a favourite is one of the more restrained ones, McCartney's emphatic '*yess*' before the solo in 'The Night Before'), but the talking left in. The Goons, almost certainly, were the reason; the comedy of voices. They are everywhere when you start to listen – Ringo's tortured outburst about his blisters, at the end of 'Helter Skelter'; the Pete and Dud intro to 'Taxman', Lennon's nonsensical mumbling at the end of 'I'm So Tired'. Much of this was accidental spill, caught on a snare mic, so it had to be included. Yet it added immensely to the music. This is one of the reasons the Beatles' songs still live and breathe. (Compare to the hermetically sealed, auto-tuned coffin of a Taylor Swift single.) But sometimes it wasn't accidental. A sinister revelation: Lennon is whispering 'shoot me' in the backing layers of 'Come Together', an allusion to his recent heroin use.

In June of 1989, an African summer took hold of London, and didn't loosen its grip until late September. Infernal, tarmac-melting heat every day – thirty-four degrees followed by a solid twenty at midnight. Hot enough to sprawl on the threadbare coverlet in the room, Soul II Soul or Neneh Cherry on Radio One. Earthquake weather, indeed. One afternoon, a girl with a South of France tan walked topless down Kentish Town Road. Sometimes I wonder if this was a heat-stroke hallucination, but, no, it actually happened. In August, the Jackson's Lane sewer in north London rose, precipitating a rat epidemic. Bins were ravaged. The cut behind the bedsit became known as Rats' Alley. One morning I saw one of these large rodents sitting on a smartly dressed woman's shoe, as she waited, oblivious, at a bus stop. I was twenty-one years old, labouring over songs in the lurid heat of my room, the band still frustratingly unsigned.

But what band? Since the demise of the Stormboys, the band was just me and my brother; us against the world, again.

Current affairs continued in some faraway unreality. China seemed to be on the brink of revolution. The photograph of the young man facing tanks in Tiananmen Square became the image of the year. The Roses '68 revolution rock was the soundtrack, in my bedsit, at least. That and the Clash, of course. I owned *London Calling* by now, the album on which 'Train In Vain' originally appeared. Listening to the song, memorising the words without effort, I identified with the lines about being alone, keeping the wolves at bay. In London, whole days – sometimes weeks – could pass without speaking to another soul. Would it all be in vain, as the song predicted? Should I just jack it in? Mick Jones's augury echoed in my mind: you'll see all your dreams come crashing down. Should I have taken the road more travelled, as my school friends Duke, Bill and Spike had? They had accepted their university places, and now, in letters, I was reading about their firsts and 2:1s. But a course had been set. There was no option but to continue in exile, making a teabag last a weekend.

The antidote to this gloom was my favourite song on *London Calling*, and it wasn't even 'Train In Vain'. I would like to say it was the portent-heavy title track, or the defiant 'Guns Of Brixton', or the political 'Clampdown', but it was in fact the entirely throwaway 'The Right Profile'. Strummer's evocative, noirish pen portrait of Montgomery Clift was the one where I edged up the volume, sent the needle back to hear it again. In his *Sounds* interview the previous year, Strummer had said: 'I want to recapture that appetite for life, that energy of being 16, when the slate hasn't been written on, y'know?'[9] 'The Right Profile' with its brass and joyful *New York, New York* Mick Jones backing vocal does just that. The tune thumps solidly along, yet is light on its feet, thrilled to be alive. There's an unexpected sax, and a superb guitar framework, too. But the real joy is Joe's vocal. Strummer, who along with Lou Reed would have undoubtedly failed *The Voice*, submits one of his finest, and funniest, vocals. It's all personality, attitude, expression, yet behind it is the skill and control of someone who has been singing for ten years. Listen to how in verse three, in character as the ruined Clift, he breaks down into a gibbering, gurgling wreck, an adult baby with his old movie stills. Like Page's calculated studio touches, or the Beatles' happy accidents, these great moments were everywhere on the Clash's records.

November '89. The Stone Roses appeared on *The Late Show*, the infamous sound-system breakdown episode where Ian Brown chants 'amateurs'. It was mesmerising, car-crash TV. In the same week, they appeared on *Top of the Pops*, alongside Happy Mondays, an unheard of coup for alternative music. The Roses' new single, 'Fools Gold', peaked at number eight. They were top group in both the *Melody Maker* and *NME* end of year polls. In less than twelve months, the black-jean brigade – groups like Birdland and the House of Love – had been deposed, chaff before the wind. Just as the Clash had helped ban flares in seventies, the new Manchester groups ushered in the next era of fashion. For the first time one was confronted by the shocking sight of indie bands in sportswear. (The revolution was, however, several years off. Anyone who lived through 1989 knows that, in the real world, it was still Sonia, New Kids on the Block, Jason and Kylie, Lisa Stansfield, Martika, the Reynolds Girls. *Jive Bunny*. All of it presided over by Radio One's Bruno Brookes and his gruesome ilk.)

With the end of the decade came an air of impending cataclysm. Old certainties suddenly gone. The Berlin Wall ripped down overnight. Violent unrest in Romania – hundreds slaughtered. China still on the brink. I listened to my Clash records; the apocalyptic imagery of 'London Calling' seemed oddly right for 1989 . . . On New Year's Eve, someone threw a party in a pine furniture shop, further up Archway Road. Passing the steamed-up window, I noticed a finger had written 'Goodbye 1980s' in the condensation. Then, underneath: 'Party into the 90s.' I crossed the street, full of hope for the new decade.

1990 would be the breakthrough year, surely?

8

Nobody Does it Better

Suede, New Glam, and 'The Drowners'

When my hypothetical grandchildren ask me, 'Granddad, what did you do in the Britpop wars?' I will answer: 'Well, kids, once upon a time your great uncle and I formed a group. Would you like me to tell you about that time? Would you like to hear the story of the band?' They will live to regret the question, of course, but I'll tell them all the same. Clear a weekend, kids; it's going to be a long haul.

You might not have heard of us. Flamingoes didn't have any hits in this country (apart from number twenty-five on the indie chart), only goodwill from the music press and a small following. Andrew Mueller, writing for *Uncut* in 2007, claims we 'built up an enviable reputation in the nineties'.[1] That's a nice thing to say, but it's perhaps an overstatement – we had our champions in the papers and a limited fan-base. Unless you were an indie kid back then, or were in the music industry, the only Flamingoes you might be aware of would be the American doo-wop group the Flamingos, whose biggest hit was 'I Only Have Eyes For You'.

Yet we happened to be active and releasing records during a fascinating period: the Britpop moment, 1993–5. A vanished world. No one had a mobile phone. Few people owned a computer. Music was still played on Walkmans. No one Facebooked or tweeted. Bands didn't have MySpace or other social media platforms as a means of disseminating their work, only the weekly music press and National Radio One. Nineteen ninety-five was also the year that pop music – for so long under the strain of its own diversity – finally began to fracture into sub-genres, a state from which it has never recovered.

But that was a long way off in 1990. The 'band' was still recording demos at Bonny Street. Pete – invariably generous with his time – would be there to help store a programme on tape, or set up a microphone. He taught us how to use the eight-track desk, the Revox tape machine, the outboard effects. And because my brother was a key holder, we were now able to record all night for free, an exceptional opportunity. In the days before everything was recorded at home on computers, this was a luxury afforded to very few. By now we were called the Shade, a studio band.

We badly needed a drummer.

When we did make the odd rare live appearance, we had to hire one. At the Subterrania in west London, we found ourselves supporting Lemongrass (later the Lemon Trees), a group fronted by a certain Guy Chambers. The soon-to-be most celebrated songwriter of the nineties – Noel Gallagher aside – approached me during sound check. Tall, confident, slightly public school, long blue-leather Gestapo coat. I, too, was in leather, a charity shop number cut in half to look like a bomber jacket. It made me appear to be two different people sewn together. 'Are you the singer then? You look like you are,' he said. I confirmed that indeed I was. One of them. Then we stood there in the empty chrome and glass venue, in our leathers, like two guys in a not very popular gay club, with nothing more to say, until he went off to fiddle with a lead.

Mostly, though, we lived in the studio. By now I was looking after Bonny Street in the week, filling the slots my brother couldn't manage: taking telephone bookings, clearing ashtrays, airing rooms that smelled strongly of men who had rocked. Then setting up the mics for the next band. After this, I'd retreat to the cramped burrow of the office, and try to read the *Melody Maker* over a sweet machine coffee, and a pilfered Hobnob (from Pete's fine stash), as crusties King Konehead pulverised the amps for hour after hour. It felt like being locked in a kind of insanity. I would dream of their racket later in bed. What must *their* dreams have been like?

The paying customers were a diverse collection of misfits and ne'er-do-wells. Roland S. Howard, ex-Birthday Party, now fronting a new group, These Immortal Souls rehearsed tirelessly at Bonny Street. (In the desk diary, in Pete's elegantly looping pencil script, every week for months ahead was: 'T. I. Souls', and the price neatly circled.) Howard, a spectral presence, seen on the stairs occasionally like an apparition, had written a classic song at sixteen, 'Shivers', and appeared in *Wings of Desire*, a film that had impressed me hugely the previous year. Then there was Eddie Tenpole, of Tenpole Tudor, robust in tweeds and a deerstalker, like some shabby earl down on his luck, rheumy eyes gleaming as I opened the cash box in the office drawer. Or Chapterhouse, pups, still with the price tags on their expensive, parentally provided Rickenbackers. At the end of the night, Pete would appear in the doorway to lock up, surprising me. Bag on his shoulder, always a smile. Then softly, almost a whisper: 'Right then . . . I'm off.'

Chris Sheehan had signed the deal with Anxious. It had been a long process, and one I'd taken care to watch close up. A demo – a suite of dark, simple songs with references to the *Marchioness* party boat disaster and the IRA – had stimulated interest. Then, a spider-like, minimalist piece called 'Letter From Heaven' had secured the contract. Most days he was up at Fundamental, Dave Stewart's personal studio at The Church in Crouch End. The era of him sitting catatonically smoking at Bonny Street, Cuban heels up on the desk, watching videos was coming to an end. Already the coolest person I knew, Chris had suddenly got even cooler. He was now a signed artist, driving a new black MG, playing the Borderline, getting reviews in the press; a skinny indie sex god with a Fender Jag.

Rob was making conspicuous progress, too. He'd appeared on television again, and at the Edinburgh Festival, and was on the radio with *The Mary Whitehouse Experience*, a comedy sketch show with Cambridge compatriot David Baddiel. The winners were going through, one by one, increasing the pressure (now located somewhere in my forehead) to achieve *something*.

Then, one afternoon in August 1990, events took a hopeful turn. The day after my twenty-second birthday, I stepped into Bonny Street's rehearsal room to jam with a ramshackle Goth outfit. Regulars, they'd told me they needed a saxophone player. I had agreed to drop by, as I'd just started on the instrument and needed the practice. And to see if they had a drummer worth poaching. The best musician, it turned out, was in fact the drummer, who was also auditioning that day. Peroxide crop, white jeans, good teeth (at this point we would have accepted a drummer with no teeth). I stayed near his ride cymbal, grooving off it. At the end of the song, I turned to him and asked how it had sounded.

'Really good!' he said, with a grin.

Hmm . . . personable and friendly, too. We smoked some blow and talked about the Stone Roses. His name was Simon Gilbert, and he worked selling tickets at ULU. I earmarked him as the possible One.

With a view to becoming better acquainted with their drummer, I started socialising with the Goth band. They lived in a squat near Angel – four darkened rooms, innumerable cuttings of film and pop stars on the wall. Mark Stewart, Gary Clail, Sisters of Mercy permanently on the ghetto blaster. They took recreational acid (especially to watch TV) and got through crates of Nuclear – Newcastle

Brown – as if Armageddon was penciled in for the next day. They weren't too serious about their group. 'You take your music religiously,' they said to me, in awe. They also told me Simon thought the Shade tape I'd given them was good.

A few weeks after the rehearsal, watching Gary Clail at Brixton Academy, everyone tripping except me and Simon, I saw my chance, and pounced. Just in time as it transpired. An ageing party girl had stuck to us, and opened her pink toy briefcase to reveal pills and crack utensils (the boys' eyes bulged). Realising I had to move straight away, before the night upended, I popped the question. He said yes immediately. Jesus. I hadn't thought he would be that easy. We might have to do a few covers, I said.

'I've always wanted to do "Jumpin' Jack Flash!"' he confessed, shame-faced.

In the weeks that followed, I saw quite a lot of Simon. We found we had much in common, especially English rock from the sixties and seventies. *Beggars Banquet* Stones, *White Album* Beatles, *Give 'Em Enough Rope* Clash.

In September came a sign of something stirring in the music scene, at last. A band called Ocean Colour Scene, playing a song called 'Sway', appeared on *The Word*, the successor to *The Tube*. The song's chorus asked the listener if they wanted a piece of the action. I did. And so, it seemed, did Simon. After the last wah-wah-drenched chord had died away, I rang him. We agreed on how stimulating they'd been. The singer wore his hair in a mod style, was dressed sharply in white, and flaunted conspicuous eyeliner, like Phil Daniels at the end of *Quadrophenia*. I couldn't remember the last time a band had referenced British pop circa 1965 so blatantly. (Forget the blustery Ben Sherman merchants Ocean Colour Scene eventually became, at this point they were exciting, honest.) A few other groups, 5.30, Fabulous, were attempting something similar. But like weak snow, nothing would stick. The time was not yet propitious. Yes, they were striking, Ocean Colour Scene on *The Word*, among the podium dancers, baseball caps, and Queen Latifah prints of 1990.

Simon made it clear to the Goths he would no longer be playing for them. I'd told him that my brother and I were nineteen (a lie), and that we'd written 250 songs (on the way to being the truth). At the first rehearsal we tried him with our 'Ziggy Stardust'/'I Fought The Law'/'Suffragette City' medley. The room exploded. Our original songs sounded even better. What a find! Strummer's Law number one (via Duke Ellington): you're only as good as your drummer. When Simon played the Shade tape in the ULU office, girls *danced*, apparently. He was fired with enthusiasm, booking us a gig there, designing the flyers, and arranging to screen the Beatles' *Magical Mystery Tour* before the performance. At last, we had found a drummer, and a brilliant one at that.

He was certainly the best drummer I'd played with up to that point. He had a heavy right foot, and was a sure, hard-hitter on the snare. But he was light, too, having lifted some funk and soul chops from his hero, Topper Headon. He was also more musically knowledgeable than most drummers. Arriving early at my bedsit one day (he always gave me a lift to rehearsals in his blue Austin Allegro), Simon found me playing a new record, 'India' by the Psychedelic Furs. 'Nothing's happening,' I said (the intro seemed to stretch on for an age). 'Yes it does – wait and see!' he said with a twinkle. He was delighted I was hearing it for the first time; I was impressed he'd heard of the Furs. Then we drove up through Finsbury Park, past the Rainbow, and talked about the Clash. I didn't know he was a fair bit older; or that he'd been in a dozen bands, and this was probably his last chance to make it.

*

Flash forward, spring 1992. A bombshell: 'Suede – The Best New Band in Britain',[2] on the cover of the *Melody Maker*. And there, with a new, Ziggy-red barnet and a twinkle, was Simon.

After the Shade's ULU show – a gig executed with amps borrowed at the last minute, cabs that couldn't be paid for, frayed, sewn-together trousers, and none of the management companies we'd approached present – Simon left the band for the east London outfit with a manager, Suede. In the months that followed, live reviews had appeared for Simon's new group; a buzz, as they say, had built. Now the *MM* had taken the enormous risk of making that famous assertion, and put a band that had yet to release a record on the cover.

With the exception of the *MM*, the music business had been sceptical of Suede. When they arrived they were extraordinarily unfashionable. If you had to formulate a career-suicide cross between two artists in 1992, it would be an amalgamation of the Smiths and David Bowie. (It was the era of Carter, Ned's Atomic Dustbin, the Wonderstuff. Fraggle.) Because of this, and Simon obviously, and the fact that their vivid, feral first single 'The Drowners' was unquestionably a classic, they gripped me like no other band had done since Roxy. In a thrilling coincidence, early photographs indicated that singer Brett Anderson resembled a youthful Bryan Ferry. Furthermore, whether they knew it or not, Suede referenced another important British group, one dear to me. They weren't the new Smiths, as everyone was saying – they were Led Zeppelin: a preening, effeminate – yet commanding – frontman; a 'dark knight' virtuoso lead guitarist; a sideburned bassist who stayed out of the way at the back; and a powerhouse drummer. (Curiously, Bowie – who had also borrowed this paradigm for the Spiders From Mars – would later remark that Anderson looked like a young Jimmy Page.) Suede's image was clearly modelled on the Smiths circa 1982, but with their long hair and the fur coat that Anderson wore in their first publicity picture, they brought to mind the Led Zeppelin of 1972. Even their choice of guitars was identical: a Les Paul and a Fender Precision bass. Live, this meant they were sonically comparable to the Zeppelin of *The Song Remains the Same*: a cold, hard, bright assault. Cocaine Rock. The Smiths had jangled; Suede had, in Richard Maibaum's phrase, a delivery like a brick through a plate-glass window. Or, rather, a Les Paul through a Marshall stack.

But there was another, more vital comparison between the two groups. It seemed to me that Suede were the first significant British guitar band since Led Zeppelin to sing about sex. For years, alternative music in the UK had been governed by John Peel's oddly sexless taste: groups such as the Wedding Present, the Field Mice and Cud. The only libidinous artist that a white, indie male was permitted to like was Prince. But Anderson was as priapic as the Robert Plant of 1975. Hearing 'The Drowners' made me feel like I was fourteen again, listening to 'Custard Pie'.

The music press had also used the term 'glam' when referring to them. Suede's masterstroke was to only hint at glam. The robust rhythmic engine of 'The Drowners' slyly referenced Bowie's 'Andy Warhol' and Roxy's 'If There Is Something'. I slipped into their Underworld gig in June 1992, wondering if they'd be wearing glitter and stack heels on stage. But they wore charity-shop shirts, and their hair just long enough to keep the grunge kids happy. (And the kids were very happy indeed. Suede received a clamorous reception that night, a portent of what was to come.) It was very clever branding, although no one called it that then. And, of course, there at the back, behind the drums, was Simon.

Surreal.

Before long, I was playing 'The Drowners' fifteen times a day. A terrible urgency took hold: surely the apprenticeship of waiting had to be over soon? We were still unsigned, still starving on the dole, still in a dreadful period of limbo. My mum sent cheques whenever she could, from her meagre nurse's pay, but when these ran out it was back to the giro. Those moments of glory were looking ever more remote by the day. My brother admitted to feeling stagnant creatively, the relentlessness of the situation undermining the work. 'I can't bear to be in the arena of songwriting for more than half an hour,' he confided, stirring a black coffee in his bedsit, looking gaunt in his old brown leather jacket from Hitchin. It was getting gladiatorial. Like me, he'd sold most of his records to buy food. 'If I don't get my copy of *Transformer* back soon, *my soul will die*,' he announced one day, not unreasonably. We were both running on fumes, thriving on an abstract notion: hope. And hope can only be sustained for so long. The extinction of the will had to be next. Was it possible all the hard work and suffering would be for nothing?

It's only in hindsight I can see how funny some of it was. Once, in a corner shop, I recall buying a loaf of bread with the usual huge plastic bag full of coppers. Jude, standing next to me, said: 'It would be less embarrassing to nick it.' The shopkeeper grinned in agreement. Or dipping a piece of bread in a cup of hot water mixed with a stock cube, reminiscing about Great Meals of Yesteryear. A seemingly endless series, with gaudy colour images, like those photographs of Death Row dinners. Sunday lunches at Uncle Chessh's, gammon and pineapple, with tender vegetables, mmm . . . wasted on a finicky thirteen-year-old. Our belief in the group was now viewed, by the few people who were aware of it, as a sort of mental problem, a derangement. At this point Harvey Keitel should have stepped into our rehearsal room and asked something like: Gentlemen, is this a good use of our time? But there was no intervention, and no question of turning back.

Finally, realising I was sick of having no money, could not actually take another day of it, I decided to stop recording all night, and get a job.

It wasn't to prove easy, however. With only two A levels, little work experience, and a recession in full swing, it was almost impossible to find even the lowliest employment. I recall cutting out a News In Brief from the local paper. 'Graduates chase mop job' it read. '50 university graduates join the rush for a job – as a pub cleaner.' At the DSS, they said they had *seventy-five* applicants for each job. During a Restart interview, an adviser attempted to coerce me into working for the council. The position? A poll-tax inspector. As someone who was being vigorously pursued for poll-tax arrears, I found this grimly amusing. Instead, I got on Norman Tebbit's metaphorical bicycle. The cab card delivery work I found that summer was secured by cold-calling taxi companies from the phone book. Eventually, there was one that would take me on.

Walking the plane tree-lined avenue of Fortis Green in the sun, 'carding' was almost enjoyable. There was plenty of time to reflect on the band's lack of progress, and what needed to be done. I had a tape of Simon Barnet's Greater London Radio show on the Walkman. My diary calls him a genius, which is perhaps a bit strong; although a man capable of playing Roxy's 'Virginia Plain', followed by World of Twist's 'Sons Of The Stage', then Zeppelin's 'Trampled Underfoot', topped by Cocteau Twins's 'Lorelei' might be deserving of the title. On one cassette was an incomplete recording of 'The Drowners'. The song begins just as Simon's 'Pretty Vacant' drum intro yields to Bernard

Butler's first massively slurred A major chord. Knowing Simon, that drum reveille would have been there to identify his allegiance to punk (and also, appropriately enough, Adam Ant's 'Press Darlings'). On headphones, I could hear detail. There was, on the chorus, what record producers call a 'builder'. It was very subtle, a single high note played on an unidentifiable keyboard. Like a dog whistle, the listener doesn't hear it, isn't aware of its presence, merely feels it. The Beatles had employed a similar trick on 'She Said She Said': a high octave in the home key, played on a Hammond organ. In 'The Drowners', the builder announces the second pass of the chorus, elevates it, then keeps it there.

It was this chorus that I was mildly obsessed with. Butler had lifted the main change from Radiohead's 'Creep', a song he confessed to being his favourite at the time. 'Creep' uses a 'pivot point' or pivot tone – B – that assists the G major (the I) to slip majestically up to B major (the III). Butler uses this unusual change, but instead of diffidently closing the sequence off with a minor IV chord, as Radiohead do – the musical equivalent of folding your arms – he follows it with the V. The Chord of Euphoria. One can imagine Butler writing it and thinking, this is not allowed, no one's done this for years; but what the hell. It lent the chorus a classic rock feel that recalled Mott the Hoople, or David Bowie. But, try as I might, I couldn't remember which song. It maddened me as I listened on the Walkman. In any event, the chorus was a glory, an imperious cyclical progression, ideally suited to Suede's trademark long outros, in which counterpoint ideas could be explored (i.e. Butler freaking out on his Les Paul).

The lyrics and music of the fade were in perfect consonance. The endlessly repeating sequence, and the words (sung in Brett Anderson's startlingly English Bowie-ese: *You're tiking me oh-vah*) hung in perfect equilibrium. Precisely what the song was doing. Slowly, delicately, reeling me in. Preparing for the real assault in the autumn.

*

'So, ah, d'ya fancy giving it a go? You and your brother on bass and guitar?'

This was Chris Sheehan, July 1992. Muswell Hill Broadway, outside his front door.

'Yeah, sure, man. I mean, of course, I'll get the songs learnt right away.'

It was a momentous question, and one that I was completely unprepared for. He was asking me to join another band, a *signed* band – Starlings. And I'd said yes. Perhaps this would be the break, the means of gaining access to the citadel. He was putting together a group to support Curve on a UK tour. It would be an experience many levels higher than anything I'd so far encountered, and surely an opportunity to get drunk and take controlled substances every night.

I visited him at The Church. Ascending the stone steps, a heavenly madrigal drifted down, accompanied by a beautifully recorded guitar figure. A feeling of intense excitement gripped me: I was going to be involved in this. Chris introduced his entourage, and we talked about the tour. He also revealed that Anxious had advanced him £50,000. 'But y'know what the funny thing was?' said Chris, languidly sucking on a dart-shaped roll-up. 'When the money finally arrived in my bank account, and I went shopping in the West End – I was so used to being broke, I couldn't think of anything to buy.' I would have had no trouble in disposing of that amount of cash. Later, as he and the engineer sat in the TV room demolishing take-aways, I eyed them hungrily, and realised they took the food for granted. I badly wanted the gig.

Chris said he'd be calling soon, in the next few weeks.

Weeks became months. But I still cleaved to the hope that Chris would ring one day, as promised. In the meantime, I moved to Muswell Hill, to keep one step ahead of my creditors. And maybe to be nearer to Chris. Pete wrote me another 'creative' full-time work reference, for the usual snooping landlord. 'Don't worry, I won't blow anything!' he reassured, with a grin. There was a gloomy, gothic air to the new place. In nearby Crouch End it always seemed to be autumn. Even in summer, there were piles of dead leaves, stacked up behind the parked cars. Pete had moved the studio to Tottenham by now. It bore a different name: La Rocka. For weeks he'd been uncertain about the change, and seemed under a cloud. The new location was remote, Transylvanian after the hub of Camden.

A few days after moving in, an odd, sweetish smell in the Muswell Hill bedsit asserted itself. When I was at school, the Dennis Nilsen story had broken. A serial killer who'd lived at nearby Cranley Gardens had been uncovered when neighbours complained about a foul odour and found, unforgettably, what they supposed were Kentucky Fried Chicken bones blocking the drains. Ever since, I'd associated Muswell Hill with mass murderers; that they just lived there, one on every street. But the smell turned out to be mould. It was everywhere: in the fridge, the cupboards, the TV. In the very air.

Whenever possible, I'd persuade my new girlfriend to stay with me in the mould-stricken room. Stella, a willowy redhead from Lancashire, was a journalist freelancing for Glasgow music magazine *M8*. We had met while I was hanging out with the Goth band, and, inexplicably, she hadn't left me. Yet. Sometimes I'd write her reviews, if she didn't have time. It became boring after a while, though, putting the boot into Londonbeat. Often, she was obliged to do phone interviews – 'phoners' – from the bedsit. The payphone in the dank, shadow-filled hallway would ring. I'd go to answer – perhaps it was Chris, for me – only to have to put my hand over the receiver and summon her.

'It's Cathy Dennis on the line for you, love.'

'OK, coming.'

At the time, I was calling five record companies a day in an effort to secure A&R names for the latest demo package. Getting past reception was always the most difficult task. When I rang Ensign, the Waterboys' label, a voice said, 'Er, there is no A&R department. Send it to Nigel Grainge, 3 Monmouth Place, off Monmouth Road, London W2.' That magical address, from the back of *A Pagan Place*. I was waiting expectantly for some of these labels to call back. But they never did. It was always for her.

'It's him from the B-52s, babe.'

'I'm drying my hair.'

'He *is* calling from the United States . . .'

'Oh, OK then. Coming.'

The band was still drummerless. At the end of the corridor lived a fellow who'd mentioned he played the drums, named Max. Gangly, gestural, unkempt, wild-eyed, early-twenties Max was like a stoner character from *The Muppet Show*. He wore his hair in an immense afro, a blond Ginger Baker. His room had mould, too; the fungal spores had destroyed a camera. Sadly, the damp was all we had in common. He blasted Nirvana's *Nevermind* out day and night. The album was the vanguard of a new sound everyone had been excited about for the past year: grunge. My first exposure had been while visiting Stella at Glasgow University, where she was studying journalism. It was here that I first heard 'Smells Like Teen Spirit', played at scarcely credible, nosebleed-inducing volume over the Union's sound system. I'd never seen a roomful of people go so utterly, completely, bananas before. Something was happening here, but I could only detect a Pixies rip-off, sung by a bellowing American.

Most days, Max's English girlfriend could be heard speaking in a West Coast accent on the payphone, a mark of how badly everyone under twenty-five wanted to come from the United States in 1992. But the search for a drummer had become so desperate I asked her boyfriend to audition. When we got into La Rocka, my spirits sank. Dave Grohl's job was safe. With little sense of timing, he rattled around every drum, as if not wanting to leave any out, each excursion more haphazard and daring than the last, rarely landing 'on the one'. The session swiftly degenerated into a haze of sloppy, skunk-fuelled jamming.

One day, Max knocked on my door unexpectedly. I'd been trying out some moves in my drainpipe white Levis (waist: 28"), and a flimsy, bottle-green Brett Anderson blouse. Eyeliner on.

He launched into a rant about the mould, then broke off suddenly, cocked his head to one side, a smile forming on his lips.

'Are you . . .?' he said, eyebrows lifting slightly.

'What?'

'Are you wearing *mascara*?'

'Of course not. Don't be ridiculous.'

I slammed the door in his face.

The pressure to achieve something, *anything*, before it was too late, was now an aviary screaming in my ears. The toxic fear of being left behind, of one's twenties slipping away with nothing to show for it, was overwhelming. I thought of writing a sign that said, 'YOU ARE 24' and sticking it to the wall, like Joyce's damning injunction to himself to write, because what else was he good for?

In the end, I didn't need to. That autumn saw the fateful 'Metal Mickey' edition of *Top of the Pops*, witnessed on my ailing black and white television. For days afterwards, absurd memories of Simon came back: him calling late at night to say such and such a song of mine was 'well 'ard'; a conversation once about record fairs; a lift to a squat party. But it was becoming harder to think of Simon as a real person, and not the new mediated being he had become. Suddenly everyone seemed to have a story about the latest messiahs of English rock. An acquaintance – a UCL contemporary of Suede – revealed Brett Anderson had been known as 'football Brett' at university, because he'd been 'baggy'; wore the loose clothing of a Happy Mondays fan. Now he was poncing around in a tight top like David Bowie, a hyper-aesthete.

In December, I bumped into Chris climbing out of the black MG on Muswell Hill Broadway. He'd found a bassist and a guitar player, the guys out of the Jesus and Mary Chain's touring band. Ah well. 'I'm too focused on my own group anyway,' I said. But I could tell he read the disappointment in my eyes.

As if further confirmation was necessary, there now needed to be a period of intense activity. For once the music scene was focused not on Manchester or Seattle, but London. The Year Zero day arrived. We ditched the set, the name – annihilated every idea from the last four years.

As 1992 drew to a close, Suedemania was peaking in the British music papers. You couldn't pass a newsstand without seeing Simon staring back. Significantly, they had also begun to permeate the mainstream press, once the sole preserve of Sting and Phil Collins. *Suede in colour. In Sky magazine. In Q magazine.* Everywhere. The sheer fervour of the adulation was extraordinary. At least it couldn't get any worse. There wasn't an even *bigger* band Simon could have joined.

In the 'inkies', Suede were on the front covers, in the centre pages, the gig reviews and the letters page. They were often the first and last name in the gossip columns, so people would read all the way through. They were starting to be cited in Musicians Wanted ads. Bowie had asked them to play at his wedding, according to *Smash Hits*. Heaven knows how Simon was acclimatising to this. He'd been blown away by a favourable local paper review of a gig we'd played at the Rock Garden. I still had his number, but something – shame, pride, fear – stopped me from using it. And the possibility he might have changed it.

Despite all this, I still had hopes for the year. (OK, there were less than thirty days left of it, but something had to give.) As a mark of how desperate I had become, I started to read my horoscope: 1992 saw Jupiter pass though my star sign. This planetary movement apparently occurs only once every twelve years. 'After a decade of patiently waiting,' I read breathlessly, 'in 1992, at last you can do whatever you want.' Wow. It made sense. *I had been obsessed with music since 1980*. This was the year it would all change. Wouldn't it?

*

'The Drowners' is the Memory Song that will forever summon up 1992. All I have to hear is Simon's Ant Music floor-tom introduction, and that first great, gouged A major chord on Butler's Les Paul, and I'm back there. It is still a perfect record: the novelistic title, the striking cover image of a body-painted Veruschka holding a gun . . . And the cyclical fade that for some reason stirred deep feelings. It would be many years before I recognised the reason for this, a most unexpected one: James Bond. The final chorus of 'The Drowners' is in fact 'Nobody Does It Better'. (The fade of that song anyway.) In 1978, the first 007 film I saw at the cinema was *The Spy Who Loved Me*. Sitting in the steeply shelved seating of the London Pavilion, Piccadilly Circus – all the better to enjoy the vertiginous, mind-blowing pre-credits ski sequence – the movie's theme tune made a deep impression on me. The rising, resolving then repeating chord sequence precipitated a curious feeling of sexual yearning. That a song (and perhaps the many naked women leaping around on screen, jumping off giant gun barrels) had done this seemed inexplicably wondrous. 'The Drowners' with its rising, resolving then repeating chord sequence pulled off the same trick, nearly fifteen years later.

Nobody did it better than Suede, in 1992, at least. The public agreed: 'The Drowners' was single of the year in both the *NME* and *Melody Maker* polls. Blanket adoration prevailed.

To make matters more confounding, Rob Newman was reaching new heights, too. He and David Baddiel played the Hammersmith Odeon (now the Apollo) in December. I'd seen the show in Gloucester with Stella; it was more like a rock gig than a comedy revue. Girls screaming 'Rob! Rob!' while their parents waited outside in Ford Mondeos to pick them up. In the lobby, on the merchandise stands, his face adorned t-shirts and huge posters. He was on the front covers of the music papers, too, a Brando-esque god.

Omnipresent. Memories of the old Rob returned. Once, back in 1985, out of school, I remembered meeting him in the sunny town, at a bus stop. He had on a yellow George Michael shirt and tortoiseshell Ray-Bans. He looked like he was in the middle pages of *Smash Hits*. His comic gifts were evident, too. One day we were in my dad's living room when he launched into a perfect impression of Rick from *The Young Ones*. I remember thinking how bold and accomplished it was. Already he couldn't be contained; needed a stage the size of the Hammersmith Odeon. I finally realised Rob was a comedy genius when we found ourselves preening in front of the same mirror in the gents of a Hitchin pub. He leaned over and intoned: 'I wouldn't bother, if I were you.'

Now he had his own TV show and was headlining the venue Bowie and the Bunnymen had made their own. Rob was inspirational: along with Simon, the first person I'd met from an unremarkable background to achieve extraordinary things.

Christmas 1992. Year Zero had arrived. I decided to write some songs in isolation. As a result, I managed to spend the entire festive season alone in a bedsit. Yet I was happier than I'd been for years, because the path ahead had been glimpsed. Perhaps the big change in '92 was merely this new direction, and the rewards from it were still to come. For two days I eked out my Xmas dinner – a tin of Irish stew – sent by my mum. And wrote lots of songs; many of which I would still be playing in European venues three years later.

Suede, and more specifically their first appearance on *Top of the Pops*, became the hinge on which nineties British music turned. (Far away in deepest Essex, on Christmas Day 1992, an about-to-be-dropped artist named Damon Albarn, driven by Suede's success and his own marginalisation, wrote a song called 'For Tomorrow'.) Those three fuzzy minutes of 'Metal Mickey' were absolutely instrumental in what happened next. Just the use of the word 'Dad' in the chorus when every other group would have sang 'Pa', trying to be American – trying to be Kurt – showed how far ahead of the competition they were. American rock was about to be dislodged by a wave of new British artists. Moreover, the so-called 'Generation X' – born between 1965 and 1979 – were teenagers in the eighties, but their most powerful memories were from childhood, the seventies. For the first time, the chief influence on British independent guitar music shifted from the sixties to the following decade.

For a few, Suede's BBC debut was akin to a previous generation's exposure to Bowie singing 'Starman' on *Top of the Pops*. Beneath the clip of 'Metal Mickey' on YouTube, comment after comment attests to this. One delirious fan writes: 'This was the moment that changed my life. I was into the Prodigy and the Shamen. The next day I went out and bought a pair of corduroy flares.' Many years later, watching the footage for the first time since it was broadcast, I was struck again by the violence of their performance. How punk they were, how hungry.

The love affair with Suede was brutally brief. To this day I only own their first three, unimpeachable singles, all on twelve-inch vinyl. When Ed Buller's production became too grandiose, I went off them, like a teenager growing out of Take That. But in the beginning they were an inexorable force. Crucially, Suede were interlopers, pioneers of a long-lost male paradigm. It was acceptable to be skinny again after the eighties' peculiar stress on muscles and money, a set of values that still prevailed in the early nineties. Now there was sanction to be a certain type of man: the scrawny band guy, the romantic outsider. (This was great news for me, who secretly wore two pairs of trousers to make his legs look thicker.) Furthermore, I realised it would be possible to embrace the music that had really sustained me throughout my teens – Roxy Music, Bowie, the Beatles; and some lesser known artists I didn't know how to fit in yet . . .

Yes, it was time for one last campaign. With money we couldn't spare, we placed a box ad requiring a drummer in the *Melody Maker* – the first influence cited was Suede – and waited for the phone to start ringing.

The second was a band called Manic Street Preachers.

9

The Other Britpop

Richey Edwards, 'Motorcycle Emptiness', and The New Wave of New Wave

History holds that the initial fission for Britpop was not a reaction against the mainstream, but another branch of alternative music: grunge. Although rather simplistic, this is broadly true. British musicians at the time seemed helplessly in thrall to the genre. It is easy to see why Blur and others, in Alex James' words, would want to make 'a deliberate attempt to embrace classic British songwriting, values and imagery'.[1] In 1992, even bands that weren't grunge, indeed, weren't even American, had the Seattle look: Doc Martens, plaid shirts, lank unwashed hair. Most importantly, they all embraced the slacker ethos, and sang with American accents.

It wasn't long before the British music papers were full of anti-US polemic. Clearly this was missing the point. Yes, we needed a few more first-rate indigenous bands to put alongside Suede, but it was futile and inaccurate to say all

American music lacked wit or glamour. The clash was between ideologies not nationalities (although 'ideologies' might be stretching it). When Nirvana were inescapable, when it was all that could be heard coming from Max's room, Cobain's line about being doused in mud from 'Come As You Are' leapt out. My initial response was: they're not for me, they're just another plaid-shirt-wearing US festival group. I wanted Antony Price suits and leopard spots; tiger-stripe lurex bomber jackets. It was the *mud*, not the fact they were American, I objected to. It was only later I began to suspect that Cobain, with his eyeliner and authentic anger, was probably more consonant with my notion of the transgressive outsider musician. My rather lofty belief was that pop should be about surfaces, ideas; but also insurrection, extremism; getting up the noses of the powers that be. In 'All Apologies', Cobain suggests that *everybody's gay*, an astonishingly subversive statement to get on the radio. It followed then that the essential groups of the era would be what I will call the 'other' Britpop: Suede, Pulp, and the Manics.

*

At the end of 1992 the most exciting band in the world was Manic Street Preachers. When they made their debut on *Top of the Pops* earlier that year, the singer's bare chest was smeared with lipstick, spelling the words 'You Love Us', the title of the song they were playing. It was a deliberate provocation to a studio audience they had correctly surmised would hate them. Large sections of the rock press hated them, too, at this point, having misunderstood the band, and, crucially, underestimated their intelligence. The Manics, all too aware they were active in a post-postmodern age – that everything in pop had already been done – decided to use their first major exposure on television sending the genre up. In three hectic, hilarious minutes they managed to include every cartoon rock shape ever thrown, including bassist Nicky Wire going down briefly on singer James Dean Bradfield's Gibson; the Ronson–Bowie move. Yet at the same time they were in deadly earnest, gave their all: they played 'You Love Us' on *Top of the Pops* as if it was the last appearance of their lives.

I fell for them that night: the Clash influence, the eyeliner, the melancholy, the contradictions, it was all just right. As was their stance of despising absolutely everything. Their anger was revitalising, and, boy, were they angry. Festivals, shoegazers, crusties, even some of my favourite bands (notably R.E.M.) took a kicking. The Manics were the definitive, nihilistic outsider band, yet somehow they seemed to be 'life-believers', in the words of D. H. Lawrence. The band member I felt most affinity with was Richey Edwards, their second guitarist, lyricist and ideologue.

A key to understanding their stance is an Edwards line from the early single, 'Motown Junk', where he admits that he laughed when Lennon was shot. I knew he didn't mean a shocked, inappropriate reaction to hearing about a death, or even my giddy excitement on the morning after John's assassination – the sort of secret thrill people have watching catastrophic news events on television, heightened by the safety of distance. No, Richey didn't give a fuck. The whole retro, Lennon-worshipping, vintage amps and guitars mindset that Oasis would soon turn into an industry meant nothing to him. Yet the line was also an index of the group's contradictions. Despite their disdain for almost all canonical rock – preferring instead a bizarre mix of Guns N' Roses and eighties indie underachievers such as McCarthy – the Manics were the ultimate portal band. They were super-fans, ardent followers. (As evinced by James Dean Bradfield's fan letter to Mike Scott. In 1985, Bradfield wrote to the Waterboys' singer; Scott discovered the missive years later in a loft clear-out.) But instead of the usual list of influences, their enthusiasms were for writers and artists, jumbled with high- and low-culture icons. The sleeve notes for their Greatest Hits, *Forever Delayed*, includes a catalogue of their reference points. Plath, Picasso, Elvis, van Gogh, Hughes, Dennis Potter, Kierkegaard, Tracey Emin, Edward Hopper, Valerie Solanas, Orwell, Beckett, Burroughs. The last page of the booklet bears a quotation from Group Material, a New York-based arts collective who explore the relationship between politics and aesthetics: 'We invite everyone to question the culture we take for granted.'[2]

The Frank and Walters they were not. But, like many people, I struggled to find a song in their repertoire that matched the image and rhetoric. Then, one day, on the radio, a gorgeous descending chord sequence, under the saddest, most moving guitar line drifted out. A thick, tubey, overdriven motif that sounded as if it had been played on a Gibson Les Paul. It was the Manics, and the tune was 'Motorcycle Emptiness'.

*

It took until early spring 1993 to find the drummer.

The phone had indeed been ringing – off the hook, as it turned out. Applicants from as far away as Doncaster came to audition at La Rocka. More often than not they would seem all right, but then let slip they thought Bowie was 'a bit arty'.

Next!

I felt like placing an addendum to the box ad: no centre partings or plaid shirts, *please*.

Finally, at the end of March, in walked a fellow wearing a crumpled, flared, black velvet charity shop suit and a peaked cap, reminiscent of the one Bowie had worn in Red Square, 1973. His features were an uncanny mixture of Brett Anderson and the Auteurs' Luke Haines, as if from some terrible midnight coupling on a bed strewn with Mott the Hoople albums. He wore a record bag across one shoulder, smeared lip balm on with a nicotined finger, and spoke in the broadest cockney accent. His name was Kevin – an incorrigible Dickensian urchin, older than us by five years. Jude had talked to him on the phone; sounded him out about Bowie already. He was cool.

Kevin hinted at a shady past in All About Eve, and Sex Gang Children. He'd also been a dustman. We ran through a few tunes. After a new one of my brother's, he put his sticks down and said: 'That's a really good song.' This was encouraging: a drummer who responded to the music. Usually they just hammered through, the tune a convenient vehicle for their own skills. The Year Zero moment of the previous December had precipitated a cache of songs unlike any we'd ever attempted. They were direct, melodically strong, intense. The key was: write about your own life and the rest will follow. Address the wound, and others out there in the darkness will respond. We were quietly confident, aware that the new tunes we'd written out of desperation were the best things we were capable of.

Already Kevin had plans for the group: no one should play anything they were unsure of; all material should be put to a democratic vote; every sartorial choice must be vetted beforehand.

We'd found our man.

Meanwhile, Suede were scaling ever-more vertiginous peaks in the UK. Brett's leaping voice could be heard on car stereos, alongside Guns N' Roses and Oleta Adams. Alarmingly, their new single, 'Animal Nitrate', had reached number seven. In February, I'd caught the end of a Radio One broadcast, a trailer for an interview with the band. Gina Morris, an *NME* journalist, had announced: '. . . and the drummer, Simon Gilbert, comes out about his sexuality.' I think I dropped my eyeliner pencil. Immediately, I embarked on a mental expedition – all the rehearsals, recordings, car journeys, gigs, parties. There had been no hint or sign. Why couldn't he have told me? Suddenly, with hot shame, I recalled a night at the Goths' squat, when Simon had still been their drummer. Watching the comedy sex scene from *The Tall Guy*, all the laddish remarks in the room. Simon had just sat there with a tight smile on his face. A new respect for him formed. Good man. He'd done a terribly difficult thing, and at his own chosen speed.

The following night, Suede appeared on television, at the 1993 BRIT Awards, playing 'Animal Nitrate'. They were stupendously exciting – out of tune and violent. Simon was up on a riser, a newly crowned gay rock god. In the weeks that followed, Suede were everywhere, on the cover of *Time Out – Brett Anderson, The Making of a Megastar* – and all the music papers. The *NME* devoted their front page to a historic meeting: Brett and Bowie. In HMV Oxford Street, one side of the window display was Suede, the other Bowie. (Had EMI invented Suede in a laboratory two years ago to rehabilitate Bowie's career? He, too, was in the midst of a renaissance. Later that year, Hanif Kureishi's *The Buddha of Suburbia* was on television, with a David Bowie soundtrack; and a new album, *Black Tie, White Noise*, was being hailed as a return to form.) Inside the shop were colourful Suede t-shirt altars and gleaming CD shrines – all their recorded work to date. A huge, magnified billboard of the week's chart confirmed *Suede* had gone straight in at number one. The fastest selling British debut album of all time. My head spun. Behind me, a kid muttered, 'It's bloomin' Suedemania.'

Shortly after the audition, I met Kevin at the Royal George, off Charing Cross Road. He was wearing eyeliner, and his tall, foxy Scottish girlfriend was in a tight Ziggy Stardust t-shirt and tan needlecord flares. Something was happening here and I *did* know what it was, this time. We talked about the surprisingly marvellous new record Blur had just released, 'For Tomorrow'. It was taken from an album,

Modern Life Is Rubbish, crowded with Kinks-like descending lines, and Bowie-esque choruses. The last time I'd heard from them they were baggy chancers, now here they were with an assured new sound, complete with handclaps and extended 'Starman'-ish outros. Kevin was good company that night, enormously loquacious, occasionally sentimental. 'I fink we should support the Kinks at the Albert 'all, get our mums a box each to show 'em it's all been worthwhile,' he said, over a pint of stout and a Silk Cut. Afterwards, at a pub called the Good Mixer, we swilled more warm Guinness and talked more music. The place was full of indie royalty, present and future. Lush, Ride, a pre-fame Jarvis Cocker . . . and Rob Newman. I found myself walking out; just couldn't face meeting him without having achieved anything in London.

The band was still nameless. In January, I'd come up with Flamingoes, taken from Roxy Music's 'Sunset', but hadn't got round to telling Jude yet. Band names are curious things, and incredibly difficult to get right. To begin with, the handle cannot be embarrassing in any way, as this will soon be evident after you've said it fifty times on the phone. It also needs to look good in a block of print, to leap out and grab the skim-reader. Flamingoes, with its proximity to 'flamboyant', did this. A good name also needs to comment obliquely on the band's stance. Flamingos, being pink, that most loaded of colours, had all the connotations of androgyny and sexual subversion I wanted for the new Roxy-influenced outfit. Cultural references could be encoded, too: John Waters' 'Pink Flamingos' was in there, as was the Flamingo, a legendary London mod club during the 1960s. Finally, it was a reference to Ferry's other mention of the bird, in 'Virginia Plain' (he observes that flamingos look identical. An apt in-joke for a band fronted by twins). I remember noting Ferry's use of it in not one but two songs during my year of Roxy, and thinking it was strangely bound up with the future. A tingle of destiny in my dad's lounge.

The first Flamingoes gig took place in May 1993, above a pub called the Charlie Chaplin, in Elephant and Castle. I'd spent the day psyching myself up, imbibing a dangerously potent glam cocktail of Suede, the Manics, Cockney Rebel and Japan. For good measure, just before we went on, our girlfriends smeared us in mascara. We played the new songs. It felt right singing them – for the first time we had something urgent to say. Surprisingly, despite the nerves, the gig was deemed a success. Afterwards, flushed with victory, I was led downstairs by Kevin, who wanted me to meet someone. 'She's the missus of a mate of mine, Keith, 'e's a record producer. I think she might want to manage us.' This was too exciting. I met Keith first. Impish, intelligent, the spit of Nik Kershaw with his upturned nose, I liked Keith immediately. He had a slightly puerile sense of humour that I warmed to at once. Sitting next to him on the wooden bench was a woman in her early thirties. Gamine, short business-like blonde bob, large, kind, empathetic eyes. She looked like a young Helen Mirren. Kevin introduced her.

'This is Deb.'

Deb was Deborah Edgely, former head of press at 4AD

records, who was indeed looking for a band to manage. Well-spoken, immediately generous and nurturing, she enthused about the gig. 'I haven't been as excited by a band for over two years. The songs . . . I mean you're obviously handsome young men,' she said with a little smile, 'but the songs are just *ace*.' We basked in the glory. Tell us more, Deborah. Despite the plaudits, however, she didn't offer to manage us that night.

The following week, we met her at Kevin's Brixton council flat. Over tea and T. Rex videos, we chatted further about the band and the industry. She admitted she'd been listening 'obsessively' to our tape. Finally, at the end of the meeting, she said: 'Can I call myself a manager then?'

I cannot convey the music of these words.

Deborah was connected to the hilt, and, within days of becoming our representative, meetings had been arranged with a raft of live agents, press companies and record labels. She'd *already* lunched with John Best of Best in Press – Suede's PR – who said he was 'intrigued'. After nearly five years of struggle, this was all it had taken to breach the citadel.

Deborah had been the partner of Ivo Watts-Russell, founder of 4AD. It was she who had persuaded Ivo to sign Pixies (he didn't want anything so 'rockist' on the label). They'd shared a large terraced house in Balham, where she now lived with her new partner, Keith. Deborah had moved in illustrious circles for the past decade. She'd dated Kevin Haskins of Bauhaus, and lived with Pete Murphy's girlfriend. A few weeks after the Brixton meeting, when she threw a birthday party, the house was packed with music business figures and indie celebrities. Bill Drummond of the KLF, the biggest selling singles act of 1991, and one-time manager of the Bunnymen, was there. I bumped into him in the pine and stainless steel kitchen, one of those awkward encounters where you both move out of the way, but choose the same path, blocking each other. Shall we dance? Drummond was tall as a giant, and wearing shapeless early nineties clothing; I was thin as a pin, and wearing a green, wide-lapelled Marc Bolan blazer. He peered down at me with a bemused expression. What was he thinking? Almost certainly: *it's 1993 you fool, not 1973*.

As I got to know Deborah better, she revealed Elizabeth Fraser and Robin Guthrie of Cocteau Twins had once camped in the spare room of the Balham house. For an indie kid like me, this was hugely impressive. It was like telling a hippy that Janis Joplin and Jimi Hendrix had been your house guests. I pestered her for stories. She clearly still had a lot of love and respect for them, and didn't reveal much. Elizabeth was a shy creature, apparently, and Robin a difficult character. Deborah was amused at my reverence, and gently indulged it. But the Cocteaus were gods, a welcome respite from the indie-boy rock of my youth. I'd lost my virginity to their album *Treasure* (I say to their 'album', actually more like between 1.10–1.20 of the first track, 'Ivo').

A week later, Deborah took the band to meet a lawyer. After intricate manoeuvres – selling albums and borrowing money off Kevin to get there – we found ourselves in a plush Westbourne Park office, with a top music business barrister offering to work for the group. I took the Tube back, out of my mind with excitement. Kaz Gill, who had brokered deals for Suede, Radiohead and PJ Harvey was now our legal representative. At last, it felt like we were 'going in'.

Deborah would often ring in the middle of the day, as I prepared a wretched repast, startling me in my pinny. 'What are you cooking?' she'd ask, an inquisitive smile in her voice. I couldn't tell her it was my signature dish, spaghetti with two fish fingers tossed forlornly on top. 'Ah, it's ah, kind of a seafood tagliatelle.' She wasn't fooled. 'Do you need feeding? Do you need food parcels?' she continued, laughing. No wonder Pixies had referred to her as 'Mum'.

A new demo was required without delay. Using her connections once more, Deborah booked the band into The Point, in Wandsworth. The studio was a converted Victorian asylum, with a private library in a glass dome, owned by Tom Bailey and Alannah Currie of Thompson Twins. One day, an unkempt traveller guy in dreads wandered in. Tom Bailey. I experienced a Technicolor flashback to 'Hold Me Now' on *Top of the Pops*, 1983. As the recording progressed, the Twins would drop into the studio. They gave good war story. Alannah Currie told us about the time she'd interviewed Lou Reed when she was a young radio journalist in New Zealand. He'd been foul to her, reducing her to tears. Many years later, he'd apologised by garlanding their backstage area at US Live Aid with flowers.

When Deborah arrived at the end of the last day, in Tom and Alannah's jeep, a sense of events becoming more dreamlike by the minute took hold. What was I doing in a converted Victorian asylum at midnight with the Thompson Twins? It was more surreal than the Dave Gahan episode. (Around this time, at Nomis Studios, helping Kevin move his drum kit to La Rocka, I found myself standing in a queue for the vending machine. In front of me was a lanky chap in a grey t-shirt and biker boots, angrily trying to get a Twix out. He was bashing and kicking the metal frame. It was Dave Gahan of Depeche Mode, currently number one in America. I toyed with taking him up on his remarks about Led Zeppelin on *The Old Grey Whistle Test* in 1984, but he probably wouldn't have wanted to hear it, especially as he eventually had to make do with a Snickers.)

In July, the band played its first gig in front of a music journalist. Deborah had told the *NME*'s Simon Williams that we looked like 'two teenage Marc Bolans'. He'd dispatched a young reporter, future *Melody Maker* editor Mark Sutherland, to see us at a dive called Euston Rails. That night, I'd taken a pre-emptive strike against the nerves by getting immensely and irresponsibly drunk. 'How many beers have you had?' asked Deborah, smiling. Those big eyes.

Luckily, we pulled it off.

A week later, on a Tuesday lunchtime, I took the bus down to Camden to buy the early *NME*. Finding a secluded spot by an infants' school, just down from Vinyl Experience on Buck Street, I flicked to the live section. The review was in.

It was a rave.

I slumped to my haunches in the July sunshine, kids in Rage Against the Machine t-shirts stepping past me, and read it, then read it again.

'*IT'S TWINS! Identical brothers Jude and James constantly pout, preen and flick their hair out of their faces, man-handling guitars with the cocky air of those that will be adored, leaving Kevin to play the Ken role in this indie-mod Bros . . . Fortunately the latest in a long line of ace faces have remembered to put some brilliant tunes in their trousers . . .*'[3] and on like that, heaping praise upon praise.

Had money changed hands? The Bros thing was regrettable, but it couldn't have been a better notice. In the school playground, children were singing a song they'd just made up.

Who wants an ice cream? Who wants an ice cream?

I wanted an ice cream! I wanted the keys to the fucking ice-cream shop. This time, I knew it was going to happen.

'They're signed to Mute, you know,' said Keith, giggling into my ear, 'it's the songs.'

We were at the Orange, Kensington, October 1993, standing in front of the support band, Rancho Diablo – bleak, serious noise merchants – watching them do their dark tuneless thing. By now it was The Song that was all-important, a result of Suede emphasising this in every interview. The press had been responsive, and had embraced the idea. That reference to 'brilliant tunes' in our *NME* review had been telling. All that mattered at this point was the work, and the unit of that work was *The Song*. Is the song good enough? If it is, the hype and frippery are justified, and you will prevail. All the glitter in the world won't conceal a deficiency in the tune department. In 1993, the imperative for bands was clear: before you leave for the studio, remember to pack the song. The few good ones were conspicuous enough. 'Showgirl', 'The Drowners', 'Motorcycle Emptiness' . . . but it wasn't just any song that was required, it was one that sounded British. Groups who had never considered songwriting to be a priority were now being called upon to write tunes that matched those of the best British artists of the past three decades: Lennon–McCartney, Ray Davies, David Bowie. And too bad if you hadn't bothered to learn your craft.

Write your best song now, while you're in your prime, I told myself. Write! Write! Write!

But it was hard, with the usual money troubles, and new demands on one's time in the form of meetings. We were being courted by a succession of 'used car salesmen', in Deborah's words – record company employees with no idea about music, just what was selling that week. There was a single exception: Simon Parker, Elektra's representative in the UK. Tall, impressively deep-voiced, educated (he'd completed an MA in Modern Literature at Queen Mary, University of London), an easy public-school charm. Funny, too. Above all, he was enthusiastic, inquisitive, and knowledgeable about music. At our first meeting – as we shook hands and took our seats in the inevitable bar in Camden Town – he asked us, 'What's your favourite T. Rex album?' We froze. Was it a trick, like Alan Partridge being asked the same question about the Beatles? (Partridge replies: 'Tough one . . . I think I'd have to say . . . "The Best of the Beatles"').[4] No, Parker genuinely wanted to know. We regained our composure and answered. *Electric Warrior*, naturally. It was a good start; maybe we could do business with the man (as he clearly wasn't The Man). Immediately he was talking about a record contract. Not just a one-off seven-inch single, but a five-album deal. Christ. *Elektra*. The label had a unique vision, and a distinguished pedigree that dated back to its legendary late sixties and early seventies signings. Love, Tim Buckley, the Stooges. It was also the Bunnymen's label. We'd have the cool 'E' logo and the little indented Warner Brothers tag, Elektra's sister company. It was overwhelming. The rock 'n' roll dream was coming true. After all the preparation and struggle, it seemed that finally, we really *were* going in.

*

When did the expression 'Britpop' first appear? The music writer John Robb claims he 'accidentally' invented the term in the eighties. The press had often used 'Brit rock' or 'British pop' or even 'Brit pop' as separate words, but the merger actually came rather late, a year after most of the key groups had begun to have hits. 'Britpop' as a kenning and compound noun appeared in editorials and reviews throughout 1994, but the first time it was used on the cover of a music paper was in early 1995. By then, all the bands loathed the term.

But as 1993 drew to a close, the unexpected resurgence in British guitar music still didn't have a name. No one knew what to call it. It was clear a great ferment was underway in London; all the early twenties musicians were at work, attempting to establish careers, fumbling towards a zeitgeist for the nineties. Many of the bands had a punky sound and look in common – the Clash, Wire, Buzzcocks – and more contemporaneously, Manic Street Preachers. An umbrella term that reflected this was needed. The best they could come up with was The New Wave Of New Wave.

By 'they', I mean the *NME*.

In order to understand the era properly, one must get to grips with the power of the national music press. It's impossible to overstate the sway they held, and difficult to comprehend in a fragmented digital age. The inkies were the government, an unelected committee of taste-makers that could literally decide if a group had a career or not. This power had been acquired in the late seventies when, probably much to their surprise, they found themselves acting as cultural arbiters. During the punk era they had created history as well as merely reporting on it. The music papers were the only forum in which punk could establish its unfolding story, its iconography and mythology. It is also easy to forget, at a time when the *NME* puts more and more heritage rock on its cover, that the music press were *news*papers. Pre-internet, they were the only way to access information on the bands of the day. Later, as musicians acquired websites, then MySpace, Facebook, Twitter and (enter the name of the latest social media network here) the decline in sales began. There were the three familiar titles: *Melody Maker*, *NME* and *Sounds*. I favoured the *Melody Maker* because they'd referred to Mike Scott as 'a fine-boned idealist', and put Suede on the cover. The *MM* had better writers, and was funnier than the *NME*, which often read like a pretentious fanzine – overly earnest, pseudo-erudite, and petrified to be seen as 'rockist'. Occupying the middle ground was *Sounds*. With its hard rock background, *Sounds* was like your slightly embarrassing mate who was still into metal. You bought it on a Tuesday afternoon when the other titles weren't available. If you had to.

This triumvirate sat in absolute authority and judgement over the music scene in the early nineties. The emerging Britpop bands would have loved to have had Paul Weller's attitude (summed up by the magnificently plosive line from 'The Modern World' in which claims he couldn't give *two fucks* about reviews), but in fact they all read the papers slavishly, from the cover to the small ads, as they knew how powerful the press were in shaping their careers.

If the music papers could be seen as the government, the PR companies were the unions. Two operations, Best in Press (later Savage & Best) and Hall or Nothing represented nearly all the major groups. Best in Press's roster included Suede, Pulp and Elastica, while Hall or Nothing acted for Manic Street Preachers, the Stone Roses and Radiohead. The latter were fiercely committed to their artists. Philip Hall, who founded Hall or Nothing, and was co-managing the Manics, had remortgaged his house to fund their early career.

Deborah was an old friend of Hall's; she invited him to see Flamingoes at an early gig. Afterwards, he expressed an excited interest in representing the group. ('I'm looking forward to working with such a good band,' he said to

Deborah, as they filed out of the Bull and Gate.) This was tremendous news for us, but there was a shadow. At the time, it was common knowledge in the industry he was very ill with cancer. His death, a mere fortnight later, at the age of thirty-four, came as a complete shock.

Two wonderful, formidable women – Gillian Porter and Caffy St Luce – ran Hall or Nothing's day-to-day business. Caffy – laid-back, sleepy charm, a gleam in her eye – was assigned as our press officer. At our first meeting, the idea of a big gig was broached, perhaps at the 100 Club, to generate interest for the new bands. Caffy also worked for These Animal Men, an intensely ambitious, Manics-influenced group that we'd supported at the Marquee. They took cheap speed, had exceptionally ugly groupies, and wore tight Adidas tops and retro trainers, like the kids you played football with at school. It was a good look, with the added bonus of being funny. They wore what I was dressed in around the time I was a Bond fan, in 1979. But it was obvious they wanted to be massive. At the time they were struggling: I'd seen them at the Bull and Gate where the number of flyer returns had been eleven.

At the end of the meeting, the plans for the gig in firmer shape, Caffy asked with a mischievous smile: 'So, are you ready to take on the world then?'

'Er . . .'

These Animal Men wouldn't have hesitated like that.

Philip Hall's funeral took place the day we played the 100 Club.

Inevitably, These Animal Men had muscled their way to

the top as headliners, leaving us to go on first. The New Wave Of New Wave gig that December – dubbed 'The New Art Riot' – was announced on Radio One. It was a momentous week for us. With Elektra's blessing, an independent label, La La Land, had signed Flamingoes for a one-off seven-inch single. We'd recorded it at Pat Collier's Greenhouse Studios, in November – as far away from residential Letchworth as you could get. Steve Lamacq played the record on the *Evening Session* to trail the gig. The 100 Club was the most important show of the band's career so far – an exposure that could secure the all-important support of the press. The day before the gig, Rob Newman played Wembley Arena, the most important show of *his* career.

At the last minute, two other unknown bands were announced: S*M*A*S*H (their name a possible reference to the Manics' cover of 'Theme from M*A*S*H') and Echobelly. In the confined and incestuous demi-monde of the British music industry, there was powerful interest and expectation.

The day of the show arrived. If pre-gig nerves had been bad before, these were like a ransacking tsunami in my stomach. I couldn't think for terror. The worst thing was that the 100 Club looked just like the pictures in all the rock books. There was the '100' in bad white letters against an orange wall – like cake decoration at a centenarian's birthday party – visible in iconic images of the Sex Pistols. I watched as the place filled with every label, journalist, plugger, PR and promoter in the land. The bands, too: Elastica arrived in a fleet of black cabs.

At precisely one minute before we were due to go on, something extraordinary happened. Two shaven-headed fellows in long coats walked up to where I was nursing a beer, and stood before me. They were backlit, so I couldn't make out their features, but they looked hard. Was it the bailiffs, finally tracking me down for those poll-tax arrears? If so I needed to tell them this wasn't a good time. No, it was Duke and Spike, with radical haircuts, and I could see now they were smiling. This was unbelievable. The last time I'd seen Spike was six years earlier, when he'd said 'pop star' to me in a Dunstable pub. Now he was going to get a chance to see if he'd been right. The last time I'd seen Duke was from the balcony of the Hammersmith Palais: he was in the mosh-pit below and gave me the thumbs up as the Waterboys' support band launched into a ragged version of 'Rebel Rebel'. Where was Bill? I wanted to catch up with my old buddies, the Desperadoes, but had to play the biggest gig of my life.

Just before setting foot onstage I caught a glimpse of Deborah, pale and drained, straight from Philip Hall's funeral. She looked as if she'd been crying for its entirety. Was it an omen?

Probably. We blew it. We weren't ready. Should have done out-of-town gigs as Elastica's management had forced them to do. And maybe not have got as drunk. During the first song, a wave of flash bulbs erupted, blinding me, and barely subsided for the rest of the set. We dashed hastily through the songs. Remember Birdland, I told myself. Ten minutes of heart-racing excitement is worth two hours of dull-witted musicianship. But it was clear we weren't even in control of our own heart-racing excitement. As I jumped off the stage, bass in hand, the singer from S*M*A*S*H accosted me.

'Was that the most fun you've ever had?'

'Yeah, with my clothes on,' I shot back.

No I didn't.

I walked to the back of the room, crushed, and watched the other acts. S*M*A*S*H were intense, committed, raw – 'We're the only band here that doesn't have guitar stands,' they sneered; Echobelly were a tight machine. With songs, too. These Animal Men preened and boomed in the background as I caught up with my old friends Duke and Spike. The industry left, having not seen the future of rock 'n' roll, but they still signed all the bands anyway. I watched Elastica leave in a fleet of black cabs.

Two weeks later, it was a subdued Flamingoes that spent 25 December at Kevin's flat. The *Melody Maker* review hadn't been as bad as I'd feared, but it was still pretty bad. John Robb wrote: '*They rushed through a psyched-out, almost mod set.*'[5] We tried to enjoy a band Christmas. After dinner, *Revolver* was taken reverently down from a high shelf, like a fine brandy. It was only a live review, but it could still be damaging at this early stage. At least there was belief in the songs. The songs would see us right; pull us through.

Around this time, Stella – still freelancing – would write pieces now and again for the music press. Occasionally, demos arrived in the post for her to review. Through Best in Press, an odd tape had fallen into her possession, a buzzed new group from Manchester, called Oasis. 'The name's a bit cruise ship, isn't it?' I said, in the Muswell Hill bedsit, lifting the makeshift cardboard flap on the ghetto blaster that was my proud repair job for the broken cassette door. I put the tape in. It wasn't very good. One of the songs was almost unreconstructed boogie – ZZ Top. Baggy boogie anyone? Not with the press genuflecting to Elastica's knowing, streamlined art-rock and S*M*A*S*H's mad-eyed, right-on racket. 'God, they're terrible!' I said. 'Worse than Whiteout. This will never catch on.'

Oh dear . . .

By early 1994, The New Wave Of New Wave was a bona fide scene, like baggy or shoegazing, only with lapel badges and much shorter hair. *Melody Maker*, not wanting to be excluded, rather feebly called it 'New Rage'. When the bands linked to the scene played, each gig was teeming with journalists. Manta Ray, proper mods from Braintree, and friends of Kevin's, were another loosely affiliated group. At a show of theirs at the Splash Club in King's Cross, Paul Moody, a writer for the *NME*, asked me, 'So are all the bands hanging out with each other now?' Such was the need for an inter-connected movement, regardless of each group's unique qualities. Elastica, only briefly and vaguely attached to The New Wave Of New Wave, had gone far beyond and were exploding everywhere: *The Word*, front covers, daytime radio.

Eventually, Elektra issued a proposal. We met with Parker at their upscale offices in Kensington. He explained the deal would go ahead if we relinquished the notion of independence in the UK. No hiding behind a major-backed indie then, as Blur were doing with Food Records. In the early nineties, credibility was still imperative for alternative bands. Kurt Cobain – a sensitive, principled man, perhaps unsuited to 'the cruel and shallow money trench'[6] of the music business, as Hunter S. Thompson memorably put it, was tortured by the idea of selling out. If the press or 'the kids' were aware a band had signed to a major label it could actually damage their sales. Before Radiohead became a national treasure, Caffy recalled an editor of a music paper hanging up the phone on her when she tried to interest him in them. When she finally managed to get them some coverage, picture editors would deliberately use photographs that showed Thom Yorke's droopy eye next to live reviews. All because they were signed to The Man: EMI. This absurd situation – a refusal to acknowledge the fact that manufacture and distribution of music requires a capitalist infrastructure – created a demand for faux-indies. Small labels, backed by major money, such as Nude (Sony), Indolent (RCA), and Hut (Virgin) enabled bands like Suede, Sleeper and These Animal Men to trade with impunity. Of course, in just over a year this would all be forgotten, sanctioned by Oasis's rapacious lust for success. But at the time it seemed as if we were the only new 'indie' band who recorded for an actual independent label.

In March 1994, the band embarked on a first UK tour. The van, from Telson's on the Holloway Road, seemed to be a vehicle more used to delivering gardening supplies than skinny rock musicians with a pronounced British sound. There was turf in the back, which I covered with the red cushions from the armchairs in my bedsit. It wasn't all glamour, though. A return to Harlow Square was made. This time there were some punters below the flying PA. We earned £100 and sold a t-shirt. Deborah was elated. *Melody Maker* awarded us gig of the week, and granted us our first interview. Pat Pope, who had photographed Suede, took the pictures.

Throughout this we were still rehearsing and demoing at La Rocka. Pete was monitoring the progress of the band with quiet encouragement. Surprisingly, his favourite songs were the raucous, punkier ones. I joked that perhaps he should have gone to that Clash audition after all.

*

'Julian and Boag from These Animal Men played it in the office for two hours non-stop. Richey loves it . . .'

The speaker was Caffy, the location the Hall or Nothing offices, July 1994. She was referring to our single.

Caffy was aware we admired the Manics, and made sure our records found their way to them. When word came back that Richey Edwards was a fan of our 45 it was immensely encouraging. The Manics were our contemporaries, but already rock royalty, years ahead in terms of what they had achieved. Occasionally, James Dean Bradfield would visit the office. I always found him slightly intimidating. Whenever I saw him walking towards me down the long drive to Hall or Nothing's Shepherd's Bush HQ, I would tense involuntarily, as I did at school when I saw the classroom tough guy in a corridor. I still did this despite the fact that everyone had assured me Bradfield was a thoroughly nice chap. Once, bizarrely, this Generation Terrorist was carrying a set of golf clubs. Potential weapons only added to his menace.

I wondered how they would fare in the new climate. The Manics, in their early incarnation, had been the direct antithesis of Britpop. In 1994, however, intellectuals, even working-class intellectuals, were not in great demand. This was a source of dismay: the fire and erudition of their interviews were exactly what I wanted from a pop group. This and the fact that they looked phenomenal. It was Roxy's balancing of opposites again. I had always needed this duality in a band to truly love them. If they had one element but not the other, I couldn't add them to my private pantheon. Richey Edwards had an antecedent, I realised: Brian Eno. Musically the least gifted member of the band, but the most intellectually curious, and the best looking. Indeed, what made Brett, Richey, and soon Jarvis, fascinating was that they all looked 'other', as in 'otherworldly', just as Bowie, Ferry and Eno had. Oasis looked like their fans, and the fans looked like Oasis. This mutuality was important, just as it had been for grunge.

That July, Richey turned up to our gig at Cardiff Hippos. I was impressed to learn that he'd paid for his ticket himself at the door. Before the show, Caffy told me he'd preferred us when we'd had longer hair. This gentle criticism, and the fact that we were being granted a visit from a genuine star, made us a little nervous in his company. In our dressing room, he introduced himself as 'Richard'. That night, the after-show atmosphere was quieter than usual. Normally, such gatherings are full of pumped, steroidal egos all competing for space. But Richey, quiet and poised, conferred decorum on the room. He was wearing a green camouflage t-shirt, work boots and a capacious pair of combat trousers that, instead of concealing his anorexia, only emphasised it. On his arms were partially healed cuts and burns – distressing purple welts under translucent skin. He incarnated the sort of mid-twenties angst that Noel Gallagher publicly sneered at. Yet, as I remember, he smiled a lot. I recall his wide, black eyes surveying the room as other people talked. He was polite, gracious and detached. He sat and listened, and was as beautiful as Elizabeth Taylor. An Andy Warhol Elizabeth Taylor. This is the point – he seemed somehow static, already checked out, a ghost: simultaneously a presence and an absence. Certainly, I'd never seen someone with such an extraordinary, waxy colour – grey as a just-delivered baby, or a cadaver. (I put this down to his smoking; he chain-smoked like everyone else present.) I wasn't aware that this was the month of his suspected suicide attempt. Later in the year, in August, *Melody Maker* announced Richey was in The Priory after a nervous breakdown. Everyone at Hall or Nothing was tight-lipped, and wore worried expressions.

Whenever I heard 'Motorcycle Emptiness' after the meeting in the dressing room, I regarded it somewhat differently. The song I'd first encountered two years earlier on the radio still had the power to surprise – the unexpected modulations of the middle eight that steer effortlessly back to the home chord, especially. And, of course, the conspicuous melancholy of the lament figure, under that opening guitar riff. (Ironically, the Manics had been the first of the new groups to employ the descending bassline that had represented sorrow in music for centuries, currently everywhere from Blur to Oasis.) But it was now the words that were unsettling. In light of what seemed to be happening to Richey, the lyrics, a list of his preoccupations, could be read as some sort of manifesto for giving up on life. Or at least life as a consumer in the late twentieth century, interested only in spending cash and cramming a house full of new possessions. (In two years' time, the film of Irvine Welsh's *Trainspotting* would revive an eighties slogan: 'Choose Life'. Of course, John Hodge, who gave Renton the line in the *Trainspotting* screenplay, meant choose a metaphorical death: the slow death of the soul, doing DIY on a Sunday morning, owning a big TV, an electric can-opener, a CD player.) Certain motifs or themes in 'Motorcycle Emptiness' leap out: pop culture, alienation, capitalism, despair, suicide. They come at you in a confusing torrent, until they are aligned by a beautifully simple five-word chorus. The image it conjures is of a lone rider at night, on an empty motorway, under neon-lit skies, escaping a baffling, blind, futile materialism. But as Richey fatalistically concedes, you can drive away from it all, but nothing changes. The most important motif is to be found in the last, ominous line of the song. There *could* be an escape from the absurdity of modern life, a pretty obvious one: the big sleep.

This was confrontational in an entirely different way from 'You Love Us'. Most people didn't want to deal with this stuff while listening to the Top 40, especially one starting to fill up with cheery Britpop. (Soon the Manics would surpass the nihilism of 'Motorcycle Emptiness' by delivering *The Holy Bible*, lyrics written 70–75 per cent by Richey, a far starker examination of some of the same themes.) The year before, a childhood friend of mine, who had struggled with anorexia and depression, had committed suicide. Like Richey, he had been troubled by conspicuous consumption and Third World poverty; had seemed to 'carry the weight of the world', as the cliché has it. But, as is often the case, the precipitants hadn't been clear. For those outside the immediate family there were many unanswered questions surrounding his death. I'd written a song, a tribute that found its way onto our debut album, but the piece of music I associated with my friend, and always will, was 'Motorcycle Emptiness'.

YouTube is predictably well stocked with Richey clips, but two in particular demonstrate how much he changed in the space of two years; the darkness that descended between 'Motorcycle Emptiness' and *The Holy Bible*. The first, an American television interview from 1992, shows Richey in a blue 'Bomb The Past' t-shirt, and bassist Nicky Wire in an enormous leopard-print jacket, playing crazy golf, and talking excitedly about success. They are both smiling, and seem happy, playful, even. It ends with Wire, in the most wonderfully soft, persuasive Welsh vowels, suggesting the entire line-up of the recent Freddie Mercury tribute concert be shot.

The second comes from two years later. An interview with grinning buffoon and ex-eighties pop star Paul King, at the *NME*'s Brat Awards. Richey is still smiling, but something has happened. He's dressed all in black, wears black mascara, and stares out into the middle distance, rarely making eye contact. His speech is far slower than in 1992, more deliberate. 'I remember you from your dubious past,'[7] he says to King, but with such charm the interviewer can't possibly come up with a retort. The conversation becomes gradually more uncomfortable. Richey intones a litany of reasons not to be cheerful. The bands that inspired you no longer do, your dog will die, your parents will die. King blusters on in a 'and-on-that-positive-note' way, not thinking that some of these things might actually have happened to his interviewee. Finally, Richey quietly and assertively steers the conversation on to a single subject: Philip Hall. He explains that, after Hall's death, the band disappeared into a room to write songs. He recalls that during their early years of sending letters to the music press and the industry, the only person to respond had been Hall. Their manager had even put the group up in his house a year after getting married. Every time King tries to move the interview to the safer pastures of the new record, Richey softly talks over him. The band would never be seen at these sort of awards shows, he assures King – 'The only reason we're here is Philip.'[8] It's an extraordinary performance, and one which inadvertently reveals all Richey's humanity.

*

Forward-wind to the following year. Amsterdam, 1995. A European tour. It was April and the city was bright, the streets lit with daffodils. We were staying in an apartment by the canal: two vast, open-plan, light-filled rooms with wooden floors. The sort of place you could leave an ironing board out and it wouldn't bother you, the sort of place that doesn't exist in London. I wanted to live there. There was an old seventies turntable and amplifier, and one night I fixed some speakers up to listen to a cache of Scott Walker records I'd discovered. A copy of *Select* sat on the coffee table. Richey Edwards was on the cover: they'd virtually written his obituary. On 1 February that year, Richey had vanished, his car – containing, among other things, a tape of Nirvana's *In Utero* – found near the Severn Bridge. He hadn't been seen since. In Paris, a French journalist had asked us about Edwards. For some reason our tour manager had answered. He'd become serious, reflected for a moment, then said emphatically: 'I think he's dead.'

Scott Walker's voice was booming now, sepulchral. 'Boy Child' poured ice down my neck. I had a presentiment, too. The previous July, as I'd watched Richey watching everyone in the dressing room, an innocuous phrase, 'a collapsed star', had been stuck in my head. There was an encyclopaedia in the flat; I decided to look up a definition. It seemed apt: 'When all its energy sources are exhausted, the star collapses under the influence of its own gravity.' Then I caught myself: I was being drawn into the same game everyone else was playing. I realised it didn't matter whether I or anyone else thought he was dead. It was merely tasteless speculation. All that was left was the memory of an iconic rock star who had bought his own ticket to see our gig, and the work he left behind, 'Motorcycle Emptiness' being among the best of it.

10

Disco 1995

Jarvis Cocker, 'Common People', and the Britpop party

I don't believe any of the bands groping towards success in 1994–5 wanted to be part of a scene called Britpop. They had all been working away, and now saw their opportunity for recognition and riches. Pulp were not going to wait another fifteen years in obscurity because they didn't want to be connected with a movement. No, they seized their chance, and would deal with the consequences of being branded with a label later. Like all generic handles, Britpop was lazy, reductive and soon to be almost entirely pejorative in resonance. As a result, it swiftly became the movement nobody wanted to belong to.

I hated the term Britpop. It was a flabby, catch-all expression designed to sell papers, just as Girl Power would be later in the decade. I understood that the press needed to confine bands taxonomically; that they were in business and had stock to shift, just as groups had – but something was starting to happen to music journalism in 1994 that made the appearance of slack coinages such as Britpop inevitable. The tabloid-ification of the music press began around this time. Only a few years before, questing intellects such as Simon Reynolds had been allowed to write about postmodernism in the *Melody Maker*. Now the writers seemed more interested in Oasis's antics on a cross-Channel ferry. It would sell papers. By 1995, the *Daily Mirror*, the *NME* and *Loaded* all seemed to be addressing the same constituency of readers.

Camden and Britpop were virtually synonymous at this point. There was, it has to be said, a tangible sense of excitement – a feeling that this was the place to be, that NW1 was Britain's exact locus of music and fashion. Guitar music with a sense of style, a great deal of it produced in Camden, was at last being allowed into the Top 40. My brother and I were residents by now. 'Our bands' were finally appearing on *Top of the Pops*. On the street, young people were dressing with more care. It was a non-guilty pleasure to put on retro Adidas sneakers, or the drainpipe white Levis, or wear eyeliner, which our girlfriends diligently applied before each gig. At first, this felt like a reversal of dressing like a hippy for much of the eighties. But in fact it was the same thing, the nostalgia artist declaring: this is my identity. Most importantly, it felt oppositional – an affront to the grunge kids with their smiley t-shirts, body odour, and beards.

If you had a sharp eye, the Ace Faces could be spotted. Camden around this time felt like a Britpop episode of

Trumpton. One could catch a glimpse of Bernard Butler walking up Parkway, looking hunted and twitchy; or Noel Gallagher, short and pugilistic – Norman Mailer-ish – heading for the Dublin Castle; or Luke Haines, standing on a corner, looking like a slightly cross woodwork teacher. Or Rick Witter from Shed Seven, loping up Kentish Town Road, a leather-clad Peperami man.

The most vivid Face was Jarvis Cocker. Once, returning from an all-night session at La Rocka, I spied him exiting a townhouse at seven o'clock in the morning. He was about to embark on the walk of shame, like a character from one of his songs. I caught his eye and he gave me a cheerful shrug. He was wearing a dagger-collared red shirt, brown cord trousers, large Jackie Onassis sunglasses, Cuban heels, and a black astrakhan fur coat. He looked fucking magnificent. Remember, this was 1994, and pretty much only Jarvis dressed like this in London. He could, on the other hand, have just been popping out for a pint of milk. I hope he was – Britpop's future song-laureate, nipping to the corner shop at 7 a.m., but remembering to dress like a star.

Jarvis didn't need the lead singer–lead guitarist dyad to function creatively, unlike Brett Anderson, or other more conventional frontmen. He'd formed Pulp in 1978 as a vehicle for his artistic preoccupations, and had been on the peripheries ever since; frustrated, invisible, out of step with the times, yet determined to succeed. He was the archetypal star-in-waiting, the personification of the Baudelairean dandy. According to Baudelaire, the dandy is always in opposition; only sure of his own existence when he can detect approval in the mirror of other people's faces. All Cocker needed was a looking glass, an audience, which he found for a brief period, 1994–7. 'To live and die before a mirror', that, claimed Baudelaire, was the dandy's slogan. For the dandy to be alone, without his reflection, was to cease to exist. Thus it was fitting that Jarvis dissolved the band when his audience started to lose interest. He pulled the plug after a poor selling Greatest Hits in 2002, because, as he noted delicately, 'I sensed the record-buying public couldn't be arsed.'

In 1994, however, large-scale success for Pulp, although tantalisingly close, still seemed somehow remote. Part of the problem was the presentation. They confused the public. Were they a joke band? I heard people ask. Jarvis had lifted some of his stage moves from Vivian Stanshall of the Bonzo Dog Doo-Dah Band. It was precisely what Suede had avoided. Of all the 'other' Britpop bands, Suede had managed *their* seventies influences adeptly, merged them carefully with contemporary elements. It would be another year before Pulp perfected their formula.

*

By spring 1994, it seemed as if we were constantly on the road. Still without major label backing – Elektra's lawyers were vacillating – our morale on these sorties was low. Usually there were just enough per diems for 20 Lambert & Butler and a Little Chef doughnut. We'd sign on, then be off once again to the vomitoriums of the north. Barrow-in-Furness, Middlesbrough, Newcastle. Places The New Wave Of New Wave hadn't as yet penetrated. The kids wore Pearl Jam shirts; and all the way there, Wet Wet Wet's 'Love Is All Around' would be on the radio. And a new cry that kept threatening to break through: *Parklife!*

With the touring came sleep deprivation, the perma-hangover, road-crash fear. An unmoored, dangerous quality to each day. Anything could happen. Always in the risky van, up and down the country again; a steady eighty on the M1, for hour after hour. Would you have a better chance in the front or the back? Death dreams invaded any sleep. Then the breakdowns, the 2 a.m. vigils on the hard shoulder for the AA flat-bed, the clutch gone or the cylinder head gasket blown. Or simply running out of fuel, as we did one tranquil dawn, homeward bound on the A1, slowing down to a graceful halt like a glider landing in a field.

Despite our first single being played on Radio One, we were still firmly in the ranks of the long-term unemployed. I cleaved to Strummer's Law number two: the dole was the true Arts Council of Great Britain. Without national assistance there would have been no Clash, Smiths, Stone Roses, Happy Mondays, Pulp, Suede or Oasis. (Or, indeed, any Creation records. Alan McGee started the label with a grant from the Enterprise Allowance Scheme.) It amuses me when politicians responsible for cutting back social security admit to being Oasis fans. Top-tier taxpayer Noel Gallagher spent, by his own admission, eight years on the dole.

In his memoir, *Life*, Keith Richards calls the social exclusion and assiduous preparation necessary to secure a record deal 'monastic'.[1] Reading his account, and other similar histories, I sometimes stop to think: they did what we did. No full-time job other than music. Just work on your craft seven days a week. For years. Whether you were in a tiny group or a massive one, the apprenticeship was the same. But that was all meant to end when you got on Radio One, right?

Lack of funds made going out almost impossible, and usually meant invitations to parties, or guest-list places to see the latest band, had to be declined. Stephen 'Tav' Taverner, the man behind La La Land, the indie label that had put out our seven-inch single, had a new signing he was excited about. One day, he played me a tape he'd received through the post, Irish lads still at school, called Ash. He suggested I see them live. 'They're sixteen, can you believe it?' said Tav, who was imposingly tall, laid-back, mid-twenties, and an optimist. 'The singer-guitar player, Tim, writes all the songs. He's a genius.' He had a look of the zealot in his eye. A genius? Steady on. All I could hear was a callow noise. But one of the tunes, 'Jack Names The Planets' *did* have a fresh, unexpected way with chords, just as Syd Barrett's early tunes had. Apparently it was Tim's first song, and was penciled to be the next release on La La Land.

Tav put me on the guest list for his new prodigies at the Falcon. Deciding to skip a day's food and spend the money on warm lager instead, I took him up. When I walked through the door of the nearly empty pub, Ash were sitting around a table with all the gaucheness of three teenage brothers in their parents' kitchen. They seemed like nice, polite boys in bad clothes, but there was something else – a strange self-possession. They seemed oddly enclosed; a band 'keep-out' force field had already been erected. I suspected they would go far.

Back in the Telson's, on the way to Deborah's, I noticed how many more guitar bands were being allowed airspace on Radio One. The previous autumn, a new controller, Matthew Bannister, had been appointed. Ever since, the airwaves had chimed with guitar-led records. Shed Seven's 'Casino Girl'; Gene's 'For The Dead', Pulp's 'Babies'. That day in the van, Oasis's first single, 'Supersonic', came on. 'The boy's no singer, is 'e!' said Kevin triumphantly, a Silk Cut wedged between yellow fingers on the wheel, crow's-feet deepening, as he dismissed the future 'voice of the nineties'. We had just rehearsed a new song of mine, and there was excitement that it could be the next single. All we needed now was a proper record deal.

When we arrived at Deborah's in Balham, however, she seemed to be suffering a nervous breakdown. The Elektra contract hadn't arrived. Having turned down all offers of work for the past year to manage the band, she'd been living on savings, and counting on her 20 per cent of the deal. Ah, it's probably just the lawyers being fastidious, I said. Better safe than sorry, eh! I phoned in our 'Ten For Today' to *Melody Maker*, ten songs you were currently listening to – a wonderfully indulgent thing, like *Desert Island Discs* – and went back to my cheerless bedsit to prepare for the next leg of the tour.

It was on the road, staying at my mother's in Keighley, West Yorkshire, that the disaster occurred. I was sitting on the deep-pile stair carpet when Deborah phoned to say Elektra had pulled their operation out of the country. That had been the reason for the delay. Apparently, Elektra UK had spent a million pounds on a British singer who had just committed suicide. Their American paymasters had decided the British wing of the label was no longer viable. The deal that had been going back and forth between Kaz Gill and the label's lawyers didn't exist anymore. It had all fallen through. The Longpigs were in a worse situation, though. They had already recorded an album for Elektra. Fuck the Longpigs! I nearly said. This wasn't some hobby, it was my life. Deborah said she had just spoken to Parker. He was in tears – he'd lost his job. I put the phone back into its cradle, and tried to assimilate the blow that had been dealt.

There was worse to come. Back in London, Deborah announced she was quitting. She'd given us a year, and couldn't afford it anymore. Kevin stayed at mine that night, for once withdrawn, morose, muttering about therapy. And at odds with all this, the joyful sound of Blur's new single 'Girls & Boys', coming out of the radio with alarming regularity.

Somehow, we managed to persuade Deborah to continue. Now it was her job to get us out of the *merde*. So sure had we been of the Elektra contract, we'd allowed the ardour of other interested major labels to cool. Now, needing to sustain momentum, it was vital to have a new record out fast. The only option was to go with the sole other company that had made a firm offer: a tiny subsidiary of an independent dance label, with no previous experience of marketing a guitar group.

I will call the label 'The Label', the label boss 'The Boss' and the A&R guy . . . Mmm, what shall I call him? 'The Ponytail', because he wore a blond ponytail, natch, and I'm going to present him in a somewhat unflattering light. Possibly say a few uncharitable things . . . all of them true. We sat in their dingy west London offices. It looked like a call centre in Hastings. What a contrast to Elektra's opulent Kensington headquarters. Deborah whispered to me, aghast at the contract on offer: 'It's a piece of toilet paper.' We hadn't told them about Elektra; they thought they were our first choice, the lunatics; that we'd gone with them out of some misguided, principled allegiance to 'indie'. Yes, if it had been Rough Trade or Beggars Banquet, not some dodgy dance operation under the Westway. For the first time in a year I was worried. The good ship Elektra had gone down with all hands, and we were on the only lifeboat. I briefly pondered the demerits of signing with a young, green, arrogant A&R man who wore cowboy boots, and who apparently only listened to hair-metal; and a middle-aged boss who only knew about dance music. But theirs was the only deal on the table.

On the day we signed with them, I looked out of the window of their rickety office and noticed, to my great surprise, a tanned Robert Plant, a blonde on his arm, strolling down a sunny Portobello Road. He was wearing a preposterous pair of brown leather trousers, but despite this he still looked like . . . if not quite a golden god, then a bronzed idol at the very least. I took it as a good omen, and signed on the badly photocopied line.

Later, The Ponytail and The Boss took us to a fancy

Chinese restaurant, in a feeble celebration of the signing. Sitting opposite me, I noticed there was something hirsutely Aryan about The Ponytail; the meaty shoulders, the blond chest hair always visible above a white t-shirt, cut off flat like the top of a privet hedge. Kevin had managed to prise a couple of bottles of champagne out of The Boss, who, assisted by his own generosity, swiftly revealed himself as a keen sexist. Dubious remarks were heard and tolerated with fake smiles. Finally, I watched in disbelief as he started coming on to our manager ('Deborah . . . that's a very feminine name'). She got up to leave, still with a PR's smile on her face – ever the professional – but Kevin yanked her sleeve and persuaded her to stay. I kept my head down, and stuffed as much of the glorious king prawn and aubergine dish down my throat as I could. It was the best food I had ever tasted in my life.

'I shan't be working with ye lads if you wear that shirt. It's an insult to The King.'

Colm, the young, skinny Irish engineer at Drugstore, the Jesus and Mary Chain's studio in Elephant and Castle, had just laid down the law. It was April 1994 – we were starting work on our new single there, and I'd made the mistake of wearing an Elvis Costello t-shirt.

I scanned his features to see if he was joking. He was not.

He ordered me never to wear the offending garment again in his presence. Reluctantly, I agreed. Colm was small, and made of pipe cleaners and black denim. He seemed to subsist on a diet of Guinness and Elvis. Although there are many contenders for the job, I think he might actually have been The King's greatest fan. Usually deferential in manner ('Awlright, Boss'), Colm had an unexpected dash of alpha in him. He could be spiky, direct, truculent even. He also had a disarmingly workmanlike approach to recording that was, nonetheless, useful. 'Producing a record is just like building a house,' he would say, as he tweaked the faders, and I've struggled since to find a better comparison. Each new verse is like an extension; something is always being added. Think of a middle eight as a conservatory, non-essential but nice to have. (Jimmy Webb, author of 'Wichita Lineman' and other burnished, immortal works, once wrote a songwriting manual, *Tunesmith*, in which he likened a song to a house. He even included a helpful diagram. The intro is the front porch, the first verse is the corridor, the chorus is the lounge, etc. He was talking about structure, but it's a good analogy for how people relate to songs. If a tune is doing its job properly the listener can walk around inside, taking what they need from it. If the song is too personal, they can't get in. And in every song there is usually a line that lets the listener in. For me, in 'Wichita Lineman' it comes in the second verse, where the protagonist admits he wants the girl for *all time*, not the more usual or expected 'for ever'.)

In Colm's mind you built upwards, and hoped by the end you would have a solid construction. I liked Colm. He had a dark sense of humour not evident from the t-shirt episode (he didn't have one at all when it came to Elvis). Moreover, he was trusted by Jim and William Reid, my teenage noise heroes, so was all right by me. He had recently engineered and produced the Mary Chain's comeback acoustic album, *Stoned & Dethroned*. The band were experiencing a resurgence of interest.

Colm took care to remind us each day that his sonic insurrectionist employers didn't approve of cigarette butts left in the coffee cups, and pointed to a sign over the sink in the kitchen. I stepped carefully around the studio, observing the rules, just in case the brothers showed up unexpectedly. One day, knowing William kept a box of scratched old effects pedals, I sneaked furtively into the guitar booth to hook some up. Instant '85 Mary Chain. I stood there with *Psychocandy* shrieking around the room, and an enormous grin.

The same month, something truly disturbing happened. Standing at the bar of the Falcon one evening, listening to Manta Ray do their New Mod thing in the shebeen next door, a friend casually dropped this into the conversation – *Kurt Cobain, what an idiot for blowing his brains out, eh?* I was stunned, speechless. Not because I was a fan, of course, it just seemed so shocking, bizarre, disgusting. No rock star of that magnitude had committed suicide before. 'Haven't you heard?' asked my friend, 'it's all we've been talking about for half an hour.' Nowadays this would be tweeted into the stratosphere; back then I went straight home and switched on *News at Ten*. There was a tiny obituary at the end of the programme, illustrating the different cultural value of Cobain and Lennon who, when he was murdered, had the whole of ITV pretty much to himself. There are some parallels between the two: both died from gunshot wounds, both epitomised the 'real' rocker, both were – that dread phrase – 'the voice of a generation'. But here the comparisons end. In 1994, pop as a single global entity was unraveling into myriad micro-genres, and Cobain's death wasn't significant to the public in general, only a certain type of music fan.

The incident is always cited historically as the green light for Britpop, like a political assassination, The Archduke Ferdinand, ushering in a new era. It *was* a pivotal moment, but at the time, in the thick of life, felt like just another destabilising event. In May, Labour leader John Smith died of a heart attack. Ayrton Senna met his end in a Grand Prix crash. In June, Hole's bass player, Kristen Pfaff, passed away from a heroin overdose. The skies seemed to be darkening, not getting lighter.

In the summer, recording commenced for our debut album. Colm had transferred from Drugstore, and drove me to Protocol Studios off the Holloway Road. In the live room stood a dirty great Ampeg rig: the eight by ten, as tall as the average Swede, and needing a team of minions to carry it anywhere. It was the Rolls-Royce of bass amps, the one all the bands used at festivals or on TV. Kevin's drums were set up in the room where Simon had played his for 'The Drowners'. A feeling that we had finally arrived was palpable. It was the Big Boys' studio, no doubt about it. At the end of the day, with several tracks in the can, Colm expressed his delight at the day's work: 'Tight as a nun's chuff on Good Friday!' he said, with a lovely lilt, rubbing his tiny hands together. An enormous pizza was ordered, and I remembered Chris demolishing his takeaway at The Church. It was my turn at last.

Around this time, I needed to pick something up from The Ponytail's flat. It was an errand I'd been dreading, but also surreally looking forward to. Would his abode be as creepy as I'd feared? He didn't let me down. In a blighted block near King's Cross, I found the address. There were posters of metal bands on the walls, and Athenas, too, real lurid, girls-splayed-on-cars stuff. Stella was with me. 'Oh my God,' she muttered when he was out of the room. (After this visit, her nickname for him was 'hairy palm'.) The whiff of batch hung heavy under low lighting. Mounds of clothes, trackie bottoms and socks, takeaway paraphernalia, empty video cases were strewn about. Weight-training equipment. Dubious tissues in florets near the unmade bed. A sense of clutter and emptiness simultaneously. I knew without looking that the only three items in the fridge were a muscle shake, a can of Grolsch and a date-expired jar of Patak's pickle. I knew he was washing up a knife and a fork, or a plate, only as and when he needed it.

The Ponytail put some Mötley Crüe on. 'If I don't like a track,' he said, 'I just programme the CD to skip, yeah?' sounding like a plummy voiced yuppie in a coffee commercial. Where was the integrity in that? You listened to *Revolver* all the way through, 'Yellow Submarine' included. I realised he didn't really like music, possibly because he got most of it free anyway.

And he was our A&R man.

*

On a hot June day in 1994, at Camber Sands, we took a break from the studio and the road to shoot a video for our new single. I'd been talked into letting the girl from the sleeve (Rebecca, a friend of Kevin's who worked the door at the Monarch) whiz around on a motorcycle as we mimed to the song. The only reason I'd agreed to the idea was the Mary Chain's 'You Trip Me Up' video: all cool leathers, LSD skies and Jim Reid's Vox Phantom stuck in the sand by its neck. But doubts were beginning to form. 'I'm just concerned it might look, y'know, a bit lame and sexist . . .' I said, to The Ponytail. 'James. What more do you need for a video than beaches, motorcycles, and chicks?' said The Ponytail, in a placatory tone.

It was an immutable rule that any promotional activity arranged by The Ponytail would be a travesty. Before one London gig, he booked the band onto a kids show for Sky TV. The interview was to take place in a crèche. It was ludicrously, laughably wrong. When we dared criticise it, The Ponytail swore at Deborah in front of all present, an unforgiveable piece of oafishness. Kevin, to his credit, stood up for her like a gentleman.

'I've never 'ad a fight with you, mate, but don't speak to Deb like that.'

It was becoming clear the Label couldn't market a free holiday in Cancún with unlimited cocaine thrown in. They had hired dance music radio pluggers for the new record, and I feared the worst. Almost as much as I did for the press ads. At the artwork meeting, when Jude made a less than complimentary remark, The Ponytail became agitated. When *I* politely suggested that the wording was wrong, that an EP wasn't a format (it read 'four-track EP and CD') he lost his temper, screwed up the artwork, and walked out of the meeting. (When the ad appeared in the paper, it read: 'four-track 12" and CD'.)

I tried to stay focused on the album. It was the thing all this had been leading up to: my life's work thus far. The Label were in favour of the singles, but didn't understand the slower, darker tunes. They didn't want this or that song, and we could only have twelve, not fourteen, on the record, for financial reasons. But this was art, surely. *Revolver* and *Psychocandy* – seven songs per side.

We had a fight on our hands from the start.

They wanted a photograph of the group on the sleeve. (The Boss had declared, without irony, that we were a teenybop band.) Oh, Parker, where were you? You would know most classic sleeves were not a photograph of the band. You would at least be aware of our references to the Beatles, Led Zeppelin, Roxy.

Now, I had, and still have, a thing about sleeves. They imprint their identity on the music. It's impossible not to; we are visual beings, after all. Because of its cover, do we not hear each song on *Revolver* in black and white, as it were; fourteen elegant, self-contained vignettes? Or U2's *The Unforgettable Fire*, with its plush, burgundy sleeve, isn't the music just somehow all *purple-ly*? No? OK, maybe it is just me then. But imagine if the cover for Joy Division's *Unknown Pleasures* was a colour image of the band eating egg and chips in a Salford caff, all 1979 tank tops and beards – a bunch of *Grange Hill* supply teachers

– and not Peter Saville's spectral, unforgettable duochrome image of radio waves from Pulsar CP 1919.

Sleeves matter. But not to The Label, it seemed.

Recording continued that August, at Falconer Studios, Kentish Town. After the drums were put down, Colm showed up every day with his copy of the *Sun*. We spent a leisurely week on basses, chatting about his plans to own a pet monkey; Elvis, of course (the ballads or the rockers?); Mike Peters from the Alarm, whom he had just finished working with, and the Mary Chain. I fulfilled a long-cherished ambition: a studio takeaway every night, alternating pizza and Chinese from north London's finest outlets.

But by now it was not a secret: we detested The Label, and Colm was starting to discover why. We'd told him The Boss and The Ponytail were two dance music con men who just wanted to make a buck out of Britpop, but his natural scepticism had held him from judgement. Then, a week into recording, the basses were deemed to be out of tune. It wasn't surprising, The Label didn't have the money to pay for proper guitars. We were still using cheap Squier copies, paid for out of giros from when we first arrived in London, six years earlier. The next day, The Ponytail appeared in the control room, chest out like an enraged rooster, tufts of hair bristling above the white t-shirt, and brushed roughly past me. 'You – in the studio,' he barked at Colm. Words were exchanged in private. When they emerged, Jude spoke up and was promptly told to shut up. He threw down the crummy Squier Telecaster he was tuning in disgust, and walked out. The Ponytail began to lecture me about how a week in an expensive studio like

Falconer wasn't cheap, and how this was his job, and how . . . I listened for a few cursory moments then walked, leaving him still talking.

Our per diems were suspended. No more studio pizzas, then. When the whole sorry scene was over, Colm said to me: 'Now get your brother to tune the feckin guitars.'

The Ponytail refused to hire a decent bass, or a proper amp. By this point I was communicating with him through Deborah. I overheard Colm talking to his manager on the phone, urging him to 'walk'. From now on, Colm would threaten to leave the project at least five times a day. At the end of the week, I took him to an Irish boozer, and, over interminable pints of Guinness, we drew up a plan. The Ponytail, dimly realising that an album without a bass guitar would sound odd, had finally agreed to release some cash to hire one. We would come in at seven in the morning, and do a week's basses in a day.

That night, I didn't sleep. I felt as if I were in the grip of a psychosis. There were pains in my chest. The following day, all the bass parts were rerecorded; one every half an hour, in a grinding, grey migraine fog. At 5 p.m. I was still playing the last one as the hire company dismantled the amp.

No one knew if we had an album.

We moved to Milo, Hoxton Square. Main guitars. At the studio, Colm was surly and offhand, as he would be from now on. And there was something else that seemed to be troubling him, though exactly what was hard to fathom. The discord had been completely preventable, I reflected;

all of it was coming needlessly from The Label. It had taken ten years to get this far, to make an album, and now each day had become an ordeal, a battle with a clueless, obstructionist record company. The feelings The Ponytail aroused in me were murderous. Every time I thought of him I was engulfed by anger, gripped by a cold fury. He should be selling socks at a car boot sale not working for a record label. I hoped he would die a humiliating death on the toilet.

The next day the trouble deepened. Or widened. It got worse, anyway. I decided not to show up at the studio. A mid-morning call from Deborah woke me, her voice trembling, saying it was all going wrong, why wasn't I at Milo? I'd never heard her in such a state.

Doubts besieged me. How to save the album? Colm seemed close to a breakdown; some obscure personal crisis of his own, that he'd hinted at darkly over the Guinness. My brother borrowed a Telecaster from Keith – the only in-tune guitar – and recorded most of his parts in one non-stop forty-eight-hour marathon, collapsing with gastro-enteritis at the end. In the midst of this, we needed to record and mix a single, have it ready in a matter of days. The deadline arrived, and we worked through the night to get it finished.

At four in the morning, after hours of unprofitable tweaking, Colm, his ears and mind gone, zeroed the board: pulled all the faders down, like someone smashing a matchstick model of a ship they'd been working on patiently for days. There were gasps in the control room.

'We haven't got a single,' he said, in defeat. The deadline was four hours away. We made it, but for some reason, the mix sounded abysmal.

The next day we were back on tour.

Derby. It all came to a head in Derby. The strain of making the album, and of playing gigs across the country, arranged around signing-on dates, for a label that couldn't afford tour support had begun to corrode the band's inner core. It was effortful and degrading, worse when there were empty venues to contend with. At Derby we outnumbered the audience, playing to the usual two Australian bar staff. Afterwards, when the per diems ran out, and with only three sandwiches between two bands and four crew, Jude decided to smash the dressing room to pieces. (It's possible he hadn't seen *This Is Spinal Tap* by this point.) Institutional chairs made short work of a long wall-mounted mirror. Guitar cases bounced off walls, gouging black furrows. Kevin and I joined in with the childish violence, relishing the feeling of release. Then we scarpered; trestle tables left upturned, concealing wood chip and glass and the three sad, flattened egg baguettes still in their cling film. It was a measure of the stress we were all under; how much we had invested in this.

I can't remember who threw the first punch. Outside, in the front seats of the parked van, my brother and I were suddenly exchanging a welter of blows. It was quite difficult to maintain, actually, with Kevin sitting between us. I got a few good right hooks in before he managed to break it up. Then, with order restored, something at once moving and bathetic occurred. Kevin suddenly slumped forward, and rested his head and hands on the steering wheel, like an imam at prayer. Words emerged. 'I love this band . . .' he said, tremulously, shoulders shaking, and I realised he was crying.

The endless tour continued, endlessly. At Chelmsford Army and Navy, Hells Angels shouted 'give up'. We spent the rest of the gig assured of our imminent deaths, but it turned out they were shouting 'skin up!' They loved the gig, and gave us rib-shattering bear hugs, before riding off, cackling into the night.

Aldershot wasn't so cosy. Squaddies screamed 'pooftahs' as we minced about the stage. Perhaps the eyeliner may have, in their minds, cast doubt on our orientation. Perhaps we shouldn't have matched them insult for insult. They threw toilet rolls, pint glasses and, finally, a hefty sanitary towel bin, which Kevin wore on his head for the remainder of the gig. We sped away, with only the van tail lights smashed.

At the Powerhaus, supporting Nova Mob, a new band fronted by Hüsker Dü indie legend Grant Hart, things got even stranger. When we were introduced, he offered us strawberries from his rider, 'In case things turn ugly later'. How we all laughed. An American musician with a sense of humour! But after the gig, packing up the gear on stage, I became aware of a terrible commotion from the shared dressing room. A raised voice, like a madman's: 'CUNTS! WHORES! GET THE FUCK OUT OF HERE NOW! EVERYONE FUCKING OUT NOW!' One by one, my tearful girlfriend, a pale Deborah, and a young, visibly traumatised female journalist, from Japan's *Rockin' On* magazine, filed out. Hart had found people in his dressing room and unexpectedly turned into a lunatic. I flashed back to the previous year, a friend's band at the same venue. We were talking in the narrow corridor backstage when an impeccable, north-eastern American voice intoned, 'Pardon me'. A handsome, Kerouac-ish figure squeezed past. It was Jonathan Richman, the headline act, on his way to the stage. Maybe Grant Hart could have taken some lessons from him in how to treat your support band.

Despite this, it was an exciting time: posters in Camden for our new single (we'd salvaged it with a new mix), sessions with Janice Long at Greater London Radio (we'd gone in at number one in their chart, the first and only time Flamingoes went in at number one anywhere). Headlining the Garage. French TV. Photos for a Saturday *Daily Telegraph* feature on mod. At the Daily Express Building, on Fleet Street, we were interviewed by Linda Duff of the *Star*, and spent a pleasant evening getting trolleyed with her and Caffy at the bar. Fan mail arrived from France, America, Japan – the latter always with superb calligraphy, little stickers and shy devotion. On Oxford Street, HMV had a Flamingoes section. (I'd waited ten years.) We had our first feature in *Melody Maker*. They still didn't know how to categorise us. 'In Glam-Mod We Trust' ran the headline. Glam-Mod? It sounded like a hamlet on the Welsh borders.

Mod culture was everywhere in London by now, the capital in the grip of a full-blown revival. This was slightly worrying, as, although nearly all my musical heroes had at one time been mods – Bowie, Ferry, Bolan, even Robert Plant – I could never bring myself to be one. I couldn't put the parka on. Blow Up, the mod mecca, was the hippest place to be. Upstairs at the Laurel Tree, you could watch the rubber floorboards heave forever to 'Itchycoo Park' as you nursed an overpriced bottle of Becks, and smoked yourself to death. Once, at a Blow Up party in Holborn, I recall studying Jarvis Cocker's long, lively, intelligent fingers as he played pinball, absorbed by the buzzers and bells, while Pete Shelley of Buzzcocks sang 'Why Can't I Touch It?' onstage with the Weekenders. It didn't seem an apposite song – Cocker was a demon. Which also didn't seem fair somehow, him being a great songwriter, too. Like being good at games *and* art.

*

At some point in 1994–5 I began to suspect the best writer of his generation, or at least the only one interested in the truth, was in fact Jarvis Cocker. The song that convinced me was 'Sorted For E's & Wizz'. Its buoyant, acoustic-driven tempo, pleasantly suggestive of floating on MDMA, punctuated by a series of dramatic accents, provides the backdrop for Cocker's story of disillusion down at the rave. The climax is the wonderful moment where Jarvis steps out of the metre to inform his mum he can't come home because he's left a vital piece of his brain in a field, somewhere in Hampshire. This is priceless, but also personifies the uneasiness at the core of the song. Surely you are meant to feel contented, loved-up at these things?

'Sorted For E's & Wizz' deals in uncertainty, the hollow feeling that can descend at festivals or large gigs. The comedown, not the high.

In the YouTube clip of the song's first performance (Glastonbury 1995, 80,000 people in the audience. You have to admire the cojones on the man), Cocker recounts the story of its inception. A female acquaintance once told him that when she saw the Stone Roses at Spike Island, shady characters had moved through the audience, asking if everyone was 'sorted'. Jarvis, wearing a well-fitting suit, his fringe somewhat disheveled, relates this to the crowd as if he's still addressing nine people at the Bull and Gate. It's here his persona is established in the public mind. One can sense from the enthusiastic cheers of the audience – many of whom wouldn't have been aware of Cocker before the gig – that they accept him. A recognition occurs. Jarvis's dour, easy humour, his self-deprecation (especially that northern self-deprecation, the absolute phobia of pretension, of getting above yourself, that he shared with the Beatles and Philip Larkin) – is manna to the crowd. Moreover, the audience embrace Jarvis because he incarnates the underdog. He announces, to a huge cheer, that it's taken Pulp fifteen years to make it to the Glastonbury main stage. 'If a lanky git like me can do it, and us lot, you can do it, too.'

After Pulp play the song, Cocker continues talking as if nothing has happened. 'I got lost at a rave once . . . all these lads that had been saying "yeah man" two hours previously wouldn't give me a lift home . . .' Then he points one of the long, intelligent fingers, and says in his impeccably lugubrious Sheffield tones: 'But I know *you're* not like that.' Perhaps this is why I warmed to Jarvis Cocker and not Damon Albarn. Cocker's unaffected charm, conveyed by the depth and naturalness of his northern accent, appealed to me. I could relate: my mother being from Yorkshire. (Cocker once narrated a documentary on John Barry; their speaking voices are remarkably similar. Not surprising: Sheffield is only fifty miles from York.)

But it is with the song they play next, 'Common People', that Jarvis really connected with me, as he did with thousands of others. 'Common People' pulls off a trick all great songs do: it seems to have been written with only you in mind. In the lyrics I recognised echoes of Bryan Ferry's wit; Brett Anderson's dedication to venery; Lou Reed's writerly approach. Jarvis, a great noticer, once said in an interview that it's the coffee ring on the table that makes it into the song,[2] the sort of diary-ish detail that proves you were there. (A lovely example is the wood chip from 'Disco 2000'.) The sort of thing that, if you don't write it down at once, disappears from your memory. 'Common People' is full of such details. It is a convincing fictive world, with well-drawn characters, and the true-to-life ambiguity that the protagonist clearly fancies the girl he's disparaging.

The music made an instant connection, too. There is a direct through-line from the Velvets to Roxy to Pulp (Chris Thomas produced both *For Your Pleasure* and 'Common People'), most obviously in the use of repetition. Jarvis was one of the few Britpop writers to consciously avoid the descending bassline, instead preferring the straight, hammering, insistent eighth-notes of 'I'm Waiting For The Man'. In a television documentary, *The Story of Common People*, composer Gary Carpenter ponders the song: 'There are no minor chords, no extensions, no inversions, no riffs, no syncopation, no modulation, no backing vocals, so why is it a good song?'[3] He decides it's because of its repetitive energy; that it would be weakened by fills and pushes, the sort of thing Status Quo might put in; and that if it didn't have what he calls a 'musical narrative' (the DA-DA-DA, DA-DA-DA accents, the rhythmic break, that occurs only twice), the song would fall apart after verse two. Agreed, but only the first point. The repetition *is* accumulatively affective, holds the attention, taps something primal like voices singing in unison. But the tune is in no danger of falling apart after verse two. The elements keep building, musical and actual narrative unfolding – the astonishing lines about life sliding out of view, the loss of meaning and control – until we're overwhelmed, convinced by Cocker's vision, and in no doubt that the song is a masterpiece.

By early 1995, it was clear something fundamental had changed in the music industry's relationship with guitar bands. In his memoir, *Adventures of a Waterboy*, Mike Scott recalls arriving in Camden that year and finding it 'insane'.[4] The phony war was over, and the opportunists – smelling easy money – had moved in. Groups that had only just learned to play their guitars were being offered million-pound advances. In the wider culture, Britpop had arrived alarmingly quickly. Union Jacks and fake cockney accents were everywhere, on television and in the tabloids.

The laddism nurtured by *Loaded* and Oasis was flourishing. The Good Mixer, the small Irish pub at the quiet end of Camden's Inverness Street – the sort of place *Fisherman's Blues* would once have played on a loop – became Britpop's locus, its embassy. Suddenly, you could read about it in the red tops as if it was the Rovers Return. When I first stepped into the place in 1991, it was empty except for a small ceilidh band playing in the corner. The mandolin player was so drunk his head rested on the instrument as he scratched away. Now the only drunks were mods in skinny tops. The pub was blessed with every London boozer cliché: old wallpaper, worn carpet, tin ashtrays, sticky beer mats. By 1995, you had to queue to get in as if it was a super-club – Fabric or the Ministry of Sound. God knows what the scenesters and tourists expected to find there. (One thing was for certain: the same carpet as 1991.)

The prevailing tenor of the period was one of rivalry, a dirty civil war between the groups. It was a turbulent time. Bandwagon jumping was endemic: groups pretending to be sharp and 'English' when a year ago they'd been playing heavy metal. Everyone seemed to hate everyone else – the musicians competing for space in the inkies; the journalists vicious and partisan, one eye on future media careers.

Apart from Suede and the Manics, where were the individualists? Only Pulp, the third group in the 'other' Britpop, seemed to be interested in following a unique path. Besides the band's obvious debt to Roxy Music, Jarvis intrigued me because he'd mentioned John Barry in interviews. I thought it had just been my brother and I who were Barry fans. Of course, the reach of the Bond films meant that the entire generation of Britpop musicians had the 007 scores embedded in their DNA. *Live and Let Die* (yes, I know the score is by George Martin) still holds the record for the most watched UK network television premiere – a staggering 23.5 million viewers in January 1980. (*The X Factor* managed about half this figure at its peak). A Bond film on TV was an event to be discussed and dissected in the playground the next day. Soon, along with Pulp, there would be an upsurge in Barry-influenced artists: Portishead, Morcheeba, Orbital, Barry Adamson, Mono, and later Robbie Williams, whose ubiquitous hit 'Millennium' sampled 'You Only Live Twice'. At the same time, John Barry's influence was detectable in the easy listening or 'loungecore' boom that was beginning to infiltrate the mainstream, starting with Mike Flowers' grisly cover of 'Wonderwall' in 1995.

A hit from Pulp's fifth album, *Different Class*, comments on the culturally regressive tendencies of Britpop, and is, perhaps, one the most important songs of the era. 'Disco 2000' is a curious song – a tune set in the past that is simultaneously about the future. As a schoolboy, the year 2000 *was* the future. Something was meant to happen, or to change. My classmates and I would gather around a copy of *2000 AD* comic, and debate what that year would be like. Of course, when it arrived, it was just like any other year. Nowadays, it's unnerving to come across the yellowed spine of 'Disco 2000' on the CD shelf, the 'future' already part of the past.

Fittingly, for a song looking backwards and forwards at the same time, 'Disco 2000' has an ambiguous key centre. It starts in E (the slashing E sus4 to E riff is an arch nod to Abba's 'Does Your Mother Know', a nice way of establishing, for the knowing nineties listener, the time and place of the song's events before its narrative begins). It then modulates to A for the rest of the verse, and stays there for a bittersweet chorus that Cocker has ensured is packed with non-chord notes, for maximum emotional heft. But before we get there, there is a catch, a nagging thought that the song keeps returning to; an itch it has to scratch. It steps up a whole tone to the contemplative plateau of B minor. The song pedals here, creating tension that is released in the chorus by going to the V (E, if we accept that the song is predominantly in A). Indie bands had disdained the Chord of Euphoria for years as too cheesy, but the Britpop writers merrily embraced it. Cocker prefaces this each time with a question for his paramour; asking her if she recalls their time together. But the most important section of this reverie is the almost throwaway reference to coming around 'to call'. To listeners of a certain age, this would evoke a gentler time, of turning up at a friend's house on your bike, aged ten or eleven, unannounced, on the off-chance they'd be in. Now we were in our twenties, no one 'called' anymore – in London at least; that would be poor manners. Everything had to be arranged in advance, messages left on new devices known as answer machines. It was this rose-tinted view of the past that was so right for the times. 'Common People', Jarvis's class-war polemic, Pulp's most celebrated hit, had connected with the public;

but in retrospect, the defining tenor of the nineties was not anger but nostalgia. As 'Disco 2000' concludes its middle eight, Cocker gets close to the mic for one of his trademark ad-libs. What he says is the essence of the song, and the decade: *I remember every single thing*.

Although some of the key songs of the era seemed to be forward-facing (Oasis's 'Don't Look Back In Anger'), or at least in the moment (the spryly optimistic 'Alright' by Supergrass), Britpop was essentially about looking back. 'Cool Britannia' was built on a false folk memory of swinging London, the 1965–6 period: *Revolver*, Mary Quant, pop art, mod fashion. It's ironic that Oasis called their third album *Be Here Now*. Rather 'be *there* now' – the past, the sixties. Cocker, reviewing Hunter Davies' book of Lennon's letters in the *Guardian* in 2012, scorns Britpop's reverence of the sixties. He points out that the Fabs did not have a blueprint or a plan to follow – 'The Beatles *didn't know they were the Beatles*' (my italics). In addition, Cocker suggests that his generation thought they had missed out on 'something amazing', and felt impelled to make it happen again, '*but exactly the same*'.[5] Thus the Britpop moment was when the injunction to generate new ideas, to push forward into unexplored territory, was finally abandoned.

*

In May 1995, Pulp appeared on *Top of the Pops*, playing 'Common People'. Unusually, I hadn't heard the song before on the radio, so it arrived as a fully formed pop-cultural moment, like Bowie's 'Starman' performance had been for a previous generation. Instantly, it was clear 'Common People' was beyond the scope of any other songwriter active at the time, Damon Albarn included. Pulp had perfected their formula, defined the zeitgeist: the song swiftly became the sound of the summer.

It was just at this point I found myself pulled in another, completely unexpected direction. With touring over for the time being, I spent most days that summer on the yellowing grass of Primrose Hill, reading – of all things – *Come As You Are*, a book about Kurt Cobain.

11

The Last Great Honest Song

Kurt Cobain, and 'All Apologies'

Step back to the previous autumn. 1994. Two albums dominated the airwaves: Oasis's exuberant, unfaltering *Definitely Maybe* and Nirvana's wrecked, defeated *MTV Unplugged in New York*. They were the two opposing poles of alternative rock; battle lines had been drawn (although, in reality, plenty of people owned both records). In the press, Noel Gallagher never missed an opportunity to remind readers that Kurt Cobain had nothing to say to him about his life. Much as I hated to admit it, I was in agreement. A depressed American bloke in a cardigan, mumbling about apologies had nothing relevant to show me either. Or had he? Kurt's lonely suicide back in April had cast a dark shadow over the year; it still disturbed me. When I took the time to listen to it, *MTV Unplugged in New York* played like one long suicide note. In a ghostly aside, before the fourth song, Cobain asks: *am I going to do this by myself?* Yes, Kurt, I'm afraid you are. It made me think, sadly, of my friend who had killed himself the previous year. Clearly, Cobain was wrestling with far weightier subjects than the hedonism then in vogue: cigarettes and alcohol, where the next white line was coming from. I still couldn't get into Nirvana, though. And, anyway, there were more pressing matters to hand.

Somehow, that autumn, despite the best efforts of The Label, we'd managed to salvage the recording of our debut album. Vocals were completed at Joe's Garage in Clapham, the Orb's studio. Colm had stepped down, burnt out. Keith took his place, cheerful as ever. ('Sold! To the man with no ears . . .' was heard every time a usable take was in the can.) Then, in October, we began mixing at Wessex Studios, in leaf-strewn Highbury and Islington. It was a converted church, where the Clash had made *London Calling* and the Sex Pistols had recorded *Never Mind the Bollocks*. Sneaking a look at the live room one day, I saw the hallowed space familiar from so many photographs. There was the spot where Lydon had stood shirtless in the vocal booth; or where Guy Stevens had hurled chairs at the Clash to make them play better. One day, Deborah introduced me to Gil Norton, producer of *Born Sandy Devotional* and the Bunnymen's *Ocean Rain*. He was recording in another studio, and was in the frame to produce our second album. We couldn't afford him.

The Ponytail was at Wessex most days, with his customary lack of self-awareness, his copy of *LOOT*, the cowboy boots up on the desk, aggravating Keith. He'd clearly missed day one of A&R school: don't hang with the band in the recording studio.

Arriving early on the last day, my heart sank when I saw The Ponytail was already there, tufts of chest hair bristling above a white t-shirt. Then Kevin arrived. My God, what had happened? He had a face like a car crash, half of it hanging off. Purple, just-healing cuts, puce and black bruises, one eye completely closed. It turned out that while queuing for a *Loaded* party the previous night, a bouncer had taken umbrage to something he'd said, picked him up by the scruff of his neck – blacking him out with some arcane martial arts grip – then let him fall face first and unconscious onto the kerb. Like dropping a kitten in a river. (Kevin needed hundreds of pounds worth of dental work, and later successfully sued the doorman.)

Slightly unnerved, we headed to the album cut, at Townhouse on Goldhawk Road. It was fascinating to watch the songs being carved by a great machine onto wet vinyl, like molasses, and the chance to write a secret message on the run-out groove . . . But even the cut was doomed to disaster. I can't remember what it was over, but I walked out. Before I knew it, I'd said, 'Have it your fuckin way' to The Ponytail and was marching down the Goldhawk Road, tranced with rage. Deborah's look as I left was worrying – I knew she was sick of the fights. At Shepherd's Bush underground, leaping blindly into a crowded carriage, I ducked my head, causing me to look down, and saw a pair of cowboy boots. Oh no. Face to face with The Ponytail. Neither of us apologised. Instead, we had a strained talk about licensing deals, during which he admitted to a fondness for Michael Bolton.

*

'I'd better drop my bombshell now.'

This was Deborah, three months later, January 1995, a band meeting at the Market Bar, Portobello Road. She had just handed us our European tour dates, before she handed us the grenade. She and Keith were leaving for New Zealand, to have kids. 'It's probably best not to tell the label, at this point,' she said, and told us she would work to find us a replacement. And, anyway, she wasn't leaving until March.

A silence gathered, and grew. At last, Jude said:

'So what are we sitting discussing this for?' pointing to the itinerary.

Then he stormed out. I later discovered he walked all the way back to Camden in tears. I stayed to the end, and left with the gig dates, spattered brown with Guinness, finished vinyl copies of the debut album (most of them scratched), and my little secret. The only consolation was the album. Finally, after over a decade, I'd achieved what I'd set out to do. And there they were, the credits: All songs by Jude/James. (You win some . . .)

Shortly afterwards, we were granted our first interview with the *NME*. A tiny feature that had taken Caffy over a year to negotiate. On the way, Kevin pulled the van over at an off-licence on Camden Road. He returned with six bottles of red wine, one each, one for the writer, two for insurance and 40 Silk Cut, in two blue bags. Had we over-ordered, possibly? The interview commenced at the World's End, Kevin refilling his pint glass under the table with red at regular intervals. Then we headed to the journalist's place, to continue. The scribe, Andy Richardson, was a gentle soul with a tidy flat. Walls of CDs. 'There are certain

Nick Drake songs that break my heart again and again,' he said, as his lounge filled with Silk Cut smoke and Kevin's ever louder and more strident pronouncements. Kevin was so drunk he'd already proudly confessed to once being a dustman. Stress is an odd thing. Like us, he knew we faced an uncertain future without our manager of two years. Then . . . In my mind, it all goes a bit wonky, a bit hazy from there. The interview is a lacuna, which is a mercy as everything surrounding the evening still makes me flinch, even twenty years later. By the end of the night, all six bottles had been sunk. And so were we, in the eyes of the *NME*, at least. Ah yes, I do have one dim memory: managing to say we wanted to be bigger than East 17. Richardson had to throw us out. Gently, of course.

The next day, I awoke with a thump of shock, as if on an electroconvulsive therapy table. An Estonian heavy metal band was sound-checking in my head. What had we done? A few weeks later, after a long recuperation, the *NME* piece appeared, with photography by Martyn Goodacre. He had taken the iconic image of Kurt Cobain in eyeliner. For our shoot, we'd stood on traffic islands in the Euston Road, while Goodacre, small and affable, smiled and snapped. All in a morning's work for the great smudge. The piece, however, was the expected disaster. The East 17 remark made it in. The article concluded, peevishly: *Drummer Kevin used to be a dustman. Keith Moon didn't.*[1]

The following week, The Boss called the band in for a meeting – predictably, he hadn't thought much of the *NME* interview. We filed into his office, like guilty schoolboys. There was going to be a conversation about respect. That morning, he was in a sanctimonious, anecdotal, expansive mood. He told us how he had started out on a market stall, with the future founder of Pepe jeans, who now earned £50 million a year. He mentioned his girlfriend, a singer, and how professional she was while touring Russia. Halfway through the sermon, The Ponytail came in with some paperwork, causing the door to fall off its hinges. A *Neighbours*-set moment to cherish. We sniggered into our leathers, but he continued, undeterred. The *NME* piece was condemned; then our live show. Apparently we didn't 'emit' onstage that we thought we were stars. We rushed the songs, didn't 'take anyone on a trip'.

'Could that be because the drummer's on speed?' I said.

Not long after this meeting, The Boss made his masterpiece. I was outside the Borderline, smoking a post-gig cigarette with Stella, when he sidled up, and with an unpleasant leer asked,

'How much did you pay for her?'

The sleazy motherfucker.

Don't judge me by your standards, I thought, and blew smoke in his face.

But at least the album was out, finally. The *Guardian*, largely, liked it. 'Glum Glam' they said. Suddenly, spirits rose. We headlined the Garage for the second time, selling it out, the biggest gig we'd played. The front rows were brimming with Japanese girls going crazy – they knew the words to all the songs. I stood onstage thinking: ten years – six of them in London – uncountable gigs, innumerable road miles. Then, on Valentine's Day 1995, I took the Tube down to Tottenham Court Road to buy the early *Melody Maker*. The album review was in. It was a love letter, a rare 'recommended' review by Jennifer Nine, an intelligent writer trusted to write notices for major releases by Sparklehorse and Radiohead. She praised the songs, her encomium ending: '*The genuine article*.'[2]

This is the Sea, and this is the one.

I was exalted, right there in front of Centre Point. I found a call box and phoned my brother. He was planning to frame the review.

Then it got even better. Charles Shaar Murray, writing for the *Sunday Telegraph*, declared: '*They wear their Beatles influences on their sleeves, but like most teenage sixties nostalgists, they hear their heroes through the veil of punk. What's especially appealing is their ability to make the venerable devices they use as charming to those who remember them from the first time around, as they do to those hearing them for the first time*.'[3] Reading this, I lifted a glass to *Revolver*, and to my dad, as any melodic facility I might have had was probably just as much a result of him playing Bach's 'Well-Tempered Clavier' for all those years. Shaar Murray added that we could 'write a sharp line' and included his favourite. Only a few years previously I'd been reading his Bowie book in my mum's lounge; now he was quoting my lyrics in a Sunday broadsheet. This must be one of those moments of glory Jude was always on about. Finally, Nick Robinson, a writer for *Music Week*, put us forward for the Mercury Music Prize. His five-star review concluded: 'The most thrilling debut of the year so far.'[4]

We set off on the European tour, and prayed the hits would follow.

*

'Who does your hair?'

Kevin again. March 1995. The borrowed high top Mercedes van was boarding the Harwich to Hamburg ferry, at the start of our European adventure with headliners Echobelly. The subject of Kevin's enquiry, a stocky German P&O marshal with a startling blond pompadour glowered in his hi-vis vest, and waved us on. Careful, Kev. Remember that *Loaded* party . . .

I had a crippling bad back from sleeping in a van for nearly a year, 'bus driver's finger' – an orange first digit on my right hand from chain-smoking, and increasingly worrying chest pains. A hangover in residence. But I was ready to play our first gigs in Europe, and readier still to get away from London, and the constant battles with The Label. After long hugs during a teary night in the Good Mixer, we had finally bidden goodbye to Deborah. She had been as good as her word, and found us another manager before setting off for the Antipodes. And there were other reasons to be cheerful. The band had signed a publishing deal with Bug Music, home to Iggy Pop and Johnny Cash's catalogue. John Leckie, the Stone Roses' producer, wanted to work with us (we couldn't afford him).

With only £3,000 tour support from The Label, we had been obliged to find the rest from our publishing advance. Spain and Italy were rubbed off the itinerary. The hot countries. They said they couldn't afford it, despite the album being already on sale there. We would be visiting Germany, France, Belgium, Holland, Denmark and Sweden only. Taking two grand out of the bank before leaving – a roll of twenties fit to choke a horse – we took the underground to Vintage and Rare on Denmark Street. There, we blew the lot on a blonde 1978 Fender Telecaster, and a black 1973 Rickenbacker 401. Proper guitars at last.

With us for the journey was a real tour manager, our first. John was large, bearish, mid-twenties. Strong Glaswegian accent. Number one crop. With his seemingly inexhaustible wardrobe of Ben Sherman button-downs, he resembled a darts champion moonlighting for an Oasis tribute band. This was ably reinforced by a slightly hooded right eye, as if he was aiming an arrow all the time. He called me Spider.

'A'right, Spider.'

We called him Big John. There was also the luxury of a tech, known as roadies back then: Sam. Small, soft-spoken, plaid shirt, permanently fixed baseball cap. A Beach Boys and Nancy Sinatra fan. That was Sam. He had actually been with us since the previous July, and was raring for adventure.

Then there was Francis, our driver. Younger than Sam, six foot, rakish, long leather coat. A ladies' man. The John Travolta of Ealing Broadway, we nicknamed him. Yes, Francis was movie-star handsome, capable and friendly.

It was a little awkward at first; I didn't know Big John or Francis. But I had a feeling I soon would. After lengthy days of tour organisation, we finally embarked on the twenty-two-hour crossing. In the ship's bar, we set about getting slowly, methodically drunk as a joyless cabaret unfolded. Then a hopeful search for food. There was only one choice on this vast, empty *Titanic*: *Wurst* and chips. The vegetarians among us – my brother and Sam – settled miserably for just the chips.

The next day, there was no question of breakfast on the boat: far too expensive. Big John had gone over some figures with me the night before, and I understood we would be touring on a very thin, very frayed shoestring. It was a fine morning, and we floated down the broad channel of the Elbe, industry and Bavarian-style houses on either side. Jude, Sam and I went up on deck, to the stern. I talked with Sam. He was a born rover, his enthusiasm for travel infectious. Finally, we docked at Hamburg.

There we found signs for St Pauli, the Reeperbahn, the legendary Star Club. This was where the Beatles had been told to '*Mach shau*!' The blackened streets were John Lennon's old manor. We were playing the Markthalle that night. It was packed to capacity. Girls asked for autographs and pictures, and wanted to know if I knew Brett Anderson. They were a minority, however. If the crowd's t-shirts were anything to go by, most of the audience still venerated Kurt Cobain. Afterwards, while calling Stella in England from the venue's production office, I noticed a hefty Glock pistol in the drawer, which the promoter quickly closed.

We roamed the streets like British tourists, a rabble, necking bottles of Pils, Big John stopping off to buy porn. The dives that showed continuous hardcore quickly acquired a nickname – 'Spunker bars' – from Big John. ('Spunker' becoming an occasional, affectionate alternative to 'Spider'.) These places were populated by hard-faced professionals, wearing all the gear under pink one-piece ski suits.

Hamburg seemed to be one big brothel. Indeed, there had been something odd about our hotel, the Nobistor. When we'd checked in I'd noticed the red table lamps and the deep vermilion carpets, but didn't think it was an actual knocking shop. This was confirmed at 5 a.m., when an agitated, shirtless bloke in cowboy boots kicked the door to my room open, looking for someone called Mona. So that's why there were mirrors on the ceiling. I just thought we had good rooms.

On the long haul to Berlin the following day, the two chief tour preoccupations – food and sleep – rapidly asserted themselves. An animal's concerns. Germany seemed to have a propensity for pizza, and Chinese food, especially. Even in the tiniest hamlet there would be a Happy Garden or a Jade Palace. No one dared suggest trying one of the rarely sighted curry houses. But with per diems restricted to 20 DM per day, and with all service station sandwiches costing over 5 DM, a firm grip on the money belt was needed. Hours of anonymous, arrow-straight autobahn passed, while I dreamed of food, trying to sleep in the bucket seat with a coat pulled up to my chin. The animal in its bedding, its burrow.

From here, the tour becomes a fragmented series of memories. Who would want to remember it all in detail?

Vignettes of insanity, boredom and the occasional near-death experience. Joining Echobelly at each venue, we would hear about their escapades. They had been on the road for months, and tour fever was upon them. In Berlin, Debbie, their second guitar player, and Alex, the bass player, were nearly relieved of their heads while sticking them out of the top of the coach, playing chicken to assuage the tedium. Debbie was round and tomboyish, a Ronald Searle character. I loved Debbie, there was mischief in her.

We drank Paulaner lager, 6 per cent volume. It had a rich sweetness, like Special Brew. The hangovers were hostile; would square up to you first thing. Each morning, trembling over a thin, black hotel coffee, with its unexpected and unpleasant back note of pepper, I would hover around the rolls and Gouda and salami from the *Fleischplatte*. An idiotic refrain in my head: *Everything takes twice as long, with the full metal trilby on.*

Cologne, Frankfurt, Stuttgart.

Each night, I watched Echobelly from the wings. They were savage and well-drilled, a strict machine, more oiled with each show. Sonya, their vocalist – sweet and approachable off-stage – was a formidable front woman. I noticed how she often nodded when she sang, an economical movement, allied with a smile. It was an affirmation the audience responded to. The show was a celebration ritual, conducted by a high-priestess lead singer.

The scam of sneaking two people for one into the hotel had failed early on, so Big John had to pay, denuding the tour budget even further. The borrowed high top didn't last long either, and had been towed away after the second gig. Waiting for the new transport on the steps of our hotel in Cologne, ignoring the cathedral resplendent in the distance, I watched guitarist Glenn's Strats and Les Pauls on their impressive single stand being loaded into the bowels of their tour bus. I was aware of a strange feeling. Not guitar envy, but *guitar stand* envy.

That night, when we returned to our hotel, we found the lobby deserted. Stupidly, someone had left a baby grand piano out. For the next four hours, Jude, Kevin, Sam and I went through every Beatles, Bowie and Velvets song we could remember, and many we couldn't. The expected manager never came to tell us to stop. Sam sang in a shaky whisper. I liked Sam, he reminded me of Bill. In fact, I sometimes called him Bill by mistake.

The new van required jump-starting every few miles on the hard shoulder. As we stood on the grassy banks, HGVs thundering past, I started to feel nervous. Spin came to mind, a band that had suffered a tour bus crash the year before, with members decapitated and mangled.

Paris. Rennes. Brussels.

The vehicle was losing oil at a ridiculous rate; there was a real danger that the engine could seize up completely.

In Rennes, the promoter, an enormous, happy Flaubertian farmer, petitioned us for an encore. Afterwards, he brought champagne to the dressing room, then a potent rum punch, and embarrassed us with compliments. How different from his English counterparts, who often begrudged you a vegetarian lasagne. Just as the night was drunkenly expiring, Jude and Kevin came walking downstairs playing acoustics, a pair of pissed troubadours, Morecambe and Wise steps. A crazy two-hour song session ensued, gratis drinks were spilled, Debbie made fun of us freely, and everyone sang. We stumbled out to look for the hotel at three in the morning. Once again, I would be wearing the trilby at breakfast.

Indeed, the hangovers were becoming untenable. You would test them, tenderly, in the first piercing shafts of daylight that peeked through the curtains, think you were all right, get up, then Bam! Another one. Big John would be rapping on the door, and you'd be frog-marched to the venue, attempting to stuff down a croissant.

Transport was now two AA Renault people carriers, 'space cruisers' (the second van had given out, as expected). Francis would be hunched over the wheel of his for ten-hour stretches, stoically, but always with good humour, while Big John helmed the other. On the epic drive to Brussels, customs officers stopped us at a toll, rudely disturbing my sleep. They ordered us to empty our pockets, then pulled us over for a thorough search. I watched them with their machine guns and pressed blue uniforms. These guys had meanness in them. You didn't say anything unless you wanted to find yourself in a strip-lit room handcuffed to a radiator. Or worse. They rifled through our luggage, easily finding Big John's shag mags, which appeared one by one, arranged in neat rows on the grass verge.

We loaded up the space cruisers and pointed them for Amsterdam. No one wanted to be in Big John's, as he drove fast, recklessly, with a seventeen-year-old's sense of immortality.

Finally, Echobelly's last night arrived – we were to continue solo through the Netherlands and Scandinavia as headliners. They threw a party at the American Hotel. Debbie gave me a going-away present, a bag of sinsemilla the size and shape of a dog's scrotum. 'Don't smoke it all at once,' she said cheerfully, 'because it will kill you.' We were on our own now. Our base was the huge apartment by the canal, the one with the Scott Walker records. We stayed for a couple of days, and explored Amsterdam. The van Gogh, Dam Square, the Sex Museum (sort of Hardcore Through the Ages). In the evenings, Big John did lines of chang with the hippy who owned the place. I could hear them, with a porn video on in the background.

Chop, chop, chop.

'Ja! Ja!'

Chop, chop.

'Jaa!'

Sam and I took the guitars into the basement, and sang songs for two hours. 'My Funny Valentine', 'Some Velvet Morning', 'In My Room'. Sam ruminated about travel freeing the soul; and how he didn't want to return to London.

Big John's management decisions were becoming ever more eccentric. Because of a new policy of booking only expensive hotels, nobody could afford breakfast. Then he would blow 70 DM on fancy sandwiches. In Copenhagen, we found ourselves in a sumptuous hotel. Why not, seeing as money was no object? After the gig, Big John stuffed the address in my pocket, and I jumped into a cab. A weird scene was taking place back at the hotel. Tour fever had taken hold. In Kevin's room – a chaos of empty Grolsch bottles, odd socks and ashtrays – Sam was freaking out, threatening to jump from the window. They were fighting over a girl. It was here I realised the opposite sex was being dealt with in substantial numbers, without me even noticing. Sam passed out. I retired to my suite. It was so grand it had its own *lobby*. But the tour fever was on me, too, and I needed to escape. Suddenly, in my mind's eye, I was racing down bright pavements, free, and singing Scott Walker's 'Copenhagen', dying my hair with the sunny streets.

We headed for Malmö, Sweden. I rode in Francis's space cruiser, to avoid Big John's mad driving. We lived on songs as much as we did motorway food. The Velvets' 'Candy Says', Lou Reed's 'Satellite Of Love' and 'Perfect Day', from *Transformer*. School memories. Sam had turned me on to *Surf's Up*, and *Nashville Skyline*'s 'I Threw It All Away'. His tour mix-tapes were a welcome escape from the Soundgarden and Nirvana singles constantly on the radio. I was exhausted, and it was an effort now to get the beer down, an immediate reflux reaction with each gulp. Ten minutes' snatched sleep at the hotel was the only rest before the gig.

In the morning, Francis confessed he'd got lucky last night, and had had one hour's sleep, so there was a good chance he would crash the car. More worryingly, it was my turn with Big John, and there was no way out. Sitting on the steps of the hotel, I wrote a pair of elegiac postcards – one to Stella; one to my mother – and looked up at the bare, black branches of two withered trees, coming to claim me. A feeling of intense foreboding.

Big John didn't let me down.

The drive to Gothenburg was executed at a steady 150km/h, a hysterical thunderstorm smashing rain across the tarmac. We hurtled into it, challenged by strong cross-winds, Big John overtaking long, looming phalanxes of articulated vehicles while lighting cigarettes, often dropping one between his knees, then looking down to rummage for it. I sat white-knuckled, stupefied with terror. But in the cosy, misted interior, with its new-car smell, I knew Big John felt safe. We chatted, or rather he did. He had a disconcerting habit of turning his head to you while he talked, ignoring the road for long moments – testicle-tightening seconds that stretched and burned into your mind. Big John would control the vehicle with only an index finger on the steering wheel. Or no-handed.

'These space cruisers drive themselves, don't they, Spider! Put a tape oan.'

If this was to be the last sound I heard, I wanted it to be a holy piece of music, a perfect song. With trembling hands, I searched the glove compartment. All I could find was a cassette of Nirvana's *In Utero*. It would have to do. I fast-forwarded to a song I had to admit I quite liked, 'All Apologies', and tried to focus on the line about feeling as one in the sun.

When we eventually arrived, three hours later, I was a wreck. A basket case. Canvassing the others, I was relieved it wasn't just me who was terrified of travelling with Big John. For the final leg, I resolved to take the train. But how? I knew he would never allow it, because of the cost, and the fact it was his job to make sure all the musicians arrived at the venue on time.

There had to be a way.

The next morning, after a shakily eaten breakfast, we embarked on the seven-hour drive to Stockholm. The last gig. My brother slept soundly in the back of Francis's car. I was with him, relieved to be out of Big John's clutches. But it would be my turn again tomorrow. I gazed out of the window. Sweden was empty and ravishing; its air, coming through the ventilation ducts, pure oxygen. When we arrived at the venue, the first person I saw was Sam. He'd been in Big John's space cruiser, and had terror in his eyes.

'I wish I'd had a set of brakes, like a driving-school car.'

That was it. I took John aside, and, as firmly as possible, told him I was catching a train tomorrow. I knew that with the drinking, the exhaustion – and the driving – I'd lost all reason, but I didn't care. His answer was an equally firm no.

Our hotel was a converted prison on an island in Stockholm's archipelago. Inexplicably, a limousine took us to the venue. We crossed a wide river on a high bridge, lights twinkling in the blackness. 'It's taken ten years to get to this,' I said to my brother. Fortunately, the last gig turned out to be one of the best. Kids chanted '*Flaming-oes! Flaming-oes!*' and afterwards everyone was in delirious spirits. We took cabs to a terrible mod club, and I made my peace with Big John, sort of.

'Look at all these women, they're checking you out, pop singer,' said John, a six-pound bottle of Becks glued to the Ben Sherman.

'I'm spoken for, but you go for it, mate.'

'Nah, Spider, I'm ugly. I'll never get things like that,' he said, ruefully.

We were sharing a room at the hotel. Before lights out, Big John announced in a slurred voice: 'You're a little pop star in the making', then turned his back, and began snoring for seven hours.

Or he could have said, 'You're a little-cocked tart in the making,' I shall never know.

I woke at dawn, and exercised furiously. But quietly, so as not to wake John – like the prisoners must have done. Then I showered and packed my case, head nipping. *Everything takes twice as long, with the full metal trilby on.* A monomaniac, there was only one thought in my mind: not to be deterred. Not to be talked out of taking the train.

I left Big John still snoring, and slipped out for the station. It wasn't easy to find without a map, but soon I was in front of a departures board. A train to Gothenburg was leaving immediately. But it wasn't to be. There were only minutes to spare when I saw Big John's football-shaped head appear in the queue. With his hooded eye he looked like a disappointed walrus. I was going to be opposed, thwarted at the last moment – but somehow he was persuaded. He stared at me with a mixture of irritation and forbearance as I bought my ticket. Then I waved goodbye to Big John, and was free.

Stockholm to Gothenburg. Then the ferry home. Semi-frozen fjords and pine forests swam by. Low, timbered houses built on islands. Members of Abba writing songs in them, almost certainly. Finally finding a seat, I still couldn't quite comprehend I was on my own at last, away from everyone. In my bag was Jude's copy of Hanif Kureishi's *The Black Album*. I read this; or I gazed out of the window, awed by Sweden; and, with no Walkman to hand, just wrote songs in my head.

*

We arrived back in England from the European tour, and returned, broken men, to our Camden flats. With the promotion for the album over, we were adrift. Whole days and weeks came loose. We rehearsed. I sent a copy of the LP to Mike, my Triffids buddy. Spike, now an Associated Press journalist in The Hague, wrote to say he'd found one in Virgin Amsterdam. He sent a copy to Duke, with the *Melody Maker* review. The record was now licensed to Europe, Japan and Australia, and would soon be out in America. At twenty-six, I'd achieved my lifetime ambition of releasing an album worldwide. Some of the teenage dreams had come true. Around this time we were put forward for a Beach Boys tribute record. Word came back that Brian Wilson was a fan of our LP. That made my decade.

I moved in with Stella, and with a shared rent had a bit of money in my pocket at last. There were people to see and parties to go to. The Britpop party however, raged somewhere else. Oasis were number one in the charts with 'Some Might Say'. At the end of their *Top of the Pops* appearance, Noel lifted the Les Paul triumphantly above his head, the Jimmy Page prizefighter move. 'Alright' was at number two. Ash were number twelve with 'Girl From Mars'. BBC2 broadcast *Britpop Now*, presented by Damon Albarn. The so-called 'Battle of Britpop' took place in August: Blur versus Oasis. It was the high water mark of the decade. The crash would arrive soon, undoubtedly.

After much persistence, The Label released some sales figures to us. We'd sold 19,200 copies of the album to date. Eighty to a hundred were selling per week. The band were number six in the video chart in Germany, number six in the *proper* chart in South Africa. There was airplay in New Zealand and Australia, where we were number sixteen. So, if we were selling records, where was the fucking money? I called a meeting with The Ponytail at the Market Bar. He was opaque on the question. Astonishingly, despite the fights, The Label was picking up our option. But he was patronising, high-handed, insulting to the last. I declined the offer of a second album.

Autumn came, the damp wind blowing leaves down Camden High Street. One day, I ducked into Record and Tape Exchange. Flicking through the albums, seeing some I'd once sold to keep afloat, and a few copies of my own LP, I felt a tap on the shoulder. It was Parker, the smile and humour still intact. Good to see a friendly face, I told him. What had he been up to? Had he found a new job after Elektra's demise? He had as many questions for me. What now after we'd parted company with our label? We repaired to the Good Mixer, uncharacteristically empty that lunchtime. The tourists must have been having a day off. As usual, the conversation was stimulating: Scott Walker's 'Duchess', Powell and Pressburger's *A Matter of Life and Death*; rarely the Industry. When I told him that Oasis had – temporarily, I hoped – spoilt the Beatles for me, he became animated. He confessed to a similar sentiment. Furthermore, ever since my moment with 'All Apologies' in the death car to Gothenburg, the only contemporary music I could listen to was Nirvana. A spectacular conversion had taken place. For months, I'd been on the Nirvana trip to end all Nirvana trips. I had been wrong all along; Kurt Cobain's voice and songwriting had unexpectedly assumed a central place in my musical life, revealing Britpop to be the hollow sham it was. I'd also gone back to my John Barry soundtracks. (In a few years' time Robbie Williams would spoil Barry – not forever, thankfully – by releasing 'Millennium'.) The end of the century, the year 2000, was approaching fast. After a couple of Guinnesses, we shook hands and went our separate ways. Outside, Camden Town was dripping in the rain. It was time for new projects, new surroundings. Get a move on, I told myself. That was the river . . .

And then, at Christmas 1995, Flamingoes finally made the decision to disband. A terrible sadness filled the days. It had been ten years since Jude and I had embarked on our kamikaze dream, and each day since had seen unwavering effort. Only two people knew what it had taken: me and my fellow traveller, my brother in arms, Jude. But the truth was, we were exhausted. From playing two acoustic guitars in pubs to selling 20,000 albums, this is what we had achieved, and now it had all come to an end. Occasionally, Deborah would call from New Zealand. 'It's good to hear your voice,' she said. But the dream was over.

I still wrote. And listened to songs. They still affected me. I still needed that private communion with the secret self, when any company had to be shut out for a few seconds, as 'You Only Live Twice' came on in a shop. Or when 'The Whole Of the Moon' trailed from a car radio. Or, with the afternoon glowing gold on a window frame, 'All Apologies', the lines about the sun, just for a moment then they're gone . . .

At this point I intended to ride out on a note of high elegy, attempting once again to put into words the ineffable properties of the Memory Song. But I'll resist the temptation. It's enough to marvel at the trick they play, the sudden breathtaking jump-cut back to the past that is effected. One doesn't know whether to laugh or weep, it's so audacious. The other day, *Revolver*'s 'Good Day Sunshine' came on – the piano, a deep comforting resonance like a good single malt on a chilly night; the lyric about the sun burning your feet as they hit the ground – and I was twelve again, in the shared bedroom with my twin brother, Mum downstairs in the kitchen, humming a tune from the radio. Wondering what life would be like when I was grown up, full of dreams of the future. The pleasures of adult life, which we were nearly ready for. The moments of glory making music.

*

I have before me a photograph. Martyn Goodacre's famous black and white shot of Kurt Cobain wearing eye-liner, the one that appeared on the cover of the *NME*'s obituary edition, and then around the world ever since on t-shirts and coffee mugs. The date is the twentieth anniversary of Cobain's death, 5 April 2014. A peculiar blue dusk, the colour of touchpaper, is descending outside my flat. I put on 'All Apologies', loud, the song Ian McCulloch once called 'the last great honest song', and consider the image with greater scrutiny. Kurt's head is tilted to one side, showing the empathy of a listener, someone engaging with you, not just having their photograph taken. His goateed jaw is firmly set, his peroxide hair disheveled, his lower eyelids heavily and evenly kohled. Much has been written about Cobain's eyes in this picture – the mixture of vulnerability and defiance – but look closer and you notice it is only the left that holds a steely challenge. The right is fathomlessly sad and questioning, partially hidden by his fringe. (Aptly, for someone so conflicted, Kurt's face is divided down the middle by a wisp of blond hair that has blown free.) But look again and they have changed places, beguilingly. It is the Mona Lisa of rock portraits . . . Despite the strain and worry in his eyes, it is striking how young he looks; like images of Lennon when he was the same age: twenty-four. The boy only just beginning to disappear from his face. With effort, I try to imagine what he and others who left early – Richey; and my friend who committed suicide a year before Cobain – would be doing now. How would they be finding early middle age? Would they be married with kids? Cobain *was* married with a kid when he shot himself, but it is impossible to imagine him enjoying the oppressive stability that phrase conjures up.

'All Apologies' is coming to an end. The incantatory coda that leads to the exhausted conclusion, the nursery rhyme simplicity of Kurt's summary phrase that somehow invokes *The White Album*, is doing its alchemical work. It's time to rewind nearly twenty years, to Primrose Hill, deep in summer, reading *Come As You Are*, the book about Kurt Cobain.

This was, it has to be said, a very odd thing to be doing in July 1995. Cobain had been dead for over a year, and his stock was the lowest it would probably ever be. The sound of the moment was Blur's 'Country House'. But 'All Apologies' had shown a way in to Nirvana. Ever since the episode in Big John's car, I kept hearing the song on the radio. One night, the DJ, back-announcing the track, was rendered speechless for a second by the power of that final incantation. He blustered and fluffed his words: this was, recognisably, something real and unaffected. The first element to connect was the austere riff, played high in a Zeppelin-like drop-D tuning. Then the words – uncomfortable truths. What else could he write? Cobain asks. Yes, gimme some truth. Then the band, like some great machine coming to life, strike up the riff: further echoes of Zeppelin, and the Beatles of 'Helter Skelter'. In fact, the *yeah yeah yeahs* before the solo were pure Fabs. Was it possible Cobain was a Beatles fan? The book confirmed he was. I should have known; there had been plenty of clues, among them the simple statement-of-the-verse-melody guitar solos, à la George Harrison.

Kurt's relationship with the Beatles was fascinating, and tied me up in knots. It's often said 'About A Girl' recalls the early Fabs. (I knew by now that Cobain had listened to *With the Beatles* for three hours before writing the song, to psyche himself up.) But it perplexed me, I could never pinpoint the actual Beatles tune. The bit people mean is where Kurt slips out of E minor to E major for two bars, when he says to his girl he can't see her every night. This sleight of hand, a trick that guitar teachers on YouTube still get wrong, is one of the most pleasing things Cobain ever put in a song. Above it, his agile melody vaults through the intervals, in fine Paul McCartney style. Eventually, I found the change on 'Honey Don't' from *Beatles For Sale*, the same E to C shift. Then I realised it *did* appear on *With the Beatles*, in 'It Won't Be Long', and in fact they had been using it ever since 'I Saw Her Standing There'.

There were other elements of Nirvana that were intriguing. Kurt had covered a Bowie song, 'The Man Who Sold The World', and, like the Dame on the cover of that album, was not averse to wearing the odd dress or two. Then there was the eyeliner. Moreover, I discovered Cobain had worn two pairs of trousers to make his legs look thicker, just as I had done. (That was the clincher, I'm afraid.) Echoes of my other top groups were in Nirvana's sound, too. The bizarre solo in 'In Bloom' adopted a similar approach to the atonal playing in the Velvets' 'I Heard Her Call My Name'. As Joe Strummer said: it's all about getting your personality through your instrument. How could I have been immune to their greatness? Previously all I'd heard was a conflation of Sonic Youth, Tad, Mudhoney; groups that held little interest. The conversion felt like a sort of cultural vertigo, an experience unsettling yet strangely exciting. Had I defected, gone over to the other side? Where did Roxy Music, and all the other British-sounding groups fit in with this New Favourite Band? Clearly, they didn't. My preconceptions had been turned upside down, and I'd learned something: don't judge an artist too hastily. I could never show my face down at Blow Up again.

Mostly, though, it was the music that compelled. It sounded fresh, whereas Britpop simply did not. Cobain used parallel chords – barres, the same shape moved up and down the guitar neck to create new and original sequences. Oddly, when he did use a descending bassline, as in the verses of 'Lithium', it sounded happy. And far from hearing a bellowing American I now heard the best rock singer since John Lennon. The lament was all in the voice, the ache of the sad fifths harmonies. Cobain, a child of divorced parents, was someone I could easily relate to. His songs were stamped by the experience, full of references to self-blame and guilt.

In the book, it was revealed that Kurt, like John Updike, had drawn cartoons as a boy, and had wanted to be an illustrator when he grew up. This is where he'd learned how to tell stories. But Kurt told stories with fragmented images, postmodern clips of language. No train of thought was ever too pointed or logical. I learned something here, too: maybe I'd got it all wrong. Songs were not short stories, they were all about *sound*, and the odd word or phrase that leapt out, not conventional narratives. Yes, Kurt was a very different storyteller from Jarvis. That glorious summer of 1995 will always be easily recalled by Cocker's carefully crafted opening lines to 'Common People', but also just as easily by one of Cobain's disembodied lines, my favourite lyric from 'All Apologies' – the couplet about feeling as one in the sun.

Take a rest

As a friend

As an old memoria

'Come As You Are', Nirvana

Outro

In 1995, the Beatles were everywhere, and not just as ghostly echoes in Nirvana songs. The *Anthology* documentary, the Gallaghers' constant name-checking, Paul Weller's *Stanley Road* with its Peter Blake sleeve, Ian MacDonald's *Revolution in the Head* . . . They were The Best Band In The World again; *Revolver* accepted as their greatest album. My boyhood Bible, *The Beatles: An Illustrated Record* (first published in 1975) had submitted the vatic assertion that *Revolver*, rather than *Pepper*, would be the more influential record. It had been right on the money. The songs on *Revolver* contain nothing less than the blueprint for Britpop. Some examples: Oasis's early sound on songs like 'Up In The Sky' was modelled on 'Dr Robert'. McCartney's high-flown bass playing from 'Taxman' was co-opted as the preferred Britpop style – suddenly all the bassists were up at the dusty end, often of a Rickenbacker. 'Setting Sun', Noel Gallagher's collaboration with the Chemical Brothers, was an unashamedly transparent rehash of 'Tomorrow Never Knows'. *Kula Shaker*. But these are only superficial citations. *Revolver*'s influence was altogether more subtle and far-reaching. It was *the* talismanic album for British indie musicians in the nineties; the classic record everyone from Paul Weller to Supergrass,

Gene to the Bluetones wanted to make. The respect for the album was extraordinary. Only the individualists – Suede, the Manics, Pulp – seemed to want to create anything other than the dry, 'timeless', monochrome music on *Revolver*. Three and a half minute pop songs, seven per side. A deeply conservative paradigm.

Ironically, the album would have been perceived as anything but conservative on its release. Pop music was still a futuristic art form in the mid-sixties, and the Beatles were taking it in a dangerous new direction. 'Tomorrow Never Knows' would have seemed as radical and seditious in 1966 as *Ulysses* had in 1922. Of course, what happened to *Revolver* in the nearly thirty-year period between its release and its discovery by the Britpop musicians was the fate of all modern art: it became assimilated, codified. The final stage of *Revolver*'s codification was the manner in which Oasis, completely missing the anti-materialist and nonconformist undercurrents on *Revolver*, took only the superficial sonic elements and turned them into a genre. Dad-rock. Noel-rock. The progressive, the revolutionary had somehow engendered the traditional, the conservative.

Although these regressive tendencies were irritating at the time, it was a shock to discover I was guilty of them myself. I had always been looking back. My childhood Bond collection – and the later Beatles fixation – could be seen as a symptom of Derrida's '*en mal d'archive*':[1] a compulsive, nostalgic, slightly morbid desire to create order from chaos through the act of collecting. Morbid because, ultimately, the archival impulse, a drive to control the uncontrollable, is a means of warding off death. When I appropriated *Revolver* from my father's house at the age of twelve, I thought it might be, in Virginia Woolf's phrase, 'an amulet against disaster'[2] – a handbook to help navigate the pitfalls of teenage romantic entanglements. John and Paul, and especially George in 'I Want To Tell You', sounded as if they knew a bit about love, that they'd been there. The world wanted The Answer from the Beatles; I just wanted answers – about writing, fame, drugs, girls. But in fact *Revolver* was an amulet against the final disaster – death. In taking the album I was starting another collection, the old archival impulse at work again.

But perhaps the most significant influence on nineties British rock from *Revolver* was the lament figure, the descending basslines on songs such as 'For No One', 'And Your Bird Can Sing' and 'Got To Get You Into My Life'. The Beatles used this venerable device – as Shaar Murray put it – which first appeared on *Revolver* (if you discount 'Michele' from *Rubber Soul*, and a handful of others) again and again; and it's arguable whether they would have quite the same emotional hold on us if they hadn't. It reached its apotheosis on the descending bridges of 'Hey Jude' – *the* template Britpop song. If you want to write a pastiche Britpop tune, start in a major key and walk down the scale. It rapidly became the cliché, the defining leitmotif of the era, the musical counterpart of a Union Jack on a guitar. 'Parklife', the bridges of 'Wonderwall', 'Whatever'.

Surprisingly, no one has investigated where the Beatles themselves took the lament figure from. In *Listen to This*, Alex Ross notes that, in pop, it arrived suddenly in 1965, seemingly from nowhere. There could have been a number of sources: the blues; Sinatra's late-night ballads; the American folk revival; even Glenn Gould's recordings of Bach's *Goldberg Variations*, popular in the late fifties. All contain the step-wise descent, which the Beatles would have absorbed from their radios. Further, the Beatles were influenced by their contemporaries: the Four Tops and the Kinks in particular. Both groups were using descending lines in 1965. It's also possible to imagine Paul McCartney at the Ashers', listening to Bach's *basso ostinatos* (literally: obstinate bass), and coming up with the baroque, eloquent 'For No One'. In any case, whatever their provenance, the assertive descending basslines on *Revolver* were the seed, the fountainhead of Britpop's central musical motif.

Crucially for the era, the descending folk lament – originally the disconsolate wailing of a bereaved mother – had, when allied to a major key, softened to allow light and dark shades. Despair was now melancholy – a sweet, safe sadness. And what is safer than the past? Experience made sense of, ordered, collected. A new kind of folk music emerged with Oasis – smiling, sunny major modes, Beatleish anthems, perfect for the fuzzy communality of the stadium experience. A descending bassline that would allow the fans to forget their troubles, like a Hamlet cigar ad.

*

About halfway through 'Smells Like Teen Spirit', Kurt Cobain sings twelve words that don't, on the face of it, make much sense. 'Our little group has always been, and always will until the end.' The gnomic absence of what we suppose is an adjective in the first clause (been what?) and a verb in the second (always will what?) is very Kurt. He's leaving it up to us to decide. On the other hand, he could just be trying to communicate his vision for the band. In interviews he claimed he only wanted Nirvana to be as big as Sonic Youth. This was the chief difference between grunge and Britpop – Oasis couldn't wait to sell millions of records. Everyone knows what became of Kurt's little group. By the time the line was heard in halls of residence in the UK – 1992, Britpop's inception year – Nirvana were the biggest band in the world.

Kurt's little group had captured me, but too late. The relentless Beatle-isation of British music had sent me in the opposite direction, towards an artist who was, ironically, just as great a Beatles fan as Noel Gallagher. But by the time I realised that Kurt Cobain was the only nineties songwriter who could properly be called a genius, he was already dead.

It's doubtful if Cobain would choose to be a musician were he to start out today. Indeed, it's arguable whether any of my favourite artists would venture into popular music, a milieu dominated by talent shows and heritage culture. Pop is ailing, while the more traditional art forms seem to be in robust health. Lennon, Page, Bowie and Ferry, who all trained as artists, might be painters or sculptors, conceptualists. Mike Scott a poet or novelist. Possibly some wouldn't even be artists at all. Richey Edwards might be an academic; Joe Strummer on the peace convoy (this is not too much of a stretch. Strummer's last years were spent around Glastonbury firesides. As the great John Cooper Clarke observed, 'Poonks are just 'ippies wi' zips.'[3]) Maybe only John Barry would be a film composer. And so, too, would Jarvis Cocker, perhaps.

At some point in the mid-nineties, I accepted Suede would only ever be as popular with the public as Echo and the Bunnymen had been in the eighties. This was a discouraging thought. It was also fairly inevitable. In the country's affections, the natural music of the outsider, which had flourished briefly during 1992–3, had been usurped by its diametric opposite. It was Oasis who inherited Zeppelin's crown and played Knebworth, in 1996. I remember the gig. I'd missed Oasis when given the opportunity to see them play to a hundred punters at the Splash Club in 1994, so decided to have a look. Before the group appeared, in front of 125,000 people, songs from *Revolver* were blasted out through the immense sound system. I experienced the hollow feeling from 'Sorted For E's & Wizz'. Predictably, there wasn't much sartorial flair in evidence that day. Most of the audience were wearing Ben Shermans and Reni hats. Not much eyeliner either, not even from the support band; a Richey-less Manic Street Preachers, promoting their new album, *Everything Must Go*. There was still a potency present, however, notably in their best song, 'A Design For Life'. Libraries, they sang, had once conferred power, but now the only thing people wanted to do was get pissed. A design for life in the nineties, and beyond. Watching the Manics, in a Hertfordshire field ten miles away from my hometown – clutching a plastic beaker of warm lager – I realised that I, post-Flamingoes, would need to redesign my life, in every detail.

*

A confession, a sin of omission. That cluster of thrilling inaugural London gigs, in autumn 1984 (R.E.M., the Bunnymen, the Waterboys), there was one missing – the Firm at the Hammersmith Odeon. The Firm were a supergroup: Jimmy Page and Paul Rodgers, and some other journeymen musicians whose names I've now forgotten. I didn't mention it because it was terrible. Well, not terrible, just not very good. But now I realise it was still Jimmy Page, still only forty, playing 'Dazed And Confused' with the violin bow in the laser pyramid, and part of 'Whole Lotta Love'. Today I cherish the memory, as Page's stature in my mind has only grown over time.

A last Zep story. Some years later, I was drinking with Chris Carr, a veteran independent PR, at a nefarious industry boozer, the Bathhouse in Soho. Chris – long white hair, amused mischievous blue eyes, never without a plastic carrier of CDs; one of the last great music-lovers in the business – was as charming and modest as ever that night. He had just been telling me a war story. Ronnie Lane trying to stab BP Fallon – publicist for Led Zeppelin and the Waterboys – in the upstairs bar at the Hammersmith Odeon. Lane had been staying at Chris's house at the time. Chris was aware of my Zeppelin obsession and found it amusing. Nick Cave and the Birthday Party used to live at his house, too, and for them Zeppelin were the enemy.

The following week, I found Chris in the same pub, sitting with an old, small, shrunken American. Tortoiseshell spectacles, shabby suit, pungent cigar.

'This is Joe.'

It was Joe Massot, director of *The Song Remains the*

Same (that is, until he had been obliged to leave the picture under mysterious circumstances). He'd also been in India with the Beatles, and directed *Wonderwall*, George Harrison's first venture into film-making. I flashed back to watching *The Song Remains the Same* with my first girlfriend, Stevenage ABC, 1985. Page reeling and twisting like a mad, punk Chuck Berry in the dragon suit, Madison Square Garden. And so began a long evening – rambling stories of debatable veracity, and an even longer line of empty Stella glasses. It may have been old age, or the Stella, but Massot couldn't remember which came first, Bath or Knebworth. *I* don't remember much about the evening now, except for knocking his specs flying when I got up to leave.

Joe Massot died in 2002. Zeppelin continue to have a long reach, many decades after they split in 1980, 'Ten Years Gone' especially. Its semi-acoustic chords and dramatic shifts became the template for the main songs on Jeff Buckley's *Grace*, the album that begat Travis, Coldplay et al. Yes, it's all 'Ten Years Gone''s fault.

*

Twelve years after our debut, in 2007, Flamingoes made a second album with a new drummer. My brother had been in touch with Rob Newman, and asked him if he wanted to contribute. Rob ended up playing ukulele on two tracks, and is now the proud owner of Barry 'Scratchy' Myers' Clash flight case from La Rocka.

Not long after this, Jude, now a novelist – despite his early lack of promise – organised a reunion with Kevin at a reading for his first book. We raised a glass, and raked through the memories. Yes, the line-up had only lasted two years, and was now peripheral to our evolving lives, but sometimes the periphery is where the most interesting stories are to be found. In the end, we sold over 20,000 albums, though we'll never know the exact figure. The Boss was dead now, and The Label hadn't accounted to us properly. There were murky tales about warehouses of vinyl in Germany. Shady deals. But when all was said and done, we agreed, slurring over the tenth San Miguel, we did something, something we could tell our grandchildren. We didn't play the Albert Hall in front of our mums, supporting the Kinks, but, hey, Brian Wilson dug the album, so there.

As for everyone else? Duke is a head of English, Spike still a journalist in Amsterdam, Bill is a cognitive behavioural counsellor living in the north of England. Simon still plays with Suede. Deborah left the music industry, and currently runs a nursery school in Devon. The Ponytail was last seen mysteriously on crutches, in Camden, not long after we left The Label, like some miscast hair-metal Richard III.

But now is not the time for dark remarks. Chris Sheehan achieved some success with Starlings, but succumbed to cancer in 2014, aged forty-nine. In 2004, La Rocka's Pete suffered a massive stroke. Pete – cheerful, positive, soft-spoken Pete who never had an uncharitable word for anyone, who neither drank nor smoked, afflicted so cruelly. He was the chief enabler of the band, assisting us to rehearse and record, to exist. He was also the reason I was able to cling on in London for so long, providing those creative references to landlords the whole city over. For many years after the stroke he lived in residential care, just round the corner from Air Studios in Hampstead. We'd bring him copies of *Mojo*, and Dylan's latest CD whenever we visited. On the wall was the legend: *Music is my religion*. I shared his faith. His speech was gone, but his essential Pete-ness was still there. He passed away in 2015. At the wake after the funeral, his family insisted we take his vinyl records. Now, whenever I play Dylan's *Basement Tapes*, or Little Walter's *Best of*, or his Bert Jansch LP, I always think of him. And, occasionally, I'll flashback to Bonny Street, Pete with his kids, fresh from seeing the Stones. Happy. Or in the doorway of the studio, a bag full of biscuits and tapes over his shoulder, ready to switch the lights off after another day of King Konehead's noise. Smiling. 'Right then . . . I'm off.'

*

When John Harris published his history of Britpop, *The Last Party*, I questioned the title. Every generation has the right to believe that *their* time is the most important one, and his title seemed to deny that. But in the light of what came after, maybe he was right. Maybe Britpop *was* the last party, the last youth movement the country will see. (Although it wasn't a movement at all, more a moment, as Harris rightly points out.) There hasn't been one since. Name one. You can't. Britpop was a conflation of all the youthquakes that had come before, from skiffle to acid house. But what came after? Nothing. Coldplay. *The X Factor. The Voice.*

And what's next? No one talks about the music of the future anymore. The reasons for this have been well documented in other books: nostalgia replaced the forward-facing gaze, resulting in diminishing cultural returns as yesterday's pop was plundered. Then, most importantly, the internet meant music could be accessed for free, and it ceased to matter as much. This stagnation, seemingly permanent, is cause for dismay. If you are obsessive about pop culture you want to see it continually evolving, showing you different things. But if you can transcend this, if you can abandon the need for significant or 'important' (important to whom?) movements or artists you are left with a piece of art – a song – that only has personal significance. And maybe that is legitimate. Sooner or later, someone will come up with a song that restores your faith in the art form. An 'I Bet You Look Good On The Dancefloor', an 'Umbrella', a 'Video Games'.

Songs are, to repurpose Larkin's phrase, where we live. Some of the time, at least. Or where we *used* to live; a song bearing us back ceaselessly into the past. Britpop can be reduced to a double CD in a service station, 'The Best of Britpop', but the songs within contain memories, lives. The trigger for a Memory Song to do its mysterious work – some banal synaptic reaction, or electrical transference – usually comes from the texture of the sounds. Yet sometimes it is just the words that transport us. In *Retromania*, Simon Reynolds muses on the record collection as a trove of memories, 'ghosts you can control',[4] from

Caruso to Cobain. Perhaps it is the other way round: the ghosts control us. Kurt's line about his 'little group' from 'Smells Like Teen Spirit' perfectly captures the quixotic ambitions of young men who form bands – brothers with broken guitars and amps hired by the hour, 'us against the world'. It sends me forcefully back to the time 'Teen Spirit' was everywhere, 1991–2. Putting the group together at La Rocka with Jude, rehearsing, recording, dreaming and scheming; knowing it was our last chance. It worked for Kurt, so why couldn't it work for us? He may be no more, but, because of the songs, his little group will be around until the end.

As Cobain sang – and will sing forever – *Memoria, memoria, memoria.*

Acknowledgements

My thanks first and foremost to everyone who subscribed to the book: without you, *Memory Songs* would not have become a reality. I would also like to thank Mathew Clayton, John Mitchinson, Jimmy Leach, Georgia Odd, Anna Simpson, Rachael Kerr and all at Unbound.

Thanks to Aki Shilz, the late Becky Swift, and Doug Johnstone at The Literary Consultancy, who were indispensable in the book's early stages.

For editorial help, thanks to Jude Cook, Samantha Ellis.

For support during the years of writing, thanks to Yvonne Enright, Ian Tuton; Geoffrey Cook, Riet Chambers, Eileen Wloch, Edith and Erhard Wloch, Caroline Franks, Stephanie France, Mike Walton, Dan Jenkins, Jon Stoker, Mike Corder, Jeff Wood, Robert Newman, Kevin Matthews, Caffy St Luce, Deborah Edgely, Simon Parker, Chris Carr, Pete Chapman, Jont, Mick and Polly Paulusma, Scott Grant, Tony Ayiotis, Jonny and Paul at FJ, Simon Williams, Mike Scott, Andreas Loizou, Richard Skinner, Houman Barekat, Eric Akoto, Andy Miller, David Wilson, Anne Aylor, Mark Hart.

Lastly, I would like to thank my dear daughter, Evelyn Marie Cook.

Copyright Acknowledgements

Notes

Chapter 1: The Two Bs

1 Alex Ross, *Listen to This* (Fourth Estate, 2010), p. 25.
2 Roy Carr and Tony Tyler, *The Beatles: An Illustrated Record* (New English Library, 1975), p. 68.
3 Ibid., p. 119.
4 Hanif Kureishi, *The Buddha of Suburbia* (Faber & Faber, 1990), p. 117.
5 Eddi Fiegel, *John Barry: A Sixties Theme* (Constable, 1998), p. 199.
6 Ibid., p. 112.
7 Simon Winder, *The Man Who Saved Britain* (Picador, 2006), p. 207.
8 Fiegel, op cit., p. 196.
9 Norman Mailer in 'Gore Vidal and his bitter feuds' by Martin Chilton, *Daily Telegraph*, 6 April 2016.
10 Fiegel, op. cit., p. 198.
11 From Noël Coward's telegram to Ian Fleming, quoted in Lee Pfeiffer and James Worrall, *The Essential Bond* (Boxtree Macmillan, 1998), p. 16.

Chapter 2: The Real Stairway

1 Jimmy Page in conversation in *It Might Get Loud* (Dir: Davis Guggenheim, 2008).

2 Ibid.

3 Roy Harper and Jimmy Page, interviewed on *The Old Grey Whistle Test*, 16 November 1984.

4 Ibid.

5 Hanif Kureishi, 'Eight Arms to Hold You' (essay), in *Dreaming and Scheming – Reflections on Writing and Politics* (Faber & Faber, 2002), p. 114.

6 Ibid.

7 *Midnight Cowboy* (Dir: John Schlesinger, 1969).

Chapter 3: Bowie's Nose

1 Ian Rankin, interviewed on *The Review Show*, BBC2, 22 March 2013.

2 Roy Carr and Charles Shaar Murray, *David Bowie: An Illustrated Record* (Eel Pie Publishing, 1981), pp. 57–8.

3 Ibid., p. 58.

Chapter 4: The Idea of Autumn

1 Mike Scott, sleeve notes, *This Is the Sea*, 2004 reissue (EMI/Chrysalis).

2 C. S. Lewis, *Surprised by Joy* (Collins Fontana, 1964), p. 19.

3 Saul Bellow, *Seize the Day* (Penguin, 1978), p. 27.

4 Matt Smith, *Melody Maker*, review of *This Is the Sea*, October 1985.

Chapter 5: Born Sandy Devotional

1 David McComb, interviewed by Lynden Barber, *Melody Maker*, 10 November 1984.

2 David McComb, from a postcard to musician James Paterson,

10 November 1984. Quoted in Chris Coughran and Niall Lucy, *Vagabond Holes: David McComb & The Triffids* (Fremantle Press, 2009), p. 116.

3 David McComb, interviewed by Adam Sweeting, *Melody Maker*, 2 August 1986.

Chapter 6: In Every Dream Home a Headache

1 Ian Penman, via Twitter.

2 Johnny Rogan, *Roxy Music: Style with Substance – Roxy's First Ten Years* (Star/W. H. Allen, 1982), p. 33.

Chapter 7: The Long Hot Summer of the Clash

1 Joe Strummer, interviewed on *Wired*, Channel Four, 1988.

2 Mick Jones, interviewed in *The Future Is Unwritten* (Dir: Julien Temple, 2007).

3 Joe Strummer, interviewed in *The Future Is Unwritten* (Dir: Julien Temple, 2007).

4 Joe Strummer, interviewed in *Westway to the World* (Dir: Don Letts, 2001). Original text from an *NME* live review of the band's Screen on the Green gig, Islington, 29 August 1976, by Charles Shaar Murray.

5 Joe Strummer, interviewed in *Sounds*, May 1988.

6 Joe Strummer, interviewed on *Wired*, Channel Four, 1988.

7 Ibid.

8 Bob Stanley, review of *The Stone Roses* by the Stone Roses, *Melody Maker*, May 1989.

9 Joe Strummer, interviewed in *Sounds*, May 1988.

Chapter 8: Nobody Does It Better

1 Andrew Mueller, Flamingoes album review, *Uncut*, November 2007.
2 *Melody Maker*, front cover, 25 April 1992.

Chapter 9: The Other Britpop

1 Alex James, interviewed in *MOJO*, April 2003.
2 Group Material, statement, 1985, quoted in the sleeve notes of Manic Street Preachers' *Forever Delayed* (Epic, 2002).
3 Mark Sutherland, Flamingoes live review, *NME*, 10 July 1993.
4 *I'm Alan Partridge*, Series One (BBC, 1997).
5 John Robb, Flamingoes live review, *Melody Maker*, 8 January 1994.
6 Hunter S. Thompson, newspaper column, 'Full-time Scrambling', *San Francisco Examiner*, 4 November 1985. Note: although Thompson was writing about the TV industry, the quote is now widely attributed to the music business.
7 Richey Edwards, interviewed on *120 Minutes*, MTV, 1994.
8 Ibid.

Chapter 10: Disco 1995

1 Keith Richards, *Life* (Weidenfeld & Nicolson, 2010), p. 123.
2 Jarvis Cocker, interviewed by Lee Brackstone, Faber & Faber, 2011.
3 Gary Carpenter, *The Story of Common People*, BBC3, 2006.
4 Mike Scott, *Adventures of a Waterboy* (Jawbone, 2012), p. 191.
5 Jarvis Cocker, review of *The John Lennon Letters*, ed. Hunter Davies, *Guardian*, 10 October 2012.

Notes

Chapter 11: The Last Great Honest Song

1 Simon Williams, *NME*, Flamingoes 'On' feature, 28 January 1995.
2 Jennifer Nine, Flamingoes album review, *Melody Maker*, 18 February 1995.
3 Charles Shaar Murray, Flamingoes album review, *Saturday Telegraph*, 4 February 1995.
4 Nick Robinson, Flamingoes album review, *Music Week*, 28 January 1995.

Outro

1 Simon Reynolds, *Retromania* (Faber & Faber, 2011), p. 28.
2 Virginia Woolf, *The Waves* (Penguin Modern Classics, 1975). 'Like amulets against disaster', p. 36.
3 John Cooper Clarke, quoted in *The Future Is Unwritten* (Dir: Julien Temple, 2007).
4 Simon Reynolds, *Retromania* (Faber & Faber, 2011), p. 313.

Bibliography

Bellow, Saul, *Seize the Day* (Penguin, 1978 [1956])

Carr, Roy; Tyler, Tony, *The Beatles: An Illustrated Record* (New English Library, 1975)

Carr, Roy; Shaar Murray, Charles, *David Bowie: An Illustrated record*, (Eel Pie Publishing, 1981)

Coughran, Chris; Lucy, Niall, *Vagabond Holes: David McComb & The Triffids* (Fremantle Press, 2009)

Fiegel, Eddi, *John Barry – A Sixties Theme* (Constable and Company Limited, 1998)

Kureishi, Hanif, *The Buddha of Suburbia* (Faber & Faber, 1990)

Kureishi, Hanif, *Dreaming and Scheming – Reflections on Writing and Politics* (Faber & Faber, 2002)

Lewis, C. S., *Surprised by Joy* (Collins Fontana, 1964 [1955])

Pfeiffer, Lee; Worrall, Dave, *The Essential Bond*, (Boxtree Macmillan, 1998)

Reynolds, Simon, *Retromania* (Faber & Faber, 2011)

Richards, Keith, *Life*, (Weidenfeld & Nicolson, 2010)

Rogan, Johnny, *Roxy Music: Style with Substance – Roxy's First Ten Years* (Star / W. H. Allen & Co., 1982)

Ross, Alex, *Listen to This*, (Fourth Estate, 2010)

Scott, Mike, *Adventures of a Waterboy* (Jawbone, 2012)

Winder, Simon, *The Man Who Saved Britain* (Picador, 2006)

Woolf, Virginia, *The Waves* (Penguin Modern Classics, 1975 [1931])

Supporters

Unbound is a new kind of publishing house. Our books are funded directly by readers. This was a very popular idea during the late eighteenth and early nineteenth centuries. Now we have revived it for the internet age. It allows authors to write the books they really want to write and readers to support the books they would most like to see published.

The names listed below are of readers who have pledged their support and made this book happen. If you'd like to join them, visit www.unbound.com.

Sandra Armor
David Austin
Jim Auton
Meena Ayittey
Julian Baldieri
Craig Baldwin
Andrea Bennett
Fiona Brell
Paul Brown
Ania Buhorah
Riccardo Cavrioli
Andrew Chesshire
Lisette Chesshire
Garrett Coakley
Geoffrey Cook
Jude Cook
Mike Corder
Anna Denton
Allison Devers
Simon Dimmock
Ana Duke
Amanda Ellis
Ezra Ellis
Lyndsey Ellis
Samantha Ellis
Jamie Fewery
Adam Foley
Clare Fowler
Caroline Franks
Hannah Gelhaus

Karol Griffiths
Simon Harper
Mark Hart
Pam Hayward
Luke Jackson
Dan Jenkins
Sally Johnston and Freddie Davis
Julie Johnstone
Nik Kealy
Hilary Kemp
Dan Kieran
Ingrid Koehler
Molly Larkin
Max Liu
Jamie Maidment
Anastasia Mania
Kevin Matthews
Ross Menzies
Peter Middleton
John Mitchinson
Clayton Moss
Aysheh Mozaffari
Carlo Navato
Richard Newman
Mick Paulusma
Bianca Pellet
Justin Pollard
Brent Quigley
Mark Rae
Jeannette Robinson
Richard Rose
Jonathan Ruppin
Johannes Schneider
Paul Schofield
Paul Simper
Kirsten Smith
Helen Southworth
Jon Stoker
Simon Swan
Emma Sweeney
Ewan Tant
Stephanie Thomason
Liza Thompson
Tanya Twigg
Jan Tyson
Haris Tzortzis
Csilla Varga
Merje Vidovich
Mike Walton
Jont Whittington
Toby Wightman
Jenny Williams
David Wilson
Eileen Wloch
Erhard Wloch
Andy Wolf
Jeff Wood
Peter Wood
Kate Wright